I0434793

Status Assessment and Conservation Action Plan for the Long-billed Curlew (*Numenius americanus*)

Biological Technical Publication
BTP-R6012-2009

Bob Gress©

U.S. Fish & Wildlife Service

Status Assessment and Conservation Action Plan for the Long-billed Curlew (*Numenius americanus*)

Biological Technical Publication
BTP-R6012-2009

Suzanne D. Fellows

Stephanie L. Jones

U.S. Fish and Wildlife Service, Region 6,
Nongame Migratory Bird Coordinator's Office, Denver, CO

Cover image: Long-billed Curlew
Photo credit: Bob Gress©

Author contact information:

Suzanne D. Fellows
U.S. Fish and Wildlife Service, Region 6
Nongame Migratory Birds
P. O. Box 25486 DFC
Denver, CO 80225-0486
Phone: 303-236-4417
Email: Suzanne_Fellows@fws.gov

Stephanie L. Jones
U.S. Fish and Wildlife Service, Region 6
Nongame Migratory Birds
P. O. Box 25486 DFC
Denver, CO 80225-0486
Phone: 303-236-4409
Email: Stephanie_Jones@fws.gov

For additional copies or information, contact:
U.S. Fish and Wildlife Service, Region 6
Nongame Migratory Birds
P. O. Box 25486 DFC
Denver, CO 80225-0486

Recommended citation:
Fellows, S. D., and S. L. Jones. 2009. Status
assessment and conservation action plan for the
Long-billed Curlew (*Numenius americanus*). U.S.
Department of Interior, Fish and Wildlife Service,
Biological Technical Publication, FWS/BTP-R6012-
2009, Washington, D.C.

Table of Contents

List of Figures

List of Tables

Executive Summary

The historical breeding range of Long-billed Curlews (*Numenius americanus*) was the western U.S. and the southern Canadian Prairie Provinces from California north to British Columbia and east to southern Manitoba and Wisconsin, northern Iowa and eastern Kansas. However, this breeding distribution has contracted and Long-billed Curlews have lost about 30% of their historical range. The eastern edge of the current breeding range is the western Great Plains from the Texas panhandle north throughout southwestern and south central Saskatchewan. Long-billed Curlews currently winter along the southwestern U.S. coast from central California, southern Texas and Louisiana south along both of México's coasts to Guatemala, and are casual along the Atlantic coast north to New Brunswick, the southeastern South Carolina and Florida coasts, and the West Indies.

Long-billed Curlews are federally protected in the U.S., Canada, and México under the Migratory Bird Treaty Act. In the U.S., they are listed as a U.S. Fish and Wildlife Service Bird of Conservation Concern: nationally, in five U.S. Fish and Wildlife Service regions, and in several Bird Conservation Regions. They are listed as a species of concern in several U.S. states. In Canada, they are on Schedule 1 of the Species at Risk Act as a "Species of Special Concern" and are "Blue Listed" in Alberta and British Columbia. In addition, they are listed as "Highly Imperiled" in both the U.S. and Canadian shorebird conservation plans. Long-billed Curlews are a protected migratory bird species but do not have an official conservation designation in México.

The high levels of concern are due to the loss of the eastern third of their historical breeding range and apparent population declines, particularly in the shortgrass and mixed-grass prairies of the western Great Plains. The Breeding Bird Survey (BBS) does not show any significant trends for Long-billed Curlews throughout much of their range; however, the applicability of BBS to adequately monitor Long-billed Curlews has been questioned. Documented declines have occurred in several portions of their range, including historical population declines, the contraction of breeding range, and reductions in the number of migrants along the Atlantic coast. Initial population declines were attributed to over-hunting and plowing of the native prairies for agriculture. Current threats include habitat loss and destruction due to urban development, grassland conversion for agricultural purposes, changes in the natural fire regime and the spread of exotic invasive species. Predation, grazing practices, energy development, diseases, and pesticides may also threaten Long-billed Curlew populations.

Long-billed Curlews breed, migrate, and winter across multiple geographical ranges; therefore, effective conservation actions will require cooperation by local, regional, and international entities. Several important steps have been taken towards identifying limiting factors affecting Long-billed Curlew populations. Current conservation needs include: population monitoring, breeding ground studies that identify local micro-habitat use, and identification of critical wintering and migration areas. The development and use of management recommendations for maintaining native grasslands, invasive species control, and water and wetland conservation are also important to the maintenance of Long-billed Curlew populations. Investigation of the effects of energy development and subsequent operations is increasingly important as the demand for alternative "green" energy sources increases. Public outreach will continue to be an important tool in the conservation of Long-billed Curlew populations. Currently, while there are very few specific Long-billed Curlew management and conservation projects on-going, there are many identified needs.

This status assessment and conservation action plan is intended to be a summary of the current state of the species, and a guide to its conservation. It is organized into three chapters. The first chapter gives the general information needed to understand the current status of Long-billed Curlews, with a focus on current threats and management requirements. The second chapter is the conservation action plan. The third chapter outlines the status of Long-billed Curlews in the states and provinces where they occur, throughout the U.S., Canada, and México.

Acknowledgments

Many individuals contributed significant time, unpublished literature, and expertise to the development of this Status Assessment and Conservation Action Plan including: Brad A. Andres, Thomas R. Cooper, Guillermo Fernández, Cheri L. Gratto-Trevor, William H. Howe, Christopher M. Rustay, Robert P. Russell, and Susan M. Thomas. State and provincial summaries were written by Alfonso Banda-Valdez, Joseph B. Buchanan, J. Nan Clarke, Miguel A. Cruz Nieto, Fabio G. Cupul-Magaña, Guillermo Fernández, Daniel Galindo-Espinosa, Martha M. Gómez-Sapiens, José I. Gonzales-Rojas, Cheri L. Gratto-Trevor, Sandra H. Johnson, Salvador Hernández-Vázquez, Catherine M. Hickey, Osvel Hinojosas-Huerta, William H. Howe, Kent C. Jensen, Armando Jiménez-Camacho, Joel G. Jorgensen, David S. Klute, David J. Krueper, Stefani L. Melvin, Gary W. Page, Allison J. Puchniak, Gabriel Ruiz-Ayma, Robert P. Russell, Irene Ruvalcaba-Ortega, Rex Sallabanks, W. David Shuford, Eduardo Soto-Montoya, Elisa Peresbabosa-Rojas, Susan M. Thomas, and Brad Winn.

Western Hemisphere Shorebird Reserve Network has been instrumental in coordinating the development of shorebird species plans which highlight site-specific conservation actions. In keeping with this goal, Guillermo Fernández coordinated the effort in México to develop and provide accounts for several states. We greatly appreciate his efforts and Manomet Center for Conservation Sciences for allowing us to incorporate this information in state summaries for this document.

We are grateful to the many reviewers, whose comments improved this status assessment and state and provincial summaries including Daniel S. Ackerman, Brad A. Andres, Doug Backlund, William H. Busby, Andrea Orabona, Mark A. Colwell, Troy E. Corman, Helen M. Hands, C. Alex Hartman, William H. Howe, Mark Howery, Kevin J. Kritz, Stefani L. Melvin, Larry A. Neel, Eric A. Odell, Lewis W. Oring, Thomas G. Shane, Julie A. Steciw, Heather C. Tipton, Sartor O. Williams III, and Eugene A. Young.

Figure 1.1 was provided by Michael Artmann, U.S. Fish and Wildlife Service, Figure 1.2 was provided by Thomas R. Cooper, U.S. Fish and Wildlife Service. Thanks to Bob Gress and Cory Gregory for use of their photos.

Chapter 1: Status Assessment

Taxomony

Two subspecies of Long-billed Curlew (*Numenius americanus*) have been identified in North America; however Grinnell (1921) disputes this.

> Class: Aves
> Order: Charadriiformes
> Family: Scolopacidae
> Subfamily: Tringinae
> Tribe: Numeniini
> Genus: *Numenius*
> Species: *americanus*
> Supspecies: *N. a. americanus, N. a. parvus*
> Authority: (Bechstein, Subspp. Bishop)

Numenius americanus americanus Bechstein 1812 is reportedly larger and has a more southerly breeding range in the western through central U.S. than *N. a. parvus*. The breeding range encompasses northeastern Nevada east through southern Idaho, central Utah, southern Wyoming, and southern South Dakota, south to central New Mexico and central southern Texas (Fig. 1.1). *N. a. americanus* was historically also found as far east as southern Wisconsin, northern Iowa, and eastern Kansas (Fig. 1.2) but is no longer found breeding east of central Kansas or east of the Missouri river in eastern North and South Dakota. *N. a. americanus* winters primarily along the southwestern U.S. coast from central California, southern Texas and Louisiana, and south along both of México's coasts to Guatemala. It is casual along the Atlantic coast as far north as New Brunswick, along the southeastern South Carolina and Florida coasts, and in the West Indies (American Ornithologists' Union 1957, 1998; del Hoyo et al. 1996; Dugger and Dugger 2002).

N. a. parvus Bishop 1910 (also known as *N. a. occidentalis*) is smaller, breeding in the northern part of the range. It historically bred from south central British Columbia east through southern Alberta and Saskatchewan to southern Manitoba and south to northeastern California, central

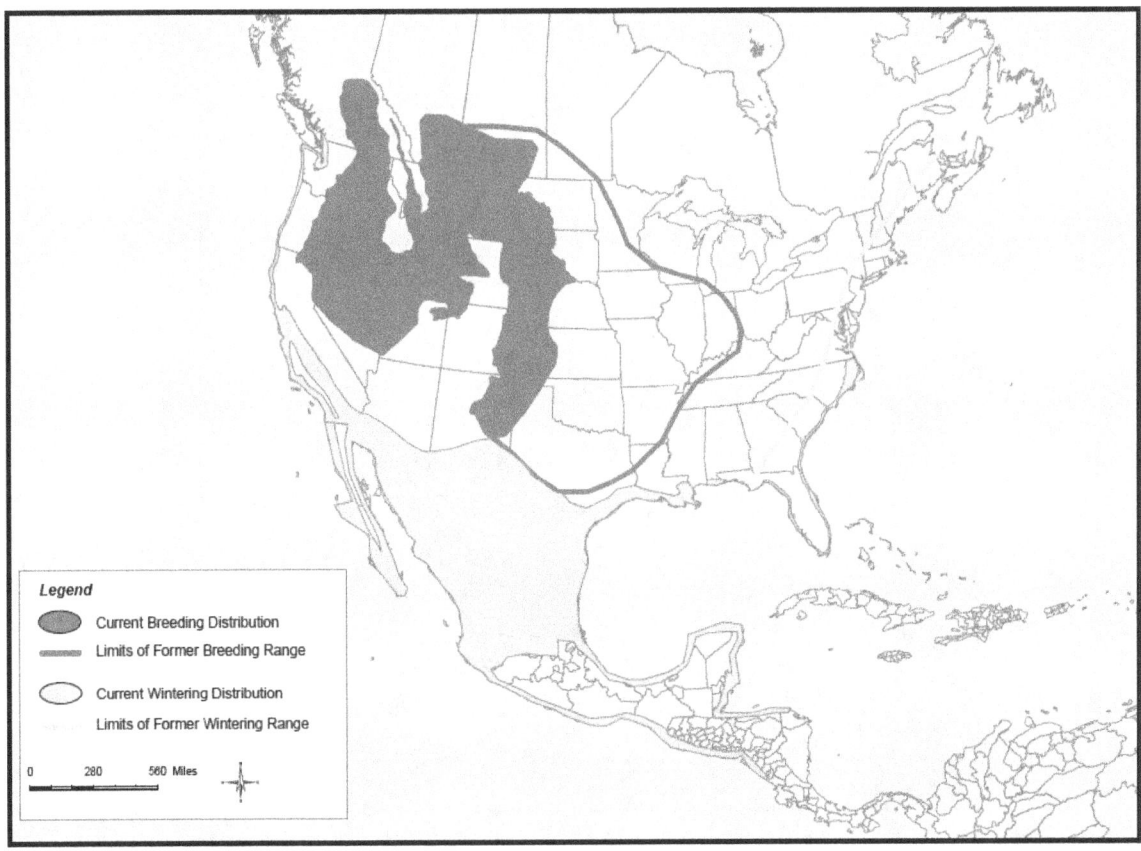

Figure 1.1. Current breeding and wintering range of Long-billed Curlews (*Numenius americanus*).

western Nevada, northern Idaho, southwestern Montana, eastern North Dakota, central Wyoming, and northwestern South Dakota. It is no longer found in eastern North Dakota or in Manitoba (Fig. 1.2). It winters primarily in the southwestern U.S. from California and Louisiana south to central-southern México (American Ornithologists' Union 1957, 1998; del Hoyo et al. 1996; Dugger and Dugger 2002; Fig. 1.1).

Numenius longirostra(is) was used until about 1900 as a synonym for the species (Blachly 1880, Dugger and Dugger 2002). Common names that have been used include Sickle Bill (Sicklebill or Sickle-billed Curlew), the French *Courlis à long bec* and the Spanish *Zarapito Americano*, (del Hoyo et al. 1996, Committee on the Status of Endangered Wildlife in Canada 2002, Dugger and Dugger 2002).

This report will address the two subspecies together since they are not well defined by either range or appearance (Grinnell 1921, Dugger and Dugger 2002).

Legal Status

Long-billed Curlews (curlews) are federally protected in the U.S., Canada and México under the Migratory Bird Treaty Act of 1918 as amended (16 U.S.C. 703-711: 40 Stat. 755; U.S. Fish and Wildlife Service 2008a). They are not listed on the

Convention on International Trade in Endangered Species list (Inskipp and Gillett 2005).

United States
Long-billed Curlews are not federally listed under the Endangered Species Act as amended (U.S. Fish and Wildlife Service 2008b); they are listed as Endangered, Threatened, or as a species of concern in several states (Table 1.1; also see Chapter 3, page 22).

Canada
The Committee on the Status of Endangered Wildlife in Canada first designated Long-billed Curlews as a species of Special Concern in 1992 and re-examined and reconfirmed this designation in 2002 (Committee on the Status of Endangered Wildlife 2002). In 2004 they were added to Schedule 1 of the Species at Risk Act as a Species of Special Concern (Environment Canada 2004). Long-billed Curlews are "Blue Listed" (provincial species of special concern due to sensitivity to human activities and natural events) in Alberta (Hill 1998) and British Columbia (Cannings 1999). They have been extirpated in Manitoba (Committee on the Status of Endangered Wildlife 2002).

México
Although Long-billed Curlews are a protected migratory bird species, they do not have an official conservation designation in México (Secretaria de Medio Ambiente y Recursos Naturales 2002).

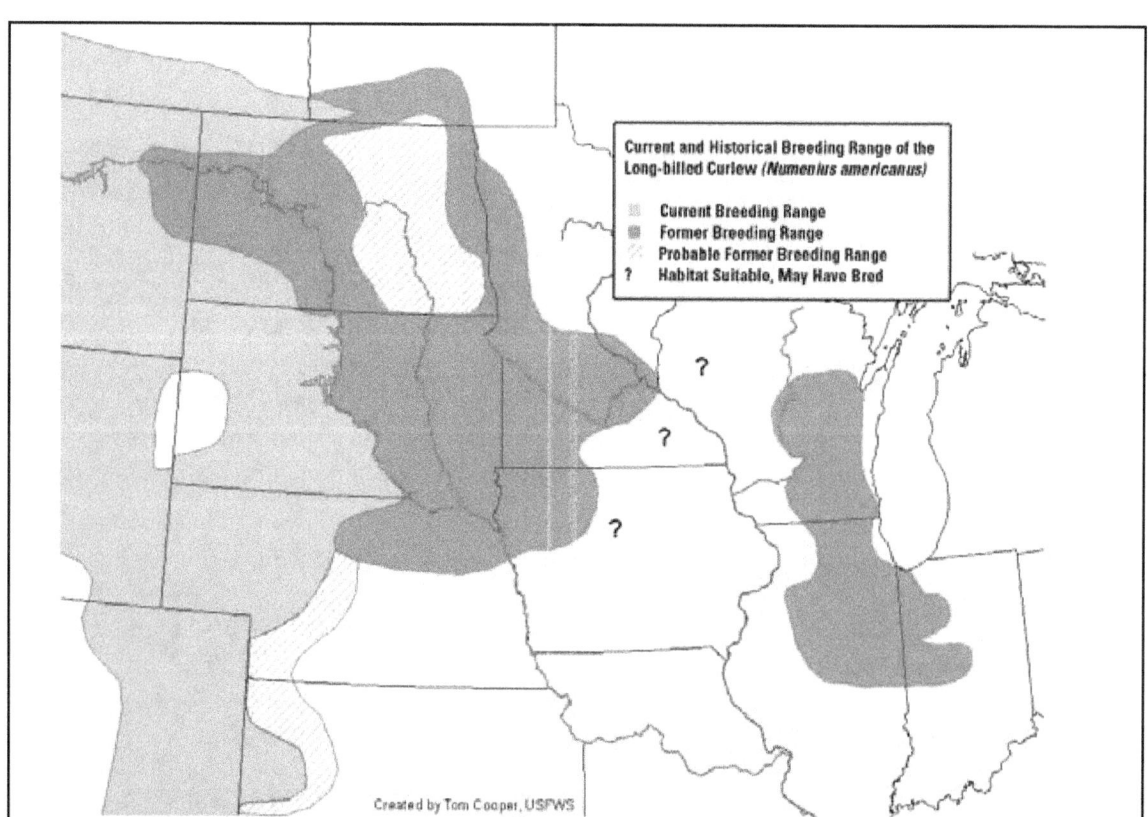

Figure 1.2. Historic breeding range of Long-billed Curlews (*Numenius americanus*) in the midwestern portion of the U.S. and Canada.

Table 1.1. State, Provincial, and Natural Heritage status, season of presence, and relative abundance of Long-billed Curlews in Canada, Mexico, and U.S.

Location	State/Provincial Status [1]	Natural Heritage Status [2]	Season of Presence [3]	Abundance [4]
Canada	COSEWIC: Special Concern	N4B		
Alberta	Blue List	S3	b, m	b: abundant; m: common
British Columbia	Blue List	S3B	b, m, w	b: uncommon; m: uncommon; w: rare
Manitoba	S/P: none	SXB, SAN	m	b: extirpated; m: rare
Saskatchewan	S/P: none	S4B, S4M	b, m	b: common; m: uncommon
México	None			
Baja California	S/P: none	Not Ranked	m, w	m: common; w: common
Baja California Sur	S/P: none	Not Ranked	m, w, o	m: common; w: common; o: uncommon
Chiapas	S/P: none	Not Ranked	m, w	sporadic
Chihuahua	S/P: none	Not Ranked	m, w, o	m: common; w: common; o: uncommon
Coahuila	S/P: none	Not Ranked	m, w, o	m: abundant; w: common; o: uncommon
Colima	S/P: none	Not Ranked	m, w	m: uncommon; w: uncommon
Distrito Federal	S/P: none	Not Ranked	m, w	sporadic
Durango	S/P: none	Not Ranked	m, w	sporadic
Guanajuato	S/P: none	Not Ranked	m, w	sporadic
Guerrero	S/P: none	Not Ranked	m, w	sporadic
Jalisco	S/P: none	Not Ranked	m, w	m: uncommon; w: uncommon
Morelos	S/P: none	Not Ranked	m, w	sporadic
Nayarit	S/P: none	Not Ranked	m, w	m: uncommon; w: common
Nuevo León	S/P: none	Not Ranked	m, w	m: common; w: abundant
Oaxaca	S/P: none	Not Ranked	m, w	sporadic
Querétaro	S/P: none	Not Ranked	m, w	sporadic
Quintana Roo	S/P: none	Not Ranked	m, w	sporadic
Sinaloa	S/P: none	Not Ranked	m, w, o	m: common; w: common; o: uncommon
Sonora	S/P: none	Not Ranked	m, w, o	m: common; w: uncommon; o: uncommon
Tamaulipas	S/P: none	Not Ranked	m, w	m: uncommon; w: uncommon
Veracruz	S/P: none	Not Ranked	m, w, o	m: uncommon; w: uncommon; o: uncommon
Yucatán	S/P: none	Not Ranked	m, w	sporadic
Zacatecas	S/P: none	Not Ranked	m, w	sporadic
U.S.	BCC: National; R1, R2, R4, R6, R8; BCR: 5, 9, 10, 11, 17, 18, 19, 21, 32, 33, 35, 36, 37	N5B, N5N		
Alabama	S/P: none; BCC: R4	S2N	m, w	m: rare; w: rare
Arizona	S/P: none; BCC: R2, BCR 33	S1B, S3/4N	b, m, w	b: rare; m: uncommon; w: uncommon
California	S/P: none; BCC: R8, BCR 5, 9, 32, 33	S2	b, m, w, o	b: uncommon; m: abundant; w: common; o: uncommon
Colorado	S/P: Species of Concern; CWCS: Tier I Species of Greatest Conservation Need; BCC: R6, BCR 18	S2B	b, m	b: common; m: uncommon
Florida	S/P: none; BCC: R4	SNA	m, w	m: rare, w: rare
Georgia	S/P: none; CWCS: Species of Concern; BCC: R4	S3	m, w	m: rare, w: rare
Idaho	S/P: none; CWCS: Species of Greatest Conservation Need; BCC: R1, BCR 9, 10	S3B	b, m	b: abundant; m: NA
Illinois	S/P: none	SXB	m	b: extirpated; m: rare
Indiana	S/P: none	SNA	m	b: extirpated; m: rare
Iowa	S/P: none; BCC: BCR 11	SXB	m	b: extirpated; m: rare

Table 1.1. continued

Location	State/Provincial Status [1]	Natural Heritage Status [2]	Season of Presence [3]	Abundance [4]
Kansas	S/P: State Species in Need of Conservation; BCC: R6, BCR 18, 19	S1B, S2N	b, m	b: rare; m: common
Louisiana	S/P: none; BCC: R4, BCR 37	S5N	m, w	m: rare; w: rare
Michigan	S/P: none	SNA	m	m: rare
Minnesota	S/P: none; BCC: BCR 11	SXB, SXM	m	b: extirpated; m: rare
Mississippi	S/P: none; BCC: R4	SNA	m, w	m: rare; w: rare
Montana	S/P: Species of Concern; CWCS: Tier I Greatest Need Species; BCC: R6, BCR 10, 11, 17	S2B	b, m	b: abundant; m: common
Nebraska	S/P: Natural Legacy Plan Tier I At Risk Species; BCC: R6, BCR 11, 17, 18, 19	S5	b, m	b: abundant; m: uncommon
Nevada	CWCS: Species of Conservation Priority; BCC: R8, BCR 9, 33	S2, S3B	b, m, w	b: abundant; m: uncommon; w: rare
New Mexico	CWCS: Species of Greatest Conservation Need; BCC: R2, BCR 16, 18, 35	S3B, S4N	b, m, w	b: common; m: common; w: uncommon
North Carolina	S/P: none; BCC: R4	SNA	m, w	m: rare; w: rare
North Dakota	S/P: Imperiled (Natural Heritage Inventory); CWCS: Level I Species of Conservation Priority; BCC: R6, BCR 11, 17	S2B	b, m	b: uncommon; m: uncommon
Oklahoma	S/P: Species of Conservation Concern; CWCS: Species of Greatest Conservation Need; BCC: R2, BCR 18, 19, 21	S2B	b, m	b: uncommon; m: common
Oregon	CWCS: Vulnerable Sensitive Species; BCC: R1, BCR 5, 9, 10	S3B	b, m, w	b: abundant; m: common; w: rare
South Carolina	CWCS: Species of Highest Priority; BCC: R4	SNA	m, w	m: rare; w: rare
South Dakota	S/P: Species of Greatest Conservation Need; BCC: R6, BCR 11, 17, 18	S3B	b, m	b: abundant; m: uncommon
Texas	CWCS: State Species of Concern; BCC: R2, BCR 18, 19, 21, 35, 36, 37	S3B, S5N	b, m, w	b: uncommon; m: common; w: common
Utah	S/P: Sensitive Species; CWCS: Tier II; PIF: Priority Species; BCC: R6, BCR 9	S2, S3B	b, m	b: abundant; m: common
Washington	S/P: Protected Wildlife; BCC: R1, BCR 5, 9, 10	S2S3B, S2N	b, m, w	b: uncommon; m: uncommon; w: uncommon
Wisconsin	S/P: none	SXB	m	b: extirpated; m: rare
Wyoming	CWCS: Species of Greatest Conservation Need, Native Species Status 3; PIF: Level I Priority Species; BCC: R6, BCR 10, 17, 18	S3B	b, m	b: uncommon; m: uncommon

1 State/Provincial Status is based on the Committee on the Status of Endangered Wildlife in Canada (COSEWIC; COSEWIC 2002); Birds of Conservation Concern 2002 and 2008 reports (BCC; USFWS 2002, 2008c); State Comprehensive Wildlife Conservation Strategy plans (CWCS; see Chapter 3 below); current State/Provincial designated classifications (S/P); and local Partners in Flight plans (PIF). BCC lists are further qualified by all which apply within state boundaries: USFWS Region (R) and Bird Conservation Region (BCR).

2 NatureServe (2006) scores: Global (G), National (N), State/Provincial (S); Breeding (B), Migrating (M), Nonbreeding (N); 5 (Secure), 4 (Apparently Secure), 3 (Vulnerable), 2 (Imperiled), 1 (Critically Imperiled), X (Presumed Extirpated), and NA (Not Applicable).

3 Typical season of current presence within State/Province: breeding (b), migration (m), winter (w); in some locations nonbreeding birds are present during the breeding season, these individuals are thought to be nonbreeding adults and/or first and second year nonbreeding birds, they are designated as over-summering (o).

4 Abundance is based on information provided for states and provinces. Breeding (b), migration (m), winter (w), oversummering (o). Measurements are relative to other sites currently reporting Long-billed Curlew and are based upon the following scale: rare (has been reported in small numbers, BBS (Sauer 2008) abundance less than 0.25, population estimates or numbers are less than 100), uncommon (population estimates or reported numbers less than 1000, localized, BBS abundance less than 0.75), common (has been reported in numbers of less than 5000, BBS abundance less than 1.25), abundant (has been reported in numbers over 5000, BBS abundance is greater than 1.25), extirpated, and N/A (information not currently available). For locations with rare, sporadic, extirpated, or no reported information, individual summaries have not been included in Chapter 3.

Description

Long-billed Curlews are the largest North American shorebird. They have a long, decurved bill and buffy-cinnamon colored plumage. They are sexually dimorphic, with females generally larger and with a longer bill than males. However, there is some overlap and the bills of juvenile birds are often shorter as well. Body length ranges from 500-650 mm, bill length 113-219 mm, wingspread 257-308 mm, tarsus 72-92 mm and tail 104-136 mm. Similar species include Whimbrels (*Numenius phaeopus*), Bristle-thighed Curlews (*N. tahitiensis*), and Marbled Godwits (*Limosa fedoa*). The plain crown and larger size of Long-billed Curlews distinguishes them from the first two species and the slightly recurved bill of Marbled Godwits will exclude curlews (Dugger and Dugger 2002).

Range

Breeding

Long-billed Curlews currently breed west of the Missouri River in the Dakotas, in west-central Nebraska, and in a few counties in southwestern Kansas (Fig. 1.1); historically they were locally common breeders as far east as southeastern Wisconsin, northeastern Illinois, and southern Manitoba (Fig. 1.2). Blanchan (1904) indicated that historically they also nested in the south Atlantic states, however; there are no current breeding records from this region (American Ornithologists' Union 1998). There are recent breeding records from east-central Arizona and south-eastern New México through the panhandle of Texas (American Ornithologists' Union 1998, NatureServe 2006).

Migration

Long-billed Curlews migrate along the Pacific Coast and throughout the central U.S. (American Ornithologists' Union 1998). Historically, Long-billed Curlews frequently occurred as far north as Massachusetts (Allen 1937) and flocks staged on Long Island, New York between July and September (Blanchan 1904). Sightings along the north Atlantic coast are now rare (Hunter 2006).

During migration, Long-billed Curlews can occur in large numbers at roost sites, a behavior that has been observed in Kansas (Shane 2005) and Texas (D. S. Stolley, pers. comm.). Birds come in to the roosts just at sunset from areas of foraging 8 to 32 km distant. In western Finney County, Kansas, an estimated 2500 individuals landed at a single roost area covering over 400 ha of agriculture fields on 29 March 2007. Most of the curlews had returned to the daytime foraging areas the next morning (T. G. Shane, pers. comm.). In Texas, records include 2261 individuals in Cameron County on 11 February 2004 (D. S. Stolley, pers. comm.). Documentation at fall migration stopover sites has led to estimates of at least 30,000 individuals using the interior valleys of California (G. W. Page, W. D. Shuford, G. M. Langham, and K. C. Molina, pers. comm.). Estimates of the number of curlews using the Delta del Río Colorado, Sonora, México during spring and fall migration are approximately 2500 and 1250 individuals respectively (Mellink et al. 1997). It is likely that there are other significant stopover sites which have not been previously documented. Length of stay by individuals at these stopover sites is unknown (T. G. Shane, pers. comm.; D. S. Stolley, pers. comm.).

Wintering

Long-billed Curlews spend the winter along the Pacific Coast, primarily from Humboldt Bay, California south through Central America, throughout Baja California, along the Gulf of México, and within the interior of northern and central México, especially within the Mexican Plateau (Fig. 1.1; American Ornithologists' Union 1998, Dugger and Dugger 2002). The population estimate of wintering birds in the Valle de la Soledad, La Soledad Natural Protected Area, Nuevo León, México is estimated to be 6392 individuals (J. I. Gonzalez-Rojas, pers. comm.). Estimates for California suggest as many as 20,000 individuals may winter inland (G. W. Page, W. D. Shuford, and C. M. Hickey, pers. comm.) and up to 5000 along the coast (Page et al. 1999). Currently, about 400 birds winter along the southeast Atlantic Coast from South Carolina to central Florida, and occasionally as far north as North Carolina (Hunter 2006). Larger numbers historically wintered in this region (Allen 1937). Birds historically wintered in the West Indies, Guatemala, Honduras, Costa Rica, and Venezuela (Blanchan 1904, McNeil et al. 1985, NatureServe 2006) and there has been a recent sighting in Peru (Senner 2006).

Population Status

Conservation Status

Long-billed Curlews have a Global Heritage Status Rank of G5 (secure; NatureServe 2006). They are a species of special concern throughout their range in North America, with both the Canadian and U.S. shorebird conservation plans listing it as "Highly Imperiled" (Donaldson et al. 2000, U.S. Shorebird Conservation Plan 2004). They are considered one of the highest priority species for monitoring among the shorebird species breeding the temperate region (Bart et al. 2005). This level of concern is due to apparent population declines, particularly in the shortgrass and mixed-grass prairie of the western Great Plains (Brown et al. 2001, U.S. Shorebird Conservation Plan 2004). The trend for the population is listed as "5" (declining) by the Canadian and U.S. shorebird conservation plans (Donaldson et al. 2000, Brown et al. 2001, U.S. Shorebird Conservation Plan 2004).

Long-billed Curlews are listed nationally as a U.S. Fish and Wildlife Service (USFWS) Bird of Conservation Concern, in USFWS Regions

Table 1.2. Primary Long-billed Curlew range, numbers, and physiographic divisions (Jones et al. 2008). Areas are described by Bird Conservation Regions (BCRs).

Name	Geographic locations	Physiographic divisions	Number (individuals)
Primary Breeding Areas			
Northern Mixed-grass Prairie	ne. Montana, North Dakota, South Dakota, Saskatchewan, Alberta	Prairie Potholes BCR (11), Badlands and Prairies BCR (17)	70,000
Shortgrass Prairie	Wyoming, Colorado, Nebraska, Kansas, Oklahoma, New Mexico, Texas	Shortgrass Prairie BCR (18), Southern Rockies/Colorado Plateau BCR (16)	30,000
Great Basin	Utah, Nevada, s. Idaho, ne. California	Great Basin BCR (9)	40,000
Columbia Basin	e. Oregon, e. Washington, British Colombia, n. Idaho	Northern Rockies BCR (10)	5,000
Primary Wintering Areas			
Atlantic Coast	Florida, coastal Georgia, South Carolina, North Carolina	Peninsular Florida BCR (31), Southeastern Coastal Plain BCR (27)	200 (estimated)
Gulf Coast	Texas, Louisiana, Mississippi, Alabama, Florida panhandle and w. peninsula	Gulf Coastal Prairie BCR (37), Mississippi Alluvial Valley BCR (26), Southeastern Coastal Plains BCR (27), Peninsular Florida BCR (31)	Texas[1]: 3,000 (estimated) Other: 100 (estimated)
Pacific Coast	coastal British Columbia, Washington, Oregon, California central valley and coast	Coastal California BCR (32), Northwestern Pacific Rainforest BCR (5)	California central valley[2]: 30,000 Coastal[2]: 20,000 (estimated)
México, Pacific[3]	Baja California, Baja California Sur, Colima, Jalisco, Nayarit, Sinaloa, coastal Sonora	Desierto de Baja California BCR (40), Sonora and Mohave Deserts BCR (33), Planicie Costera, Lomeríos y Cañones de Occidente BCR (43), Marismas Nacionales BCR (44), Planicie Costera y Lomeríos del Pacífico Sur BCR (45)	25,000 (estimated)
México, Gulf[3]	Tamaulipas, Veracruz	Gulf Coastal Prairie BCR (37)	500 (estimated)
México, Inland[3]	e. Sonora, Chihuahua, Coahuila, Nuevo León, Durango, Zacatecas, San Luis Potosí	Sierra Madre Occidental BCR (34), Chihuahua Desert BCR (35), Tamaulipan Brushlands BCR (36)	Unknown (could be 60,000)

[1] B. Ortega, pers. comm., [2] PRBO data (D. Shuford, pers. comm.), [3] G. J. Fernández, pers. comm.

1 (Pacific Region, mainland only), 2 (Southwest Region), 4 (Southeast Region), 6 (Mountain-Prairie Region), and 8 (Pacific Southwest Region). They are also listed in Bird Conservation Regions 5 (Northwestern Pacific Rainforest), 9 (Great Basin), 10 (Northern Rockies), 11 (Prairie Potholes), 17 (Badlands and Prairies), 18 (Short Grass Prairie), 19 (Central Mixed Grass Prairie), 21 (Oaks and Prairies), 32 (Coastal California), 33 (Sonoran and Mojave Deserts), 35 (Chihuahua Desert), 36 (Tamaulipas Brushlands) and 37 (Gulf Coast Prairie; U.S. Fish and Wildlife Service 2002, 2008c).

Population Numbers

Recent work has suggested that there are considerably more Long-billed Curlews than the previous rangewide estimates of 20,000 (Brown et al. 2001, Morrison et al. 2001) or 55,000 individuals (54,873, range 32,700–62,500; SLJ). These estimates were derived from a compilation of expert opinion and most results were from surveys considered to be of poor or unreliable accuracy. A later estimate incorporating the rangewide survey coordinated by USFWS and U.S. Geological Survey (USGS; Stanley and Skagen 2007, Jones et al. 2008), estimated the population at 123,500 (range 65,000–163,500; Morrison et al. 2006). The 2004-2005 range-wide survey followed a statistically valid design, occurred

over two years and counted breeding Long-billed Curlews in 16 western states and three Canadian provinces (Stanley and Skagen 2007, Jones et al. 2008). In this survey, total curlew population size averaged across the two years was 161,181 individuals (range 120,882-549,351; Jones et al. 2008). Estimates for the U.S. were 166,244 for 2004 and 96,276 for 2005; estimated for the three Canadian provinces combined were 16,988 for 2004, and 42,856 for 2005 (range 11,999-72,152 individuals; Jones et al. 2008; Table 1.2).

Population Trends

Breeding Bird Survey (BBS) data for Long-billed Curlews presently consists of 280 survey routes containing curlews; 220 of these routes are in the U.S. and 60 are in Canada. Survey-wide analysis from 1966-2007 based on these 280 routes averaged 1.37 individuals per route (Fig. 1.3). BBS trends are significant and negative only in the Central BBS Region (-2.5, $n = 87$, $P = 0.00$) and USFWS Region 6 (-1.7, $n = 114$, $P = 0.04$). Trends are significant and positive in Oregon (8.2, $n = 26$, $P = 0.05$) and USFWS Region 1 (3.2, $n = 79$, $P = 0.01$; Sauer et al. 2008; Fig. 1.4).

In general, species are considered adequately monitored by the BBS if the standard error (SE)

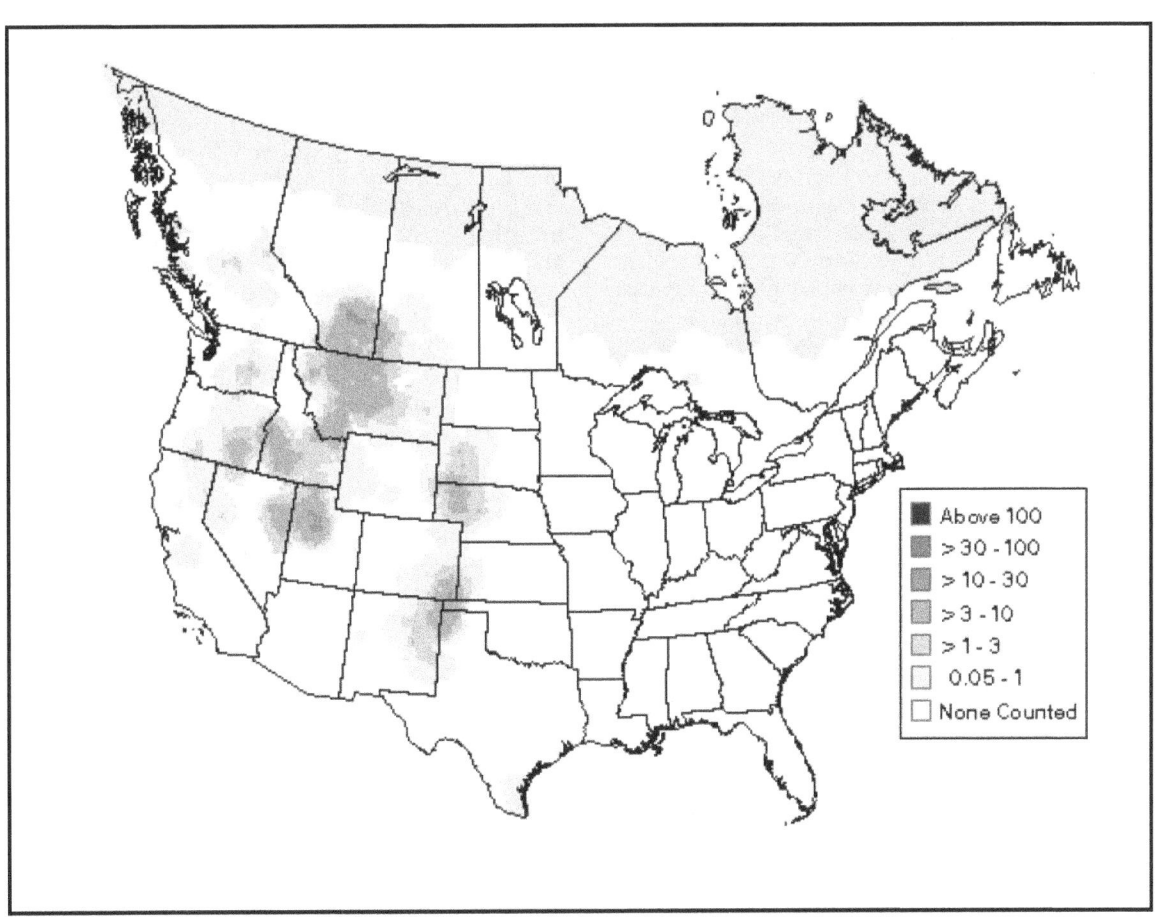

Figure 1.3. Breeding Bird Survey abundance map (1994–2003; Sauer et al. 2008).

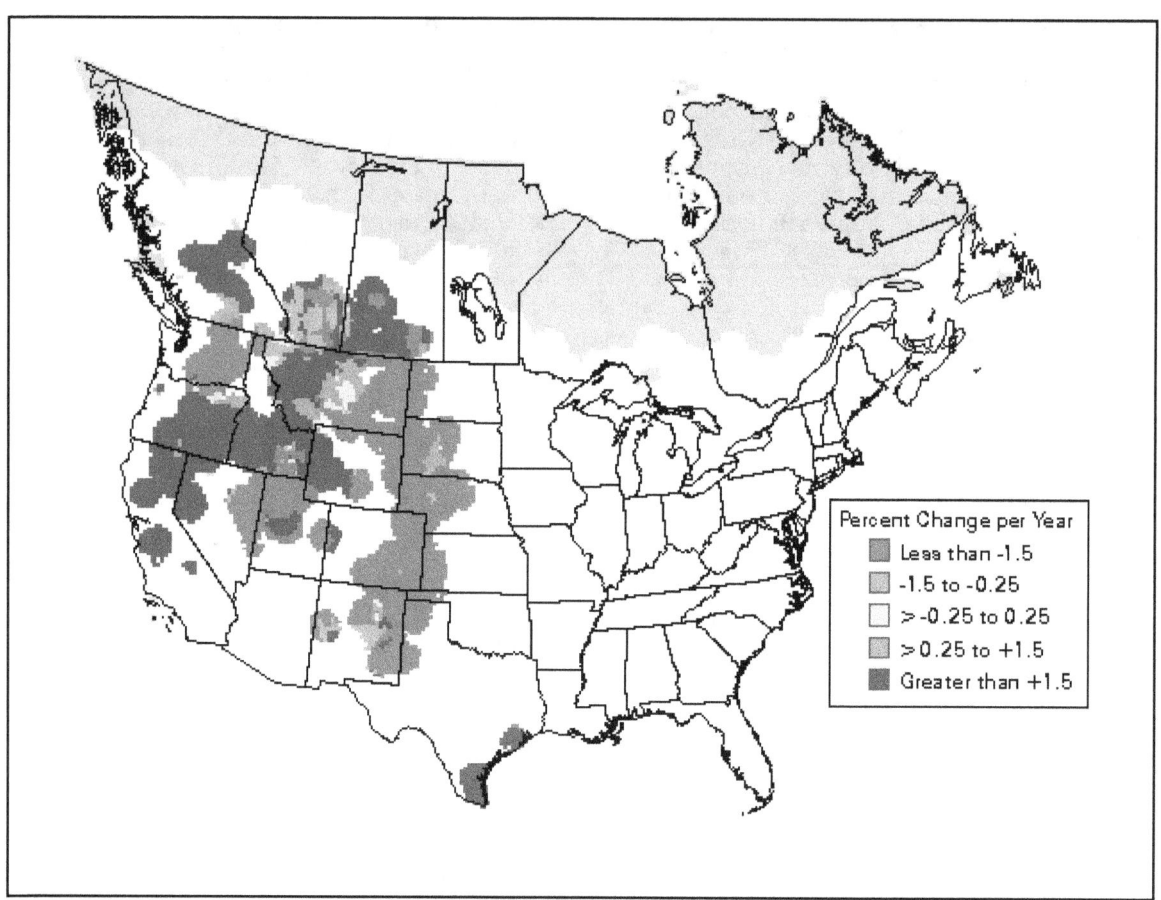

Figure 1.4. Breeding Bird Survey trend map (1966–2003; Sauer et al. 2008).

of the estimated rangewide trend is < 0.90 and if there is no reason to believe that bias (e.g. roadside, detectability, and survey timing) is especially large (Bart et al. 2005). Using BBS data, Long-billed Curlews have a SE of 1.10 (Bart et al. 2005), which indicates that the BBS may not adequately monitor Long-billed Curlew trends. An increase in the number of BBS routes with Long-billed Curlews could potentially lower the SE below the 0.90 threshold. However, since BBS routes are surveyed in June, when Long-billed Curlews are largely inconspicuous (C. L. Gratto-Trevor, pers. comm.), there seems to be a bias introduced by the timing of the BBS which an increase in the numbers of routes would not address. This bias may be substantial and; therefore, the BBS may not adequately reflect Long-billed Curlew trends (see Chapter 2, page 15).

Habitat Requirements

Breeding
A literature review by Dechant et al. (2003) reported that most studies documented Long-billed Curlews avoiding trees, tall weedy vegetation, and tall dense shrubs during the breeding season, and that they nested in the simplest, most open habitat available. Water availability, minimum block size, vegetation height, density, structure and species composition are characteristics whose

importance has been debated. Generalizations may be meaningless though as foraging, nesting, and brood rearing habitats used throughout the breeding season generally require different features and these differences are not always taken into consideration when generalizing studies over a large range. Geographical variability in Long-billed Curlew habitat reflects both availability and diverse environmental conditions throughout their range (e.g. King 1978, Pampush 1980a, Foster-Willfong 2003, Hartman and Oring 2006a).

Water.--The need for open water in proximity to nesting areas is not clearly defined and creates diverse opinions (Dechant et al. 2003). The actual role which standing water plays for Long-billed Curlews may be based on geographical range, local environmental conditions, and age of curlews. The ephemeral nature of water across much of their range, coupled with their high degree of site fidelity and long life expectancy (Redmond and Jenni 1982, 1986), may result in annual and seasonal differences in the amount of water at any particular breeding site used by curlews (McCallum et al. 1977).

Although not statistically significant, Gratto-Trevor (2000, 2006) found Long-billed Curlews used natural wetland basins more frequently than managed wetlands in southeastern Alberta. Within these natural wetland habitats, curlews were more commonly found on drier transects which had ≤ 5% of their length along a wetland (Gratto-Trevor 2000). Foster-Willfong (2003) found radio-tagged chicks in Saskatchewan moved toward wetland areas as they grew and prepared for migration. In Colorado and Texas, most observations of curlews were found within 1.6 km of intermittent or standing water (King 1978).

It has been speculated that wet areas may be more attractive to foraging curlews due to the loosened substrate making it easier to probe for food items as well as attracting more prey items to the area (Gillihan 1999). In addition, intense livestock grazing around watering structures may provide the low vegetation profile preferred by curlews (Gillihan 1999). In Nevada rangelands, agricultural expansion has created approximately 4000 km² of irrigated hayfields and pastures, producing Long-billed Curlew breeding habitat and resulting in a breeding range extension (Oring and Hartman 2006).

Habitat block size.--Block size of suitable habitat has also been considered an important factor for nesting Long-billed Curlews. Several minimum block sizes have been recommended for habitat management planning purposes; however, currently there are few studies which provide data which could be used to develop meaningful rangewide minimum block size recommendations.

In South Dakota in 2005, mean home ranges equaled 1.87 km² (range 0.70-4.89 km²) and 0.75 km² (range 0.52-1.00 km²) during breeding and brood rearing periods respectively (Clarke 2006). In 2006, a drought year, mean home ranges were 7.71 km² (range 1.15-29.11 km²) for the entire breeding season and during the brood rearing period 4.8 km² (Clarke 2006). Based on these measurements, minimum block size requirements could be dependent upon stage of breeding (nesting or brood rearing) and could show annual differences based on local annual weather conditions (Clarke 2006).

Vegetation structure during nesting.--Height, density, and structure of vegetation have also been investigated as important factors determining Long-billed Curlew nesting habitat. In Saskatchewan, pastures of crested wheatgrass (*Agropyron cristatum*) were more likely to be used if they had been grazed prior to the nesting season (Foster-Willfong 2003). In the Columbia River Basin of Washington, Allen (1980) found birds nested in fields of cheatgrass (*Bromus tectorum*)/Sandberg's bluegrass (*Poa sandbergii*) where the average heights were < 10 and 20 cm, respectively. Pampush and Anthony (1993) found annual grass habitats and open shrubs in Oregon, with a mean effective height of 16 cm, were preferred over bunchgrass for nesting. In northeast Oregon, Pampush and Anthony (1993) found significantly higher nest density in cheatgrass habitats. These cheatgrass habitats provided the most open habitat available in the area (Pampush and Anthony 1993) which may demonstrate a preference for open habitat and not

a selection of cheatgrass. Within the Teton Valley, Idaho, Long-billed Curlews nested in heavily to moderately grazed grasslands but used denser cover for brood-rearing (Cavallaro 2006). In South Dakota, on unbroken native mixed-grass prairie rangeland, nest sites averaged 55% grass cover and 47% forb cover (Clarke 2006). In addition, Clarke (2006) found that there was significantly less shrub cover at nest sites than at random sites. A natural range fire during the fall, followed by low precipitation, led to a reduction in vegetative cover during the 2006 nesting season, where curlews selected nest sites in significantly shorter vegetation than available (Clarke 2006). Nest sites dominated by a greater proportion of junegrass (*Koeleria macrantha*) and buffalograss (*Buchloe dactyloides*) had higher success rates during both years of the study (Clarke 2006). Nesting habitat in Wyoming consists of grass < 30 cm (Wyoming Game and Fish Department 2005). The sandsage prairies of western Nebraska rarely exceed one meter in height (King 1978, Kingery 1998, Sharpe et al. 2001) and host high densities of breeding Long-billed Curlews (Sharpe et al. 2001). King (1978) found that the average height of the tallest vegetation at chick hatch was 11 cm (range 4-23 cm) in Colorado and Texas. Measured at three meters from the nest site, the average was 20.6 cm (range 7-34 cm).

Vegetation structure during brood rearing.--Foster-Willfong (2003) noted a shift of use from tame pastures and native prairies during the nesting period to spring and summer crop fields which were used during the brood rearing period. Annual grass habitat dominated by cheatgrass was preferred for brood rearing in Oregon as it provided a profusion of grasshoppers for young to feed on. Fallow ground and cropland with a low profile, such as potatoes, wheat, and alfalfa were used as long as crops did not exceed 30 cm in height. Expansive stands of bunchgrass were avoided by adults with broods in Oregon (Pampush 1980a, Pampush and Anthony 1993). In South Dakota, broods used habitats with a greater proportion of six-week fescue (*Vulpia octoflora*), Indianwheat (*Plantago patagonica*), junegrass, and American vetch (*Vicia americana*) than random points. Creeping spikerush (*Eleocharis palustris*) was found in greater proportion in brood use areas than at random points as well (Clarke 2006). In Texas and Colorado young birds concentrated their activity in short and mixed grass habitats (King 1978).

Winter

Coastal sandy beaches, intertidal mudflats, salt marshes, coastal and inland pastures and farmlands, freshwater wetlands, salt ponds, and agricultural pastures are used by wintering Long-billed Curlews (Page and Gill 1994, Colwell and Sundeen 2000, Colwell and Mathis 2001, Colwell 2006). Variations across the nonbreeding season from fall through spring, as well as daily variations make generalizations about winter habitat difficult. Tides also affect the availability of foraging and loafing areas at coastal areas (Colwell and Mathis 2001).

During the late fall, curlews were foraging on mudflats of Humboldt Bay region of northern California at intermediate and low tides, in the surrounding agricultural fields at intermediate and high tides when mudflats were not available, and were not observed using salt marshes in significant numbers (Long and Ralph 2001). Pasture use increased by mid-winter in the region to the point that most curlews were feeding there even at low tide (Colwell and Mathis 2001). They hypothesized that availability of earthworms in pastures, coinciding with the seasonal onset of rains, is an important condition in determining the number of nonbreeding curlews in the Humboldt Bay region (Colwell and Mathis 2001). Curlews were found to use intertidal territories or pastures only during daylight hours and used the bay at night (Leeman and Colwell 2005). Some curlews may use agricultural pastures for winter foraging habitat independent of tide (Leeman and Colwell 2005). Proportionately more Long-billed Curlews were observed roosting, rather than foraging, on pastures during high tide. This may reflect a need for inland high tide roosts rather than an immediate need for feeding areas (Leeman and Colwell 2005). Winter use was greater on estuary sites which ebbed earlier and tended to be more channelized. Long-billed Curlews flew directly from their high-tide roosts to the tidal flats and then dispersed to feeding territories as the sites became exposed by the outgoing tide (Danufsky and Colwell 2003). Farther south along the coast, Stenzel et al. (1976) observed curlews feeding on the tidal flats during low tide or occasionally feeding in the salt marsh but not along the coast or in neighboring pasturelands in their study of wintering birds at Bolinas Lagoon, California.

In winter, curlews in Arizona and New México were found using plowed, harvested, and grassy agricultural fields, flooded fields, desert grasslands and cut-over alfalfa fields (Monson and Phillips 1981; Corman and Wise-Gervais 2005; W. H. Howe, pers. comm.). In Nevada, wintering birds have been observed using emergent marshes and flooded saltgrass (*Distichlis spicata*) or mudflats (L. A. Neel, pers. comm.). During the nonbreeding season inland birds in southern Texas used grasslands and brushlands (Igl and Ballard 1999). Long-billed Curlews wintering in Jalisco, México roost in high-elevation mangroves at Barra de Navidad lagoon and in sandbars and dunes at high tide in Agua Dulce lagoon (S. Hernández-Vázquez and F. G. Cupul-Magaña, pers. comm.).

Migration
Little information is available on specific habitat characteristics used by Long-billed Curlews during migration. Individual birds may remain year round at some sites so it is often impossible to distinguish migration habitat from wintering and over-summering habitat.

Staging areas include coastal and inland sites in both managed and natural habitats (Paulson 1993,

Davis and Smith 1998, Rivers and Cable 2003, Shane 2005). Long-billed Curlews migrating through the interior of North America use fallow, plowed, wheat, and alfalfa fields, sparsely vegetated areas such as prairie dog colonies, low grassland fields, shallow wetlands, and lake and reservoir edges for foraging and roosting (Paulson 1993; Shane 2005; D. S. Stolley, pers. comm.; E. A. Young, pers. comm.). Many agricultural sites used by curlews have center pivot irrigation systems (Shane 2005). In the southern Great Plains, curlews use farmed playas (Rivers and Cable 2003) and saline lakes to a lesser extent (Davis and Smith 1998, Andrei et al. 2006). Long-billed Curlews were observed in greater numbers on agricultural fields in California's Imperial Valley than on the shorelines and river deltas of the Salton Sea (Shuford et al. 2002a). In Indiana, migrating Long-billed Curlews occurred on isolated wet prairie habitats (B. McCoy, pers. comm.).

Pacific Coast migrants are found along beaches, mudflats, deltas and other wetlands (Campbell 1972, Paulson 1993). Along the southern Atlantic and eastern Gulf coasts, migrating Long-billed Curlews are found on beaches and mudflats associated with creek inlets and barrier islands (S. L. Melvin and B. Winn, pers. comm.) as well as on manicured lawns (B. A. Andres, pers. comm.).

Threats

Initial population declines were attributed to over-hunting and plowing of the native prairies for agriculture (Oring 2006, Oring and Hartman 2006, Russell 2006). Current rangewide threats include habitat loss and destruction due to urban development, grassland conversion for agricultural purposes, changes in the natural fire regime, and the spread of exotic invasive plants (Pampush 1980a, Pampush and Anthony 1993, Oring 2006, Askins et al. 2007). At the local level, predation, grazing practices, energy development, diseases, and pesticides and contaminants are potential threats (Clarke and Jensen 2006, Johnson 2006, Oring 2006). Destruction of nests and human disturbance have also been considered a threat (King 1978).

Over-utilization
Long-billed Curlews were heavily exploited during the commercial market shooting period in the U.S. (Oring 2006, Russell 2006). Curlews were easily brought into shooting range using decoys and they responded to distress calls by flocking towards wounded birds which resulted in large numbers being harvested in a single shooting event (Blanchan 1904). Although currently protected by the Migratory Bird Conventions between the U.S. and Canada and México (U.S. Fish and Wildlife Service 2008a) illegal shooting may still occur, although probably at low levels (Cannings 1999).

Habitat Loss

Destruction of prairie grassland habitat and increased agricultural use has altered the historical breeding distribution of Long-billed Curlews (King 1978, Hartman and Oring 2006b, Oring 2006). Extensive loss of habitat has been documented throughout their historical range (Dahl 1990, Pampush and Anthony 1993, Knick et al. 2003). Urban development (Oring 2006), plowing of grasslands for crops (Pampush 1980a, Russell 2006), a shift in agricultural use from grazing to farming (King 1978, Pampush and Anthony 1993), the subsequent loss of native prairies in the midwest region of the U.S. (Russell 2006), and changes in the natural fire regime (Pampush 1980a) have all led to habitat loss and fragmentation across the breeding range of Long-billed Curlews.

Introduced invasive plant species have altered the physical and community structure of many western grass and shrubsteppe habitats (Pimentel et al. 2005). Extirpation of Long-billed Curlews from their historical eastern range may be attributed to the spread of exotic species following the loss of American bison (*Bison bison*) and the plowing of native prairie in the midwest region of the U.S. (Russell 2006). Exotic invasive species such as diffuse knapweed (*Centaurea diffusa*) are thought to be avoided by breeding curlews (Committee on the Status of Endangered Wildlife 2002).

Cheatgrass is an invasive grass now found throughout the breeding range of Long-billed Curlews. Although Long-billed Curlews are known to nest in cheatgrass-dominated habitats in high densities (Pampush 1980a), Allen (1980) found them only using mixed cheatgrass/Sandberg's bluegrass when the cheatgrass component was < 10 cm tall. This is an issue in the Columbia Basin region of eastern Oregon and Washington, where National Wildlife Refuges (NWR) are replanting native vegetation in areas where Long-billed Curlews breed in relatively high densities (S. M. Thomas, pers. comm.). Land managers in Utah have also noted a high density of nesting curlews in cheatgrass (K. A. Hersey, pers. comm.).

Long-billed Curlew chick. Cory Gregory©.

Historically, regular fires and grazing maintained the grasslands used by breeding Long-billed Curlews in a relatively treeless condition (Askins 2007). Large blocks of planted trees (such as shelterbelts or windbreaks) are often planted to protect tilled areas from the effects of wind and lessen soil erosion (Dronen 1984). This addition of trees to grasslands is a threat to suitable breeding habitat for Long-billed Curlews (Dechant et al. 2003).

Invasive species also pose a potential threat to Long-billed Curlew habitat along migratory routes and in wintering areas. Cordgrass (*Spartina alterniflora*), is an introduced invasive species found in the tidal marsh plains, channels, and mudflats of the San Francisco Bay estuary of California. This threat could reduce Long-billed Curlew use of the bay substantially during both the spring and fall migration (Stralberg et al. 2004).

Predation

Mammalian and avian predators have been linked to decreased local breeding success of Long-billed Curlews. Coyotes (*Canis latrans*; Oring 2006, Oring and Hartman 2006), red foxes (*Vulpes vulpes*; Paton and Dalton 1994, Gorrell et al. 2005), badgers (*Taxidea taxus*), long-tailed weasels (*Mustela frenata*; Redmond and Jenni 1986), Prairie Falcons (*Falco mexicanus*; Oring and Hartman 2006), Northern Harriers (*Circus cyaneus*), Short-eared Owls (*Asio flammeus*; Clarke and Jensen 2006), gopher or bullsnakes (*Pituophis catenifer*; Kingery 1998), and corvids such as crows (*Corvus* spp.), magpies (*Pica* spp.; Pampush 1980a, Redmond and Jenni 1986, B. Olson, pers. comm.), and Chihuahuan Ravens (*Corvus cryptoleucus*; King 1978) have been documented as predators of Long-billed Curlew chicks and eggs. Researchers inadvertently attracting predators to nest sites have also been noted (Allen 1980). However, intensities and sources of predation are extremely variable and often contradictory throughout the breeding range (Pampush 1980a, Paton and Dalton 1994, Oring 2006) and more information on their impact is needed (Paton and Dalton 1994, Oring 2006).

Grazing

In Colorado and Texas, the overall direct effects of cattle (*Bos taurus*) grazing were found to be minimal (King 1978). In South Dakota, 75% of Long-billed Curlew nest loss was attributed to trampling by bison (Clarke and Jensen 2006). Domestic sheep (*Ovis aries*) in Idaho were responsible for some nest loss (Redmond and Jenni 1986). Deterioration of native grasslands by extensive cattle and sheep grazing has also led to the fragmentation of prairie grasslands and introduction of invasive species such as cheatgrass in some locations (Pampush 1980a).

Energy Development

Energy development, such as oil and gas and mining activities occurs throughout Long-billed Curlew breeding range (Knick et al. 2003). Oil and gas shipping along the Pacific and Gulf coasts poses a potential threat from oil spills which could destroy habitat and food resources for nonbreeding Long-billed Curlews (U.S. Coast Guard 2003). The recent increase in demand for renewable energy resources may present an additional threat since much of the area targeted for wind power development is within the central prairies and western grassland and shrublands that comprise the primary breeding range of Long-billed Curlews (U.S. Department of Energy 2008). Threats to Long-billed Curlews from wind energy may be due to either or both the loss and fragmentation of breeding habitat or due to direct hits on the wind towers. The intensity of the threat could be related to wind farm location and times of operation (Stewart et al. 2007).

Long-billed Curlews may be vulnerable to direct mortality due to strikes from rotor blades (W. H. Howe, pers. comm.), increased predation associated with the added structures and incursion into grasslands, disruption of aerial breeding displays, disturbance caused by increased human activity during both the development stage and during general maintenance of the wind farm, and habitat fragmentation (Erickson 2006, Johnson and Shaffer 2006, Robel 2006, Strickland 2006). It is unknown if Long-billed Curlews exhibit avoidance to the towers and would thus be affected by the mere presence of a windmill. Winkelman (1992 *in* Stewart et al. 2007) showed a significant decrease in local populations in coastal Holland of the European Curlew (*Numenius arquata*), a species with similar habitat requirements.

Biofuels, such as corn-derived ethanol, have lead to the increased conversion of native prairie and rangelands to corn production (Stubbs 2007, Scharlemann and Laurance 2008). Several of the primary areas in North America for corn production coincide with the breeding range of Long-billed Curlews. Ethanol production has the potential to directly reduce wildlife habitat (DeLuca 2007, Secchi and Babcock 2007, Stubbs 2007) and could increase threats to Long-billed Curlew breeding populations in these areas.

Disease
Aspergillosis, a respiratory tract infection caused by fungi, was responsible for the deaths of chicks in Idaho (Redmond and Jenni 1986). Other diseases have not been reported.

Pesticides
Blus et al. (1985) collected eggs in 1978 in Oregon to test for organocholorine-induced mortality in Long-billed Curlews. Although eggs were determined to have DDE residues and low levels of heptachlor epoxide, oxychlordane, and PCB residues, there was no significant egg shell thinning (Blus et al. 1985). In the early 1980s, oxychlordane, heptachlor epoxide, and dieldrin levels in the brains were within levels associated with mortality in experimental birds (n = 3; Blus et al. 1985). DDE, DDT, PCBs, and several other chlorinated hydrocarbon pollutants were also detected (Blus et al. 1985).

Recently, a 20% failure of egg hatch in Nevada has led to a contaminant analysis of eggshell thickness and comparison with pre-DDT (prior to 1944) specimens (Oring 2006). Significant eggshell thinning was determined to have occurred. As most uses of pesticides containing organochlorides have been banned in the U.S., it is suggested that Long-billed Curlews are being exposed to organochloride pesticides on their wintering grounds (Oring 2006, Blus et al. 1985).

Spraying for grasshoppers (suborder Caelifera, order Orthoptera) and Mormon crickets (*Anabrus simplex*) is conducted throughout much of the Long-billed Curlew breeding range when cricket numbers reach high levels (Animal and Plant Health Inspection Service 2003). Currently carbaryl, diflubenzuron, and malathion are the most commonly used pesticides for control in the U.S. (Animal and Plant Health Inspection Service 2003). It is unknown if these pesticides or this spraying constitute a threat to Long-billed Curlews.

Other
Vehicles.--Vehicle traffic, for recreational, commercial, and scientific purposes, was documented in the direct loss of Long-billed Curlew nests and eggs (King 1978). Farming practices such as field fertilization, dragging for cow manure in grazed pastures (Committee on the Status of Endangered Wildlife 2002), and plowing wheat stubble also led to nest destruction (King 1978).

Disturbance.--King (1978) noted that in areas where there were low levels of disturbance, such as overhead planes or vehicular traffic along roadways, incubating Long-billed Curlews maintained a crouched posture and did not respond as if unduly threatened. However, low level (150 m) military aircraft flying training maneuvers did elicit alarm responses in birds in Texas (King 1978), while regular intense activity at a military bombing range in Oregon did not elicit an alarm response (Pampush 1980a). Nesting curlews seemed to have become acclimated to the disturbance and did not treat it as a threat (Pampush 1980a).

Recommendations

Although the population is higher then previously thought, Long-billed Curlew populations are lower than historically and their range continues to contract. We believe that high levels of concern for Long-billed Curlews are warranted, particularly in the shortgrass and mixed-grass prairies of the western Great Plains. The only existing long-term monitoring program, the BBS, shows negative population trends throughout much of the breeding range, although in many areas these trends are non-significant (Sauer et al. 2008). Documented declines have occurred in several parts of the continent, including the reduction of breeding range and fewer migrants observed along the Atlantic coast. The effects of energy development, including wind power and bio-fuel development, in the Great Plains and throughout the west, may become significant forces in changing current habitat and resulting in the displacement of Long-billed Curlew breeding populations. Current population level threats, including habitat loss and fragmentation, encroachment of woody vegetation, urban development, the spread of exotic invasive plants, and threats due to contaminants such as pesticides, continue to affect the species on both the breeding and wintering grounds.

In Chapter 2, we present a Conservation Action Plan for Long-billed Curlews. We believe that the conservation of this unique and amazing species should continue to be a high priority throughout the continent. We hope that this document will direct and contribute to their long term conservation.

In Chapter 3, we present more detailed summaries on the status of curlews in states and provinces throughout their range.

Chapter 2: Conservation Action Plan

Introduction

The Conservation Action Plan (Plan) for Long-billed Curlews was developed and prioritized by a diverse group of partners interested in Long-billed Curlew conservation. This Plan includes a prioritized list of actions and needs that we believe will assist us to achieve long-term rangewide conservation of Long-billed Curlews (Table 2.1). Implementing effective conservation measures will require the cooperation of a coalition of local, regional, national, and international partners (Harrington et al. 2002). Since micro-habitat use by Long-billed Curlews varies within and across seasons and geographic areas, management will require local and seasonal components (Colwell and Sundeen 2000, Foster-Willfong 2003). In addition to this Plan, several states have developed objectives and actions designed to address state-wide conservation of Long-billed Curlews as part of their State Wildlife Grant programs (Hagen et al. 2005, Idaho Department of Fish and Game 2005, New Mexico Department of Game and Fish 2006).

The goal of this Plan is to identify appropriate management techniques to halt and, hopefully, reverse population declines in this species. To achieve this goal, several important steps have been taken towards identifying limiting factors and creating a prioritized rangewide Plan. The first step identified to achieve this goal was to estimate the rangewide breeding population size of Long-billed Curlews and determine how populations were distributed within their breeding range (Jones et al. 2008). A survey in Alberta of breeding Long-billed Curlews (Saunders 2001) and the subsequent rangewide survey in 2004-2005 were the first broad-scale attempts towards achieving a defensible population estimates for Long-billed Curlews (Stanley and Skagen 2007, Jones et al. 2008). In addition, current and historical breeding-range studies have begun to identify local habitats used by Long-billed Curlews (Hartman and Oring 2006a, b; Redmond and Jenni 1982), and these characteristics can be used in landscape planning efforts. The Long-billed Curlew Symposium at the 2006 Western Hemisphere Shorebird Science Meeting in Boulder, Colorado, helped to facilitate discussion among Long-billed Curlew scientists and land managers (Oring 2006). Subsequent discussions have led to identification and prioritization of the needs outlined in this Plan.

Results from the rangewide breeding survey indicated that the overall population of breeding Long-billed Curlews is greater than previously thought (Table 1.2; Morrison et al. 2001, 2006; Jones et al. 2008). These results also indicated that breeding birds are generally evenly distributed throughout their present range (Jones et al. 2008). Because of this distribution, there are no broad-scale threats that have been identified that are negatively affecting the entire population and require immediate action or study. However, current indications are that landscape changes, which led to the approximately one-third contraction in their historical breeding range, may still be limiting population growth of Long-billed Curlews in parts of their range.

Therefore, we recommend that conservation actions be prioritized as follows:

(1) Evaluate monitoring methods, specifically those issues related to the BBS. We must ascertain if the trends produced from the BBS are reliable, particularly with regards to timing of the survey and precision (or bias). We need to know the current status of the species, and the direction and magnitude of any trend.

(2) Identify the types and intensity of current threats, on breeding, migration, and wintering grounds. It is important to identify exactly where and what level of risk perceived threats pose to Long-billed Curlew populations.

(3) Identify critical migration staging areas and determine if threats there (e.g. development, alterations to hydrology, contaminants, and disease) are limiting Long-billed Curlews' ability to gain weight and successfully complete migration. Reduction in stopover quality might also negatively affect survival and subsequent reproduction.

(4) Identify critical winter areas and specifically determine how Long-billed Curlews are distributed throughout their wintering range.

(5) Determine the causes of the breeding range contractions and identify those factors that continue to limit population growth throughout the breeding range.

(6) Determine if Long-billed Curlews are positively responding to management actions designed for their conservation.

(7) Assess if environmental factors on the wintering grounds could be limiting Long-billed Curlew population growth.

Priority Actions

Population Monitoring and Assessment

BBS data suggest a population decline, although the results are not statistically significant (1966-2007), except in USFWS Region 6 and the Central BBS Region (Sauer et al. 2008), where range contraction is still occurring. Precision of trend estimates is poor, which is probably related to the low numbers of Long-billed Curlews detected on each route (rangewide = 1.37 individuals/route; Sauer et al. 2008). The priorities are to evaluate the adequacy of the BBS to monitor breeding populations.

1.0. Inherent BBS assumptions should be tested to see if they are valid for Long-billed Curlews.

1.1. *Detectability*. A basic BBS assumption is that there is no relationship between detectability and density (i.e. a constant proportion is always detected, and the proportion detected is a function of the number of birds present). This can be examined using the rangewide survey dataset, since detectability was estimated using double-observer and time-removal methods.

1.2. *Road Bias*. A preliminary analysis (Stanley and Skagen 2007) determined that Long-billed Curlew numbers did not vary as a function of distance from road. Another issue with roads would be to determine if trends along roads mirror the broader landscape for suitable Long-billed Curlew habitat. This could be examined by assessing habitat similarity near and away from roads using GIS. There may be regional differences in this effect. Densities of Long-billed Curlews on roads versus off-roads would likely be different, but that would not be an issue if the trends are the same and a constant proportion is detected (the detectability assumption specified above is being satisfied).

2.0. Currently, the BBS cannot be used to monitor Long-billed Curlews due to the low precision. This can be addressed two ways.

2.1. *Increase the number of routes*. This could be achieved by augmenting the number of BBS routes surveyed, along the lines of the current project in Canada that is conducting additional grassland routes (B. Dale, pers. comm.). We would statistically evaluate this by increasing the number of routes and investigating the periodicity (e.g. every 5 years), which they would be run.

2.2. *Time-of-year*. Perhaps the biggest concern regarding Long-billed Curlew monitoring is the timing of BBS surveys, which typically occur in June. This time period corresponds with the latter stages of breeding when Long-billed Curlews are most inconspicuous (late incubation period or, in some areas, after the young have already fledged and birds have departed the breeding area). This may create two potential problems: a) clumped distributions in June could lead to greater variance (lower precision) in estimates and b) lower detectability of curlews on routes, since Long-billed Curlews are more likely to be less visible and not as vocal. These problems could be examined by comparing data collected on the range-wide survey and the BBS. This assumes that inherent BBS assumptions are still being satisfied and that increased sample size does not mitigate these problems.

Long-billed Curlew's wing, July 3, 2008. Cory Gregory©.

Long-billed Curlew, Galveston Island, Texas. Bob Gress©.

Currently, a survey is being conducted in north and east North Dakota to use the BBS routes to survey grassland and marshland breeding shorebirds (N. Niemuth, pers. comm.). This survey will be expanded in 2009-2010, and will survey approximately 15-45 routes in portions of South Dakota, North Dakota, and eastern Montana between 1–15 May. This project will use BBS techniques to improve our understanding of the population status of breeding shorebirds, including Long-billed Curlews, Willets (*Tringa semipalmata*), Marbled Godwits, Wilson's Phalaropes *(Phalaropus tricolor)*, Wilson's Snipe *(Gallinago delicata)*, and Upland Sandpipers (*Bartramia longicauda*; SLJ and N. Niemuth, pers. comm.).

Migration Staging and Wintering Areas

Although work has been completed on estimating population size and determining breeding distribution, we have still not identified all of the important sites used by wintering and staging Long-billed Curlews, particularly in México. As a general strategy, we believe we should initially emphasize identifying critical migration and wintering areas, assessing their functional ability to support Long-billed Curlews, and then, if warranted, develop conservation actions and evaluation measures for these areas (Table 2.1).

Habitat Assessment and Management

While many threats have been identified, there has been little work on Long-billed Curlew responses to suggested and implemented conservation and management interventions. For example, there is some evidence that human activity can alter use of ocean beaches by shorebirds (Pfister et al. 1992). However, whether or not Long-billed Curlews are similarly affected by this type of disturbance has not been determined. Concomitantly, it is unknown if Long-billed Curlews would positively respond to

beach closures if this action was taken. The effects of energy development on Long-billed Curlews are not fully understood. Pre-project investigations should be made a priority in areas suggested for wind power or oil and gas development (Texas Parks and Wildlife Department 2005). Consequences of increased biofuel production on Long-billed Curlews are unknown but could likely decrease breeding habitat in the eastern portion of their range. Knowledge of the response of breeding Long-billed Curlews to invasive species, such as cheatgrass, and the effects of both timing and method of eradication actions are needed to make informed management recommendations. Grazing, haying, and prescribed burning are all recommended management tools for maintaining native prairie grasslands for breeding Long-billed Curlews (Hagen et al. 2005). Determining the best timing and intensity of these management tools are important to maximize benefits and reduce disturbance (Hagen et al. 2005). However, recommendations can vary across the curlew's range, and management of other high priority wildlife species (e.g. prairie-dogs) could conflict with recommendations developed for Long-billed Curlews (Clarke and Jansen 2006; Foster-Willfong 2003; Montana Fish, Wildlife and Parks 2005). This spatial variation and possible management conflicts reinforce the need for local evaluation of management actions that can then be integrated into a rangewide perspective (Table 2.1).

Research

Research needs were identified and prioritized by the Long-billed Curlew Working Group. Research needs are focused on information gaps that could be helpful in identifying limiting factors and the risk posed by perceived threats. Also, priority research needs were identified to focus on data that is required for population modeling exercises (Table 2.1).

Table 2.1. Recommended prioritized conservation actions for Long-billed Curlews (LBCU) throughout their range. This list serves to identify conservation action items that could lead to the conservation of this species. Where "Lead Party" has been identified it is not meant to obligate any party to provide funding or implement the action. In a few cases, potential partners and costs have been identified; in most cases that needs to be completed.

Task	Action Group	Annual Cycle	Action Item	Lead Party	Potential Partners	Cost (K) per year	Cost (K) Total	Duration	Comments
1.0	Population Monitoring and Assessment	Breeding	Test inherent assumptions of the BBS.	FWS					
1.1	Population Monitoring and Assessment	Breeding	Detectability as a function of density, i.e., is the proportion detected a function of the number of birds present.	FWS	USGS, state agencies, NGOs	10	10	1yr	
1.2	Population Monitoring and Assessment	Breeding	Road bias. Do trends along roads mirror the landscape in general for LBCU?	FWS	USGS, state agencies, NGOs	10	20	2yr	
2.0	Population Monitoring and Assessment	Breeding	Test/develop methods to improve the poor precision of the BBS. This project will include 2.1 and 2.2, below. The area of this project is ND, SD, e. MT.	FWS	State agencies, NGOs	21	42	2yr	N. Niemuth, and S. Jones, in 2009-2010
2.1	Population Monitoring and Assessment	Breeding	Increase the number of routes and evaluate the effect.	FWS	Above				Above
2.2	Population Monitoring and Assessment	Breeding	Time-of-year. Examine by comparing data collected in rangewide survey vs. BBS data. BBS routes will be run during 1-15 May.	FWS	Above				Above
3.0	Population Monitoring and Assessment	Migration	Identify and map migratory pathways and important stop-over sites between breeding grounds and the wintering grounds.	FWS, state agencies					
4.0	Population Monitoring and Assessment	Migration	Determine movements of birds to and from breeding sites; timing, locations of critical migratory stop-over; and length of stay.						
5.0	Population Monitoring and Assessment	Migration	Determine micro-habitat requirements for migration sites.						
6.0	Population Monitoring and Assessment	Wintering	Complete a map of current Long-billed Curlew wintering range and habitat.	FWS, state agencies, México					
7.0	Population Monitoring and Assessment	Wintering	Assess the importance of wintering sites through LBCU range.						
8.0	Population Monitoring and Assessment	Wintering	Determine important areas that support winter roosts.						
9.0	Population Monitoring and Assessment	Wintering	Determine distribution, abundance, and habitat use of LBCU wintering at inland and coastal sites.						

Table 2.1. continued

Task	Action Group	Annual Cycle	Action Item	Lead Party	Potential Partners	Cost (K) per year	Cost (K) Total	Duration	Comments
10.0	Population Monitoring and Assessment	Wintering	Assess existing levels of conservation protection for wintering habitats.						
11.0	Population Monitoring and Assessment	Wintering	Conduct research on Long-billed Curlew wintering ecology.						
12.0	Population Monitoring and Assessment	Wintering	Determine importance of water, and required distance from wintering areas.						
13.0	Population Monitoring and Assessment	Wintering	Determine threats and limiting factors on the wintering grounds.	federal agencies	WHSRN, JVs, state agencies				
14.0	Population Monitoring and Assessment	Wintering	Quantifying the effects of disturbance on coastal wintering grounds e.g. human recreational activity, particularly on foraging rates and habitats.	Universities, NGOs	FWS				
1.0	Habitat Assessment and Management	Breeding	Determine micro- and macro- habitats across the breeding range, using data from rangewide survey.	FWS	Texas A & M	10	10	1 year	Completed, Saalfeld et al. 2008.
2.0	Habitat Assessment and Management	Breeding	Improve LBCU breeding habitat in North America, including publishing recommendations as Best Management Practices.	Shorebird Temperate Grp; JVs	FWS, USGS, NGOs				
2.1	Habitat Assessment and Management	Breeding	Improve LBCU breeding habitat and Best Management Practices - Northern Prairies.	JVs	FWS, USGS, NGOs	10	10	1 year	
2.2	Habitat Assessment and Management	Breeding	Improve LBCU breeding habitat and Best Management Practices - Great Basin and sagebrush grasslands.	JVs	FWS, USGS, NGOs	10	10	1 year	
2.3	Habitat Assessment and Management	Breeding	Improve LBCU breeding habitat and Best Management Practices - shortgrass prairies.	JVs	FWS, USGS, NGOs	10	10	1 year	
3.0	Habitat Assessment and Management	Breeding	Determine minimum habitat requirements.						
4.0	Habitat Assessment and Management	Breeding	Determine effects of energy development, particularly oil and gas and wind farms; determine appropriate mitigation recommendations.						
4.1	Habitat Assessment and Management	Breeding	Assess effects of wind power and oil/gas development - habitat fragmentation.						
4.2	Habitat Assessment and Management	Breeding	Assess effects of wind power and oil/gas development - infrastructure.						
4.3	Habitat Assessment and Management	Breeding	Assess effects of wind power and oil/gas development - nesting success.						

Table 2.1. continued

Task	Action Group	Annual Cycle	Action Item	Lead Party	Potential Partners	Cost (K) per year	Cost (K) Total	Duration	Comments
4.4	Habitat Assessment and Management	Breeding	Assess effects of wind power and oil/gas development - interference with breeding/territorial display/defense.						
4.5	Habitat Assessment and Management	Breeding	Assess effects of wind power and oil/gas development - strike hazard.						
5.0	Habitat Assessment and Management	Breeding	Assess effects of invasive species (e.g. cheatgrass) on LBCU nesting success, across the geographic and habitat range of the species.						
6.0	Habitat Assessment and Management	Breeding	Determine the best timeline for habitat restoration, seed mixtures, and the response to restoration, across its range.						
7.0	Habitat Assessment and Management	Breeding	Determine if collisions are a threat and methods to reduce/mitigate risks from collisions (e.g. wind farms, communications towers).						
8.0	Habitat Assessment and Management	Migration	Protect, restore, and protect migration and staging habitat.		WHRSN, JVs, state agencies				
9.0	Habitat Assessment and Management	Wintering	Protect and improve LBCU habitat in wintering grounds.						
1.0	Research	Breeding	Reduce critical knowledge gaps regarding demographics, population size and trend, adult survival, and life history.	Researchers, USGS	Universities, NGOs, state agencies				
1.1	Research	Breeding	Estimate reproductive success and breeding habitat use in geographic areas where information is lacking.	FWS	State agencies, NGOs				
1.2	Research	Breeding	Determine adult and juvenile survival rates across breeding range and in a variety of micro-habitats.						
1.3	Research	Breeding	Increase knowledge about dispersal patterns (juvenile and adult) and factors affecting dispersal.						
2.0	Research	Breeding	Assess potential effects of various non-habitat limiting factors.						
2.1	Research	Breeding	Assess role of water in different areas, and at different stages in the reproductive cycle.						

Table 2.1. continued

Task	Action Group	Annual Cycle	Action Item	Lead Party	Potential Partners	Cost (K) per year	Cost (K) Total	Duration	Comments
2.2	Research	Breeding	Evaluate the effect of predation across a wide geographic range.						
2.3	Research	Breeding	Evaluate the effect of cattle/bison grazing at different stocking rates and rotation timing.						
2.4	Research	Breeding	Evaluate the effects and timing of other disturbances (e.g. haying, fire).						
3.0	Research	Breeding	Compile information on reproductive success from across the breeding range, for an evaluation for a population viability analysis.						
4.0	Research	Breeding	Assess how important and extent of colonial and semi-colonial nesting.						
5.0	Research	All	Assess importance of contaminants such as pesticides, heavy metals.						
6.0	Research	Breeding	Investigate correlations between climate changes, timing of spring arrival of LBCU on breeding grounds.						
1.0	Education and Outreach	Breeding	LBCU projects for education and outreach on the value of conserving intact native shortgrass and mixed-grass prairie.						

Education and Outreach

Development of education and outreach tools were recurring themes in every category of the recommended conservation actions. Long-billed Curlew conservation will require public and landowner education and outreach on the value of conserving intact native shortgrass prairie. Long-billed Curlews are large, conspicuous birds and are a good flagship species of prairie grassland ecosystems. As such, they can be effectively used to introduce prairie conservation into classrooms and communities (Table 2.1).

Other Species Covered

Many grassland management actions, such as increasing dense nesting cover to increase waterfowl nesting, have the potential to negatively affect habitat use by breeding Long-billed Curlews (Prairie Habitat Joint Venture 2000). While a number of grassland breeding shorebirds overlap with Long-billed Curlews in range and general habitat use, this species may not be a good indicator or umbrella species for habitat management. However, many of these species will be covered in the monitoring survey discussed above. Marbled Godwits, Willets, and Upland Sandpipers generally use similar habitats in portions of the Long-billed Curlew's range, but significant portions of their ranges do not overlap with curlews. In addition, micro-habitat needs (i.e. gradients of grass density and wetness) for Willets and Upland Sandpipers do not overlap well with Long-billed Curlews. Mountain Plover (*Charadrius montanus*) habitat requirements are generally quite different from those of Long-billed Curlews, although their ranges do overlap. In areas where Long-billed Curlews are a component of the breeding bird community, habitat managers should try to integrate adequate curlew habitat requirement needs into their management plans.

Priority Populations and Regions

Long-billed Curlews can be divided into ecological groups, based on vegetation regimes, ecoregions, and political boundaries (Table 1.2). Within each physiographic region, Long-billed Curlews appear to have some different micro-habitat requirements which need to be taken into consideration when implementing management actions. Population numbers have been estimated for these divisions (Table 1.2).

Conservation Strategy

This Plan is a product of a diverse group of agencies, organizations, and individuals with an interest in Long-billed Curlew conservation. The conservation strategy outlined here will address threats to both breeding and non-breeding habitat and assess potential threats from non-habitat factors. During 2001 and 2002, the Temperate Breeding Group (Bart et al. 2005) of the shorebird monitoring group, Program for Regional and International Shorebird

Monitoring (PRISM), initiated work on a number of the conservation actions for Long-billed Curlews. In February 2006, a workshop was held on Long-billed Curlew research and conservation and management needs, which provided the basis for the conservation needs identified here. The conservation strategy for this species includes maintaining an active Long-billed Curlew Working Group, developing a broad-based partnership to deliver Long-billed Curlew and temperate breeding shorebird conservation, increasing available funding for Long-billed Curlew research, and increasing partner attention to the habitat needs of the species.

Completed and On-going Conservation Actions

Since its inception in 2001, the Temperate Breeding Group (Bart et al. 2005) of PRISM has initiated, and completed, work on a number of the conservation actions identified for Long-billed Curlews.

(1) Completed the rangewide survey (Stanley and Skagen 2007, Jones et al. 2008).

(2) Analyzed the population size estimates, including those in Canada (Jones et al. 2008).

(3) Analyzed habitat and distribution data from the rangewide survey (Saalfeld et al. 2008).

(4) Designed, and planning to conduct in 2009-2010, a BBS-based monitoring survey in portions of South Dakota, North Dakota, and Montana (SLJ and N. Niemuth, pers. comm.).

(5) Conduct research on various aspects of the life history and ecology (Hartman and Oring 2006a, b; Oring 2006).

(6) Established a Long-billed Curlew ListServ.

(7) Established a web site to exchange current reports on Long-billed Curlew research (http://www.fws.gov/mountain%2Dprairie/species/birds/longbilled%5Fcurlew/).

(8) Convened two workshops to discuss Long-billed Curlew conservation and status (LaCrosse, Wisconsin, in 2002 and Boulder, Colorado, in 2006). These workshops were attended by a wide range of agencies, organizations, and individuals. Participants at these meetings developed strategies and recommendations for specific actions needed to achieve the conservation of the species. In some cases, lead agencies, partners, and costs have been identified; in many cases, the scope of the action is unknown and will only be known after initial development of projects have been completed (Table 2.1).

(9) A third workshop is planned for the 2009 Western Hemisphere Shorebird Group meeting in México. It is hoped that this meeting will provide an opportunity for researchers from México to be involved, to share their research, and to further implement the identified priority wintering and migration needs.

Chapter 3: State and Provincial Summaries of Long-billed Curlew Status

Introduction

This chapter presents the individual status assessments for U.S. and Mexican states and Canadian provinces where Long-billed Curlews are currently found in large numbers (Table 1.1). State and provincial status, along with information about ocurrence are given. Status assessments have been combined where Long-billed Curlews have either been extirpated (Illinois, Indiana, Iowa, Michigan, Minnesota, and Wisconsin) or have only a few wintering or migrating individuals yearly (Alabama, Florida, Georgia, Louisiana, Mississippi, North Carolina, and South Carolina).

No status assessment is included for the Canadian province of Manitoba; breeding Long-billed Curlews have been extipated from this province and there is no information available.

Most of the accounts for México were developed from materials submitted for the Western Hemisphere Shorebird Reserve Network's (WHSRN) site-based conservation plan project. Individual state status assessments have not been included for the states of Chiapas, Durango, Guanajuato, Guerrero, Morelos, Oaxaca, Querétaro, Quintana Roo, Yucatán, Zacatecas, or the Distrito Federal, since data are sporadic and largely anecdotal. No records of Long-billed Curlews occurring in Aguascalientes, Campeche, Hidalgo, Estado de México, Michoacán, Puebla, San Luis Potosí, Tabasco, and Tlaxcala were found.

The status assessments presented here all follow the same format. Where no information is available or is not relivant to the state or province that section may be omitted. Many of the states and provinces have limited information on Long-billed Curlews and this is reinforced in these summaries.

Long-billed Curlew chick with transmitter. Cory Gregory©.

Long-billed Curlew. Cory Gregory©.

UNITED STATES

Arizona

SUMMARY: Long-billed Curlews are a rare breeder in Arizona. The only breeding recorded was in 1993 in the White Mountains area. It is an uncommon to locally and irregularly common migrant and is generally rare to locally uncommon in winter in southern Arizona, but is possibly increasing.

STATUS:
State: Long-billed Curlews do not have a state designated status.

Natural Heritage Rank: Arizona rank S1B (Critically Imperiled Breeder), S3S4N (Vulnerable to Apparently Secure Nonbreeding); *National rank:* N5N, N5B (Secure Nonbreeding, Breeding); *Global rank:* G5 (Secure; NatureServe 2006).

TRENDS:
North American Breeding Bird Survey (BBS) trends and abundance data: Long-billed Curlews were not detected on any routes (Sauer et al. 2008).

Christmas Bird Count (CBC): The first Arizona CBC was conducted in 1910, with 1-7 counts conducted irregularly into the 1960's. Number of count circles gradually increased from then to the 2005 level of 33 circles. Curlews were undetected in 69 years out of the 85-year history of Arizona CBC. First recorded on a CBC in 1975 (1 individual). Fewer than 10 recorded in 11 of the years since then. Peak numbers were from the years 1986 (90 birds, Elfrida CBC), 1988 (74 birds; 71 Elfrida CBC, 2 Gila River CBC, 1 Patagonia CBC), 2003 (122 birds; 106 Gila River CBC, 15 Elfrida CBC, 1 elsewhere) and 2005 (81 birds, Gila River CBC). Recorded in 6 of the 10 years from 1996 to 2005 (National Audubon Society 2006). The increase in occurrence may be due to greater observer coverage and knowledge of where to look for them rather than actually representing a true increase in winter numbers.

RANGE:
Breeding: One pair with three small young were located approximately 2.4 km west of Eagar, Apache County on 21 June 1993 at approximately 2176 m elevation, for the first and only confirmed breeding in the state (Corman and Wise-Gervais 2005). Additional summer observations have occurred within a few miles of Eagar since 1993. Two pairs were also seen displaying approximately 6.4 km west of Eagar near a prairie-dog town in April 2006 (T. E. Corman, pers. comm.). Breeding is also suspected near the Springerville/Eagar airport, where adults were observed mobbing a Ferruginous Hawk (*Buteo regalis*) by the airport in either 1994 or 1995 (T. E. Corman, pers. comm.). Big Lake, Apache County may represent another potential breeding location. Historically, one individual was observed in late June 1915 (Goldman 1926); a pair was also observed

in this area in mid-June 1993 (Corman and Wise-Gervais 2005).

Migration:
Approximate timing: Spring migrants arrive in the lower Colorado River Valley in early March, peaking in April; small numbers persist through May and early June. Fall numbers start increasing in mid-June and could represent fall migrants or failed breeders. Their numbers peak from mid-July through early September and numbers are less through mid-October (Rosenberg et al. 1991). Records suggest migration peaks in March and July; most of these observations are from outside the lower Colorado River Valley (eBird 2008).
Location of staging areas: Long-billed Curlews occur statewide in appropriate habitats but are most numerous in the lower Gila and Salt River Valleys and along the lower Colorado River. There are no known predictable staging areas.
Numbers, particularly high counts: Maximum counts are of 124 near Mesa (Maricopa County) on 3 April 1952 and 125 at the same location on 12 March 1964 (Monson and Phillips 1981); 190 were reported at San Luis (Yuma County) on 28 September 1974 (Rosenberg et al. 1991).

Winter:
Approximate timing: Long-billed Curlews are found throughout the winter in Arizona.
Locations: Most consistent in the Gila River Valley from Phoenix downstream to the lower Colorado River Valley in Yuma County (T. E. Corman, pers. comm.). They are also recorded regularly in the Arlington Valley near Buckeye and on the Paloma Ranch near Gila Bend (Maricopa County). They are occasional but not annual in higher-elevation agricultural fields in the Sulphur Springs Valley of southeastern Arizona (e.g. near Elfrida, Cochise County) and occasionally found elsewhere.
Numbers, particularly high counts: 106, Gila River CBC, 27 December 2002; 140 in Arlington Valley on 26 December 2005 (T. E. Corman, pers. comm.); "several hundred" wintering near Yuma in recent years (H. Detwiler, pers. comm.).

ABUNDANCE AND POPULATION: There has only been one documented case of breeding in Arizona.

HABITAT: Long-billed Curlews in Arizona primarily are found below 305 m elevation in agricultural fields, especially in flooded fields or cut-over alfalfa fields during winter. They use "fields" (Monson and Phillips 1981), plowed or grassy agricultural fields, and are occasionally observed roosting on sandbars and lakeshores (Rosenberg et al. 1991) during migration.

THREATS: Threats include loss of grasslands through conversion to agriculture or urbanization.

Submitted by William H. Howe
Reviewed by Troy E. Corman

California

SUMMARY: Long-billed Curlews occur in California year round, with lowest numbers in May, but status varies considerably seasonally and regionally. The breeding population is relatively small and restricted to the northeastern region of the state. California is an important area for wintering and migrating curlews, with the lowland areas in the interior of the state supporting the bulk of the population, likely between 10,000-20,000 individuals. Important areas to wintering and migrating curlews in the interior of the state include the Central Valley, Imperial Valley, and Carrizo Plain. Agricultural land, particularly dry and irrigated pastures, alfalfa fields, and post-harvest rice fields, are the most important inland habitats in winter and migration. Several thousand curlews occur on the California coast during fall migration and in winter; primary coastal habitats are wetlands, beaches, and (locally) pastures. Urbanization of agricultural land, changing agricultural practices, and intake of contaminants such as pesticides and herbicides are potential serious threats. Overall trends in curlew populations in California are unknown, and the species is poorly monitored in the state.

STATUS:
State: No official status. Formerly considered a California Bird Species of Special Concern (California Department of Fish and Game 1992), but no longer given this designation (Shuford and Gardali 2008).

Natural Heritage Rank: California rank: S2 (Imperiled); National status: N5B, N5N (Secure Breeding, Nonbreeding); Global rank: G5 (Secure; NatureServe 2006).

TRENDS: Overall trends in curlew populations in California are unknown.

North American Breeding Bird Survey (BBS) trends and abundance data: Trend and relative abundance are analyzed from 8 routes in California. Relative abundance equaled 0.57 individual per route. Data suggest a positive trend in California from 1966-2007; however, the trend is not significant (22.8% per year; P = 0.48; Sauer et al. 2008). Credibility of the BBS is poor, with a BBS Credibility Indicator equal to Red (data have important deficiency, such as low abundance and low sample size; Sauer et al. 2008). The BBS may include data from the Central Valley, where curlews do not breed, and the June timing of the BBS overlaps with Long-billed Curlew nonbreeding movements (G. W. Page, W. D. Shuford, and C. M. Hickey, pers. comm.).

Christmas Bird Count (CBC): Statewide, the number of Long-billed Curlews reported per party-hour has increased on the CBC from 1960-1961 through 2005-2006 (National Audubon Society 2006). However, this is associated with an increase from 14 to about 40 in the number of CBC circles reporting Long-billed Curlews (National Audubon Society 2006). The available analyses on the Audubon website are not sufficient to assess recent trends in winter curlew abundance in California.

RANGE:
Breeding:
Approximate timing: Small numbers of Long-billed Curlews breed from April to July in northeastern California.

Breeding atlas or lat-long locations: Not available.

Counties recorded: Inyo, Lassen, Modoc, Mono, Plumas, Shasta, Sierra, and Siskiyou (G. W. Page, W. D. Shuford, and C. M. Hickey, pers. comm.).

Migration: During migration, Long-billed Curlews occur widely in California, particularly along the coast, in the Central Valley, in the western Great Basin, and in the southern deserts.

Approximate timing: Spring migration generally extends from mid-March through mid-April. Fall migration occurs primarily from mid-July through mid-October. Peak numbers are seen in early spring, from 1 March through 1 April and in the post-dispersal period 1 July through 15 November (eBird 2008). Patten et al. (2003) reported fall migration peaks in the Imperial Valley in July and August.

Location of staging areas: Because Long-billed Curlews occur at many of the same coastal and inland locations in fall, winter, and spring, it is difficult to distinguish if there are migratory staging areas and if so, whether they differ from wintering areas. Further obscuring knowledge of staging areas is that small numbers of non-breeding curlews spend the summer in the same areas where they migrate and winter (G. W. Page, W. D. Shuford, and C. M. Hickey, pers. comm.).

Numbers, particularly high counts: Patten et al. (2003) reported 7,890 curlews on 28 July 1987 and Shuford et al. (2004) also reported 7,476 on a single day in August 1995 in the Salton Sink. The numbers of curlews migrating in autumn is around 10,000-20,000 individuals (G. W. Page, W. D. Shuford, and C. M. Hickey, pers. comm.).

Winter: Long-billed Curlews are present along the coast from Humboldt to San Diego counties and in the interior of the state in the Central Valley, Imperial Valley, and Carrizo Plain (Fig. 3.1). Small numbers of birds also winter locally in valleys within the Coast Ranges and in the southern California deserts.

Approximate timing: Wintering birds begin arriving 21 June in the Elk River estuary of Humboldt Bay (Colwell and Mathis 2001) where about 300 curlews are resident from June to April (Colwell 2006). Females arrive as early as late June, with males and juveniles arriving later (Colwell 2006). Individual birds typically depart to breeding areas in early April (Colwell 2006). In other areas, departure from wintering areas extends from late March to early May (Jurek 1973), with the majority

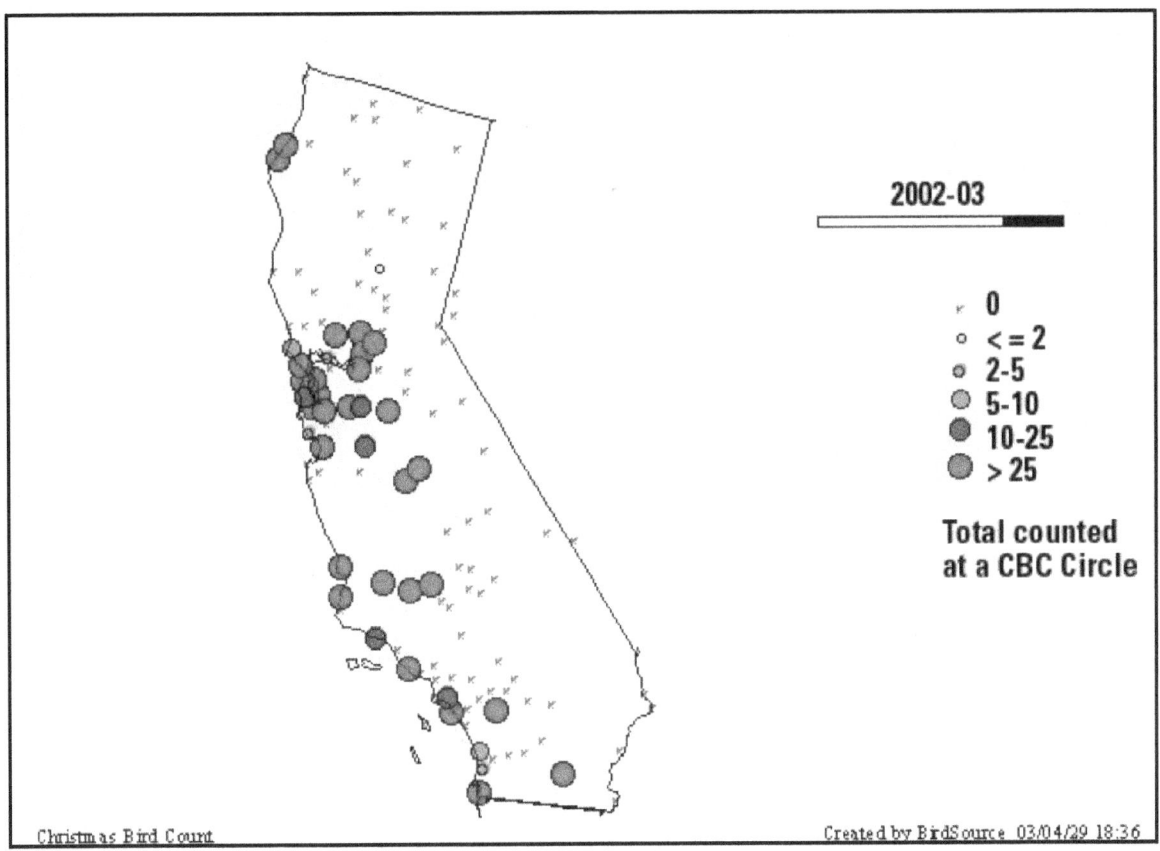

Figure 3.1. Christmas Bird Count data for the California region for 2002-2003 (National Audubon Society 2006).

of birds departing in the first half of April (Shuford et al. 1989).

ABUNDANCE AND POPULATION: Anecdotal observations and data from broad-scale and site-specific surveys suggest the breeding population is around 100-200 pairs (G. W. Page, W. D. Shuford, and C. M. Hickey, pers. comm.). The numbers of curlews migrating in autumn statewide are probably around 10,000 individuals (G. W. Page, W. D. Shuford, and C. M. Hickey, pers. comm.). The wintering population ranges from 1000-5000 individuals on the coast (Page et al. 1999) and is likely 10,000-20,000 individuals inland. Statewide CBC early winter totals from 1995-1996 to 2005-2006 averaged 7838 individuals (SD = 2013; National Audubon Society 2006). The highest and second highest totals were 11,082 (2004-2005) and 10,666 individuals (1995-1996; G. W. Page, W. D. Shuford, and C. M. Hickey, pers. comm.).

HABITAT:
Breeding: At Lower Klamath NWR, Siskiyou County, Long-billed Curlew nests were found in various low grass-forb communities (Brown 1986). Also, there are anecdotal observations of breeding in heavily grazed pastures, wet meadows, and salt grass (W. D. Shuford, pers. comm.).

Migration: On the coast, Long-billed Curlews are found in wetlands, on beaches, and in grassy areas. In the interior, curlews forage primarily on agricultural lands. Roosts of curlews have been found at water treatment ponds, agricultural waste water ponds, managed wetlands, and saline lakes (Shuford et al. 2002b, 2004).

Winter: Primary foraging habitats are tidal mudflats, sloughs, and salt marshes in coastal wetlands (Stenzel et al. 1976, Colwell and Mathis 2001, Colwell et al. 2002), wet pastures (Colwell 2006) and some outer coast beaches (Lehman 1994). At low tide, curlews aggregate on bay tidal flats (Colwell 2006); at one site with particularly high curlew densities, 10-15 curlews were recorded defending low-tide feeding territories ranging in size from 0.2-4.7 ha. The residency of individual curlews varies greatly (12-71% of 130 daily low tide observations made between June-April; Colwell 2006). Winter rains create supplemental foraging habitats in pastures adjacent to the bay, where they feed on earthworms and other invertebrates (Colwell 2006).

Non-wetland habitats used near the coast include wet and dry pastures and grasslands (Colwell and Mathis 2001), sewage ponds, and active and fallow agricultural fields (Shuford et al. 1989). In the Central Valley, curlews forage on agricultural lands including dry and irrigated pastures, dry and flooded post-harvest rice fields (Elphick and Oring 1998), alfalfa and other hay fields, fallow fields, and occasionally tilled fields (G. W. Page, W. D. Shuford, and C. M. Hickey, pers. comm.). In the Imperial Valley, curlews favor agricultural fields (Patten et al. 2003). Along the Salton Sea shore, they roost in shallow impoundments (Patten et al. 2003, Shuford et al. 2004).

MONITORING: Monitoring has included Point Reyes Bird Observatory's (PRBO) 1988-1994 surveys of coastal and interior wetlands in California and PRBO's 1971-2006 counts of wintering waterbirds at Bolinas Lagoon in Marin County. Habitat and geographic coverage by these surveys was not widespread enough to determine population size or trend for Long-billed Curlews in California.

RESEARCH: Because of the large numbers of indiviuals wintering in California, most work has focused on non-breeding birds, particularly at the northern limit of the species' winter range in Humboldt Bay (Colwell 2006). Other research in California has been on diet, particularly in coastal wetlands (Stenzel et al. 1976, Colwell and Mathis 2001, Leeman et al. 2001), and wintering territory habitat use and spacing (Colwell and Mathis 2001, Colwell et al. 2002). Only one study has been completed on seasonal abundance, nest site characteristics, and timing of curlew nesting in California (Brown 1986).

Long-billed Curlews establish and defend nonbreeding feeding territories in coastal wetlands (Colwell 2006), with the number of territorial curlews declining from fall into winter (Colwell and Mathis 2001). Curlews feed for similar proportions of time in summer (84%) and winter (88%). Summer diets differed because curlews ate many bivalves on 2 of 8 territories; diets also differed in numbers of shrimp, crabs, and worms. During winter, diets were similar among three territories (Colwell et al. 2002). Further work has examined the importance, use and distribution of non-breeding curlews, in a coastal estuary (Mathis et al. 2006), in rain-soaked pastures in the coastal environment (Leeman and Colwell 2005), and in post-harvest rice fields in the Sacramento Valley (Elphick and Oring 1998). Further research on wintering habitats, timing and use; breeding natural history; and effects of contaminants are important areas of research for the conservation of Long-billed Curlews in California.

CONSERVATION ACTIVITIES (ONGOING): None specific to Long-billed Curlews.

THREATS: Loss of habitat, including agricultural land to urbanization, and changing agricultural crops and practices are pressing threats. Pesticide and herbicide contamination, excessive grazing, and disturbance are other potential threats in California (G. W. Page, W. D. Shuford, and C. M. Hickey, pers. comm.).

Submitted by Gary W. Page, W. David Shuford, and Catherine M. Hickey
Revised by Stephanie L. Jones
Reviewed by Mark A. Colwell and Susan M. Thomas

Colorado

SUMMARY: Long-billed Curlews breed in the Central Shortgrass Prairie Region of eastern Colorado. Although there currently are no monitoring, conservation, or management activities specifically aimed at curlews, they may benefit from some of the grassland nesting bird initiatives and activities being conducted throughout the state.

STATUS:
State: Long-billed Curlews are a Species of Concern in Colorado and have been ranked as a Tier I Species of Greatest Conservation Need (Colorado Division of Wildlife 2006).

Natural Heritage Rank: Colorado rank: S2B (Imperiled Breeding); *National rank:* N5N, N5B (Secure Nonbreeding, Breeding); *Global rank:* G5 (Secure; NatureServe 2006).

TRENDS:
North American Breeding Bird Survey (BBS) trends and abundance data: Long-billed Curlews are reported on 15 routes. Relative abundance equals 1.24 birds per route. Data suggest a nonsignificant negative trend from 1966-2007 (-6.0%/yr; $P = 0.22$) within Colorado. Credibility of the BBS is poor, with a BBS Credibility Indicator equal to Yellow (data have a deficiency such as low abundance, low sample size, or significantly different sub-interval trends; Sauer et al. 2008).

Christmas Bird Count (CBC): Long-billed Curlews are not present in Colorado during winter (Andrews and Righter 1992).

Long-billed Curlew. Cory Gregory©.

RANGE:

Breeding: Long-billed Curlews are found primarily in the Central Shortgrass Prairie as well as on the Front Range, Southern Rocky Mountains, and Wyoming Basin regions of Colorado (Colorado Division of Wildlife 2006). The Colorado Breeding Bird Atlas (Kingery 1998) documented the highest statewide density of breeding curlews in extreme southeastern Colorado, in Baca and Las Animas Counties, primarily east of the Purgatoire River. Relatively high breeding density also occurs north of the Arkansas River, from El Paso and Pueblo Counties, east to the Kansas border. Lower densities of curlews occur sporadically throughout east-central and northeastern Colorado (Kingery 1998). There are few West Slope records (Bailey and Niedrach 1967). Low densities of breeding curlews likely exist in northwestern Colorado as breeding was suspected in Moffat and Mesa counties (Kingery 1998). Surveys conducted in 2004 and 2005 by Rocky Mountain Bird Observatory documented curlews only in southeastern Colorado (Sparks et al. 2005, Sparks and Hanni 2006).

Approximate timing: Kingery (1998) provided limited information on phenology. Courtship activity was reported as early as 19 April. Nesting activity was reported primarily in May and June. Fledged young were reported as early as 11 June and as late as 15 July. King (1978) observed mating activities between 12-15 April but thought that they were nearing completion.

Breeding atlas or lat-long locations: Evidence of breeding in Colorado was documented primarily on the eastern plains of Colorado (Kingery 1998). Breeding evidence was "confirmed" in 24 atlas blocks, "probable" in 21 blocks, and "possible" in 33 blocks.

Migration: Andrews and Righter (1992) described Long-billed Curlews as a rare spring and fall migrant in western valleys, mountain parks, and on the eastern plains of Colorado. They are regular migrants along the reservoirs in eastern Colorado (Bailey and Niedrach 1967). No large staging areas are recorded.

ABUNDANCE AND POPULATION: Breeding population was estimated at 943-3233 individuals based on Breeding Bird Atlas data (Kingery 1988). Populations are thought to have declined from historical levels, but few data are available to estimate the size of the historical or current population.

Surveys conducted by Rocky Mountain Bird Observatory in 2003 did not produce a sufficient number of observations of Long-billed Curlew in Colorado to estimate density within the study area (Hanni and McLachlan 2004). During 2005, a graduate research project was designed to estimate occupancy and abundance of rare grassland breeding birds in eastern Colorado (H. C. Tipton, pers. comm.). Occupancy surveys conducted between 1 May and 30 June resulted in detection of Long-billed Curlews on 18 of 282 randomly selected plots. Abundance surveys conducted 19 May through 6 June using double-observer sampling methods resulted in the detection of seven Long-billed Curlews on a total of six of the 282 plots. Data were insufficient to estimate occupancy, abundance, or density of Long-billed Curlews in eastern Colorado (H. C. Tipton, pers. comm.). Colorado was one of 16 western states involved in the 2004-2005 Rangewide Long-billed Curlew Breeding Survey conducted by the U.S. Fish and Wildlife Service and the U.S. Geological Survey. During the two-year survey, twenty-one 32-mile long road-based routes were run within the state's known breeding range. Long-billed Curlews were not detected during the survey on any of the routes (SDF). None of the above-mentioned survey programs were designed to specifically provide population estimates for curlews in Colorado.

HABITAT: Long-billed Curlews are found primarily on shortgrass prairies, playas, and in open water. They also use mixed-grass prairies, dryland and irrigated crops, Eastern Plains rivers and streams, grass- and forb-dominated wetlands, and sand dune complex grasslands (Colorado Division of Wildlife 2006). They Curlews were observed in highest densities within native prairie on sites with 3% or less shrub cover (Hanni and McLachlan 2004). During a study of breeding grassland birds in eastern Colorado in 2005, Long-billed Curlews were observed using grassland, dryland agriculture, and prairie dog colony plots (H. C. Tipton, pers. comm.).

MONITORING: There are no current Long-billed Curlew-specific monitoring programs in Colorado. Section-based surveys were conducted by Rocky Mountain Bird Observatory in 2003-2006 throughout the shortgrass prairie region in Colorado (Hanni and McLachlan 2004, Sparks et al. 2005, Sparks and Hanni 2006). Long-billed Curlews were observed during these surveys; however, the number of observations were low and the section-based monitoring program is likely inadequate to monitor population trends of this species.

Based on survey projects conducted between 2003 and 2005, the following recommendations were made for future monitoring of curlews in eastern Colorado: 1) employing a stratified sampling frame and/or one with unequal inclusion probabilities to increase sample size within the core curlew habitat while still sampling throughout the plains but at a relatively lower intensity; 2) tailoring plot size to Long-billed Curlew biological requirements; 3) timing occupancy visits closely together in May; and 4) do not survey on roads (H. C. Tipton, pers. comm.). However, based on data from the 2004-2005 rangewide survey (Jones et al. 2008) surveys would be more effective if conducted during mid-April in eastern Colorado to coincide with the local preincubation period. No obvious road-bias was demonstrated during the 2004-2005 rangewide survey (Stanley and Skagen 2007).

RESEARCH: King (1978) investigated habitat use of breeding Long-billed Curlews in Baca County. She was able to document breeding behavior, time of nesting, nest characteristics, and habitat use by breeding and foraging Long-billed Curlews.

CONSERVATION ACTIVITIES (ONGOING): There are no Long-billed Curlew specific conservation activities in Colorado at this time. Several specific conservation actions have been suggested to maintain and restore habitat and address other threats within the state (Colorado Division of Wildlife 2006). Avoiding destruction of large tracts of native prairie, providing incentives such as conservation easements, re-seeding with native, site-appropriate species, and use of compatible grazing management practices will help protect breeding habitat for Long-billed Curlews. Restoring playas and reducing groundwater pumping will also have wide-ranging benefits to wildlife in the region.

THREATS: Colorado Division of Wildlife (2006) assessed threats and concluded Long-billed Curlews were subjected to disturbance from motorized and non-motorized recreation and proximal non-recreation sources, habitat loss due to conversion of grasslands to cropland and native shortgrass prairie degradation, and general water pollution as well as concerns about pesticide spraying and run off.

MANAGEMENT: There are no Long-billed Curlew specific management actions currently taking place in Colorado. For nesting curlews, the Playa Lakes Joint Venture has developed habitat recommendations based on population objectives and modeling efforts. These efforts call for an increase in acreage of large blocks of shortgrass prairie with a focus on central eastern Colorado and the counties north of the South Platte River (Playa Lakes Joint Venture Landbird Team 2007). Their habitat recommendations include: 1) large blocks of grasslands at least 530 ha in size, 2) located within 1.6 km of a water source, 3) less than 81 ha of shrub, 4) less than 8 ha of woodlands, and 5) less than 20 ha of roads (Playa Lakes Joint Venture Landbird Team 2007).

Submitted by Suzanne D. Fellows and David S. Klute
Reviewed by Heather C. Tipton

Idaho

SUMMARY: There are low numbers of breeding Long-billed Curlews found in the state. Sporadic short term monitoring projects have been conducted. Idaho researchers were among the earliest to look at breeding biology, productivity, and habitat needs in Long-billed Curlews. As in most parts of their range, habitat loss is the biggest threat; however disturbance from recreational vehicles has also been documented.

STATUS:
State: Long-billed Curlews are classified as a Species of Greatest Conservation Need in the Idaho Comprehensive Wildlife Conservation Strategy (Idaho Department of Fish and Game 2005).

Natural Heritage Rank: Idaho rank: S3B (Vulnerable Breeding); *National rank:* N5N, N5B (Secure Nonbreeding, Breeding); *Global rank:* G5 (Secure; NatureServe 2006).

TRENDS:
North American Breeding Bird Survey (BBS) trends and abundance data: Twenty-four routes have Long-billed Curlews. Relative abundance equals 1.82 birds per route. There is a non-significant increasing trend from 1966-2007 (2.1; $P = 0.14$). Credibility of the BBS is good, with a BBS Credibility Indicator equal to Blue (Sauer et al. 2008).

RANGE:
Breeding:
    Approximate timing: Long-billed Curlews appear to begin breeding in early to mid-April throughout much of Idaho.
    Breeding atlas or lat-long locations: Long-billed Curlews breed at various locations throughout southern Idaho, including Camas Prairie Centennial Marsh, the Snake River Birds of Prey National Conservation Area, Magic Reservoir, Camas NWR, and the Teton Basin. They are also found in the Palouse Prairie and Boundary County in northern Idaho (Fig. 3.2).

Migration: Information on staging locations, timing, and numbers for curlews in Idaho is currently unavailable.

ABUNDANCE AND POPULATION: As of 1980, there were an estimated 3000–5000 pairs nesting in southern Idaho (Pampush 1980b). Current population size of this species in Idaho is unknown.

HABITAT: Long-billed Curlews use grasslands/wet meadows and shrub-steppe habitats for nesting.

MONITORING: The Teton Regional Land Trust monitors breeding curlews in the Teton Basin, using the regional protocol proposed by Jones et al. (2003). Starting in 2006, this protocol is also being used to survey curlews in the Boise District (Four Rivers Field Office) of the Bureau of Land Management (joint effort between BLM and Idaho Department of Fish and Game). Between 1977 and 1983, Redmond and Jenni (1986) monitored curlew populations in southwest Idaho. Sporadically throughout the 1980s and 1990s, roadside surveys were conducted on the Boise District of the BLM.

RESEARCH: Productivity of curlews in southwest Idaho was examined by Redmond and Jenni (1986) from 1977 through 1979. Adult survival was estimated at 85%, but because of limited data,

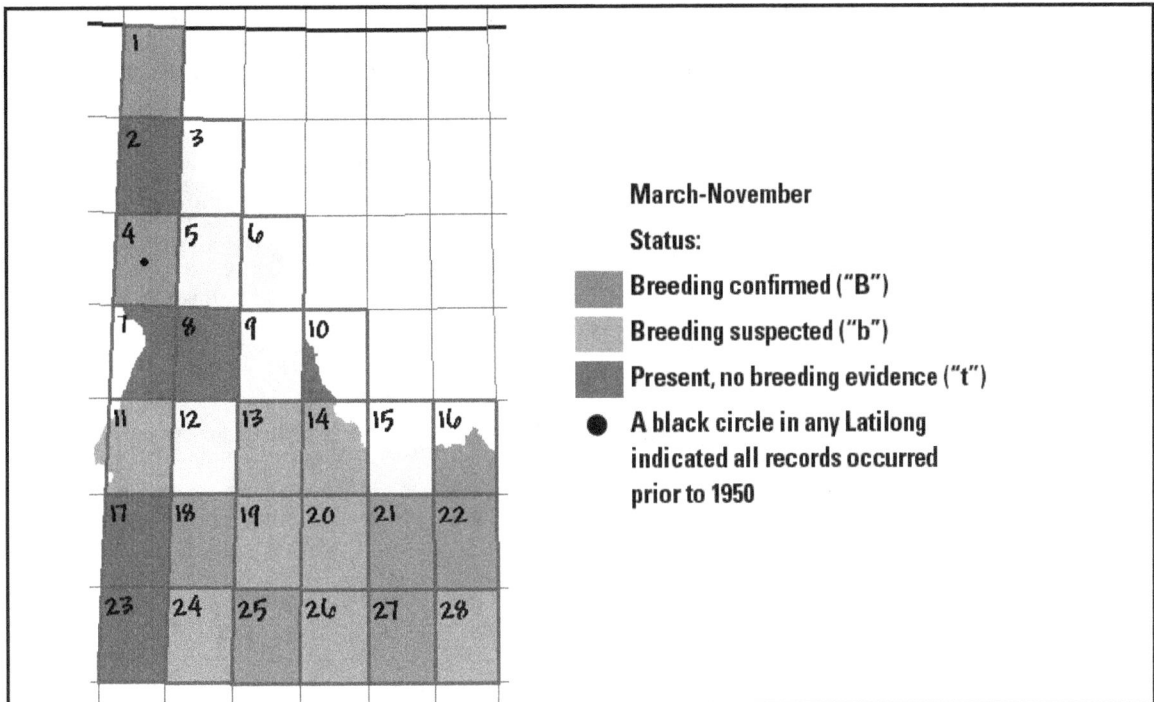

Figure 3.2. Breeding locations (lat-long) for Long-billed Curlews in Idaho. Period of presence is March-November (migration and breeding; R. Sallabanks, pers. comm.).

survival rates of subadults/juveniles could not be determined (Redmond and Jenni 1986).

CONSERVATION ACTIVITIES (ONGOING): Work by the Teton Regional Land Trust biologists has led to conservation actions such as local monitoring of Long-billed Curlews and the development of a landowner conservation working group. By using conservation easement agreements and restoring habitat, the Trust and its landowner partners have been able to protect nesting and brood rearing habitat for Long-billed Curlews and other species in the Teton Valley (Cavallaro 2006).

THREATS: The greatest threat to Long-billed Curlews in Idaho is loss of habitat. Conversion of grasslands to croplands, development of residential communities, increasing recreational use, and deposition of refuse have all resulted in loss of suitable habitat in Idaho (Jenni et al. 1981). Disturbance from excessive vehicle traffic (particularly off-road vehicles) and recreational use can be a substantial problem for nesting Long-billed Curlews, particularly during brood-rearing (Jenni et al. 1981). Pesticides can have detrimental effects on Long-billed Curlews, and pesticide poisoning has been documented in neighboring Oregon (Blus et al. 1985).

Submitted by Rex Sallabanks
Reviewed by Susan M. Thomas

Kansas

SUMMARY: Long-billed Curlews are known to breed in small numbers within Kansas, primarily in shortgrass and sandsage prairies of the southwestern third of the state. Migratory flocks, some in excess of 1,000 individuals, and regular observations of birds indicates Kansas contains significant habitat important to this species. There are no specific conservation actions aimed at curlew populations or habitat within the state. Management actions for shortgrass prairie, wetland management and shorebirds in general may benefit curlews if they are timed correctly.

STATUS:
State: Long-billed Curlews are a State Species in Need of Conservation.

Natural Heritage Rank: Kansas rank: S1B (Critically Imperiled Breeding), S2N (Imperiled Nonbreeding); *National rank:* N5N, N5B (Secure Nonbreeding, Breeding); *Global rank:* G5 (Secure; NatureServe 2006).

TRENDS: Data are insufficient to determine trends in Kansas.

North American Breeding Bird Survey (BBS) trends and abundance data: Long-billed Curlews have been recorded on only three routes in Kansas. Relative abundance equals 0.16 individual per route. There is a non-significant negative trend between 1966 and 2007 (-7.0%/yr; *P* = 0.56). Credibility of the

BBS data are poor, with a BBS Credibility Indicator equal to Red (data have important deficiencies such as low abundance and low sample size; Sauer et al. 2008).

Christmas Bird Count (CBC): No records (National Audubon Society 2006).

RANGE:
Breeding:

Approximate timing: The following breeding season chronology is inferred by back-counting, using the information which has been reported for Kansas as well as data collected in studies from neighboring Baca County, Colorado and Cimarron and Texas counties, Oklahoma. Males may arrive on territories as early as late March or early April (Thompson and Ely 1989, King 1978) and begin pairing upon the arrival of females. Egg laying may commence as early as 1 April and is most likely completed by mid-May (Cable et al. 1996, King 1978, Shackford 1994). Successful nests may hatch as early as the end of April; however downy chicks were reported through the end of May (Shackford 1994, King 1978).

Breeding atlas or lat-long locations: Breeding has been confirmed in the southwest corner of the state within Stanton, Morton, and Finney counties. Breeding is also suspected to occur in Hamilton, Greeley, Sherman, Logan and Rush counties (Busby and Zimmerman 2001; Thompson and Ely 1989). The Cimarron National Grassland (NG), the largest federally owned property in the state (Busby and Zimmerman 2001), is the main area where curlews are found nesting within the state. Cimarron NG covers over 43,700 ha in Morton and Stevens counties.

Migration:

Approximate timing: Migrating Long-billed Curlews pass through the state during spring migration between mid-March and the third week of April (Shane 2005). Adult Long-billed Curlews begin to be seen in groups in early July. Most birds have left the state by late August. In 1989, a particularly warm and dry fall, a late fall migrant was seen on 11 November in Morton County (C. D. Hobbs, pers. comm.).

Location of staging areas: As of April 2006, Long-billed Curlews have been observed in 53 of Kansas' 105 counties (Otte 2006). For the most part, numbers are not large and sightings are irregular throughout the state. Current migration is primarily through the western half of Kansas. Large flocks have been seen in southwestern counties during spring migration (Shane 2005). Quivira NWR and Cheyenne Bottoms are two sites where single or small groups of nonbreeding curlews are occasionally found (Thompson and Ely 1989). There are a few migration records in the south-central counties of Cowley, Sumner, and Sedgwick, despite extensive shorebird studies in the region (E. A. Young, unpubl. data).

Numbers, particularly high counts: Shane (2005) reviews migration of Long-billed Curlews

sighted in Finney and Kearny counties. High counts include sightings of 90 on 25 March 2005 flying over Garden City (Finney County); at least 346 in a foraging flock in Finney County on 2 April 2005 (Shane 2005); 1322 in 65 flocks (1-125 individuals) in a roost flight along the Kearny/Finney County line on 4 April 2006; the largest roost flight flock estimated at 320 in Finney County on 2 April 2006 (Shane and Shane 2006); and 105 in Gray County on 1 April 2006 (T. G. Shane, pers. comm.). A flock of 24 were reported to have spent two days on a Morton County farm pond on 12 August 1978 (Cable et al. 1996).

ABUNDANCE AND POPULATION: Long-billed Curlews are considered uncommon breeders within Cimarron NG; although they are hard to find and easily missed, 1-10 individuals can be seen and territorial adults indicate a small number of yearly nesters (Cable et al. 1996). Breeding population estimates range between 50 and 250 pairs (L.W. Oring, pers. comm.) to 168 pairs extrapolated from Breeding Bird Atlas data (W. H. Busby, pers. comm.).

HABITAT: Long-billed Curlews breed primarily in the High Plains physiographic region of Kansas. Shortgrass prairie and cultivated agriculture are the principal habitat types found in this region (Busby and Zimmerman 2001). Large, often disjunct, parcels, characterized by riparian, shortgrass prairie, sage-yucca or sandsage prairie, and croplands are managed for livestock grazing, energy development, recreation, and conservation by the U.S. Forest Service in the extreme southwest corner of the state; curlews primarily use the shortgrass and sand-sage prairies during the breeding season (Cable et al. 1996, Busby and Zimmerman 2001). Habitats used by staging curlews in the Quivira NWR and Cheyenne Bottoms areas include wetlands and burned areas (SDF). In southwestern Kansas, prairie dog towns (SDF) and dry upland pastures (Thompson and Ely 1989) are noted as being used by curlews. Most staging curlews near the Arkansas River Valley of Finney and Kearney counties have been seen feeding predominantly in alfalfa fields, fallow fields, recently plowed or disked corn and milo, or in cultivated wheat and alfalfa fields (Shane 2005). Many of these sites are in conjunction with, or in near proximity to, center pivot irrigation (Shane 2005). Sitings in south-central Kansas are in conjunction with lake edges, plowed fields, alfalfa fields, and wetlands (E. A. Young, pers. comm.)

MONITORING: Although there are no current Long-billed Curlew specific monitoring programs, Kansas Department of Wildlife and Parks (KDWP) monitored shorebird numbers and chronology throughout the state between 2002-2006 (Hands 2008). Section-based surveys in 2003 did not produce a sufficient number of observations of Long-billed Curlews in Kansas to estimate density within the study area (Hanni and McLachlan 2004). Kansas was one of 16 western U.S. states involved in the 2004-2005 Rangewide Long-billed Curlew Breeding

Survey conducted by the USFWS and USGS (Stanley and Skagen 2007, Jones et al. 2008). During the two-year survey, eight 32-mile long routes were run within the state's known breeding range. Long-billed Curlews were only detected during the survey on a single route in Morton County in 2005 (SDF). None of the above mentioned monitoring programs were designed to specifically provide population estimates for curlews in Kansas.

RESEARCH: There are currently no Long-billed Curlew specific research studies being conducted within Kansas. However, recent sightings of large numbers of spring migrants highlight the need for studies on length of stay, monitoring of numbers, habitat studies, questioned the role of farming practices to curlew conservation (Shane 2005).

CONSERVATION ACTIVITIES (ONGOING): There are currently no Long-billed Curlew specific conservation activities in Kansas. Conservation activities which would benefit the large flocks of spring migrants should be supported (W. H. Busby, pers. comm.).

THREATS: Conversion to agriculture and the changing of grazing and burning practices are identified as two threats to grassland breeding habitat of Long-billed Curlews. Very little intact native shortgrass prairie remains within the Kansas breeding range (W. H. Busby, pers. comm.). Near misses with electrical transmission lines have been observed (Shane and Shane 2006). Wetland degradation by siltation and polluted runoff as well as draining, filling, conversion to agriculture and excavation are also threats to wetland habitats used by migrating curlews (Playa Lakes Joint Venture Shorebird Team 2007). Although current chemicals used in alfalfa and other agricultural crops are reported to be safe, affects on Long-billed Curlews should be monitored (Blus et al 1985; T. G. Shane, pers. comm.). It is unknown if there are any implications, such as increased heavy metal or other contaminant levels, on Long-billed Curlews who forage for earthworms in areas served by center pivot irrigators (W. H. Busby, and T. G. Shane, pers. comm.).

MANAGEMENT: Habitat management activities within the Kansas breeding range should emphasize conservation of native shortgrass species and management techniques to maintain grasslands in as pristine a condition as possible. Where necessary, reseeding should be done with native shortgrass species. Current CRP buffer practices, which allow planting of tallgrass species, should be avoided in southwestern Kansas. The Cimarron NG is currently undergoing a revision of its grassland management plan. Long-billed Curlews have been identified as a regional U.S. Forest Service Sensitive Species and are listed as a Management Indicator Species for Grasslands. Under the current draft management plan, habitat improvements and management are proposed which would provide and manage for curlew breeding habitat (U.S. Forest

Service 2005a, b). Breeding habitat management issues for Kansas are addressed by the Playa Lakes Joint Venture Landbird Team (2007). They suggest the following: 1) large blocks of grasslands at least 530 ha in size, 2) located within 1.6 km of a water source, 3) less than 81 ha of shrub, 4) less than 8 ha of woodlands, and 5) less than 20 ha of roads (Playa Lakes Joint Venture Landbird Team 2007).

According to the Playa Lakes Joint Venture, foraging habitat is the major limiting factor for migrating shorebirds in the region. Their objective is to increase current migrant Long-billed Curlew use-days from 966 to 1376 within Kansas Bird Conservation Region (BCR) 19. They have recommended wetland management actions such as increasing the percentage of time wetlands hold water and managing existing wetland to better address the foraging needs of shorebirds and achieve these objectives (Playa Lakes Joint Venture Shorebird Team 2007). As there were no data available to determine use days in BCR 18 at the time the Playa Lakes Joint Venture was developing management recommendations, recommendations were not developed for BCR 18 (H. Hands, pers. comm.). The specific habitat requirements and timing of Long-billed Curlew migration will require management be more species-specific than what is sufficient for shorebirds in general.

Submitted by Suzanne D. Fellows
Reviewed by William H. Busby, Helen Hands, Thomas G. Shane, and Eugene A. Young

---

Montana

SUMMARY: Long-billed Curlews are found across Montana between March and September. They nest in native shortgrass prairies and are found on wetlands and around reservoirs during migration. There are no specific monitoring, conservation, research or management actions currently directed at curlews within the state.

STATUS:
State: Long-billed Curlews are a State Species of Concern and classified as a Tier I (Greatest Need) in Montana's Comprehensive Fish and Wildlife Conservation Strategy (2005). Montana Partners in Flight also ranks Long-billed Curlews as a Priority Level II, (Species in Need, lesser threat or stable/increasing population; Casey 2000).

Natural Heritage Rank: Montana rank: S2B (Imperiled Breeding); *National rank:* N5N, N5B (Secure Nonbreeding, Breeding); *Global rank:* G5 (Secure; NatureServe 2006).

TRENDS:
North American Breeding Bird Survey (BBS) trends and abundance data: Long-billed Curlews are reported on 31 routes. Statewide, relative abundance equals 2.29 birds per route. There is a non-significant negative trend from 1966-2007 (-0.07;

$P = 0.70$). Credibility of the BBS is marginal, with a BBS Credibility Indicator equal to Yellow (data have a deficiency such as low abundance, low sample size, or significantly different sub-interval trends; Sauer et al. 2008). Further analysis of the BBS data trends map suggests the species is declining in the eastern third of the state, while increasing in the western portion of the state. The results in the central portion of the state are less clear.

Christmas Bird Count (CBC): Long-billed Curlews are not found in Montana between September and March.

RANGE:
Breeding:
    Approximate timing: The majority of nesting takes place during the last two weeks of May and into mid-June (Davis 1961; S. J. Dinsmore, pers. comm.). There are less than 10 records which describe breeding behavior earlier than 1 May (D. Casey, pers. comm.). Silloway (1900) collected eggs in the Lewiston area which he estimated had been laid at the end of May as well as those he estimated had been laid several weeks earlier.
    Breeding atlas or lat-long locations: Long-billed Curlews are found across the state although they are more common east of the Rocky Mountains. On the Rocky Mountain Front, curlews are known to return to the same breeding areas from year to year.

Areas that appear to have higher breeding densities include the Rocky Mountain Front, Phillips, and Beaverhead counties, north Valley County (Lenard et al. 2003, 2006), and north central Montana in areas of remaining native prairie. The Montana Birds Distribution Database contains observation records submitted by volunteer contributors from across the state (Fig. 3.3). The Natural Heritage Program also keeps records of individual observations (Montana Natural Heritage Program et al. undated).

Migration:
    Approximate timing: On the Rocky Mountain Front, curlews arrive on their breeding grounds in mid-April and depart for the wintering ground in late July to August (D. Casey, pers. comm.). In the Bozeman area, spring migration periods are from 15 April to 5 May. Records of migration between 1995 and 2000 at Bowdoin NWR indicate that arrival dates ranged from 9 April to 16 May, although they arrived most consistently in mid-April (D. M. Prellwitz, pers. comm.). Generally fall migration statewide is from mid-July to September, with peaks in early August (A. J. Puchniak, pers. comm.).
    Location of staging areas: Freezeout Lake Wildlife Management Area (WMA; Putnam and Kennedy 2005), Bowdoin and Benton Lake NWRs, Lower Veseth and Nelson reservoirs, and Dodson Dam WMA regularly report fall migrating Long-

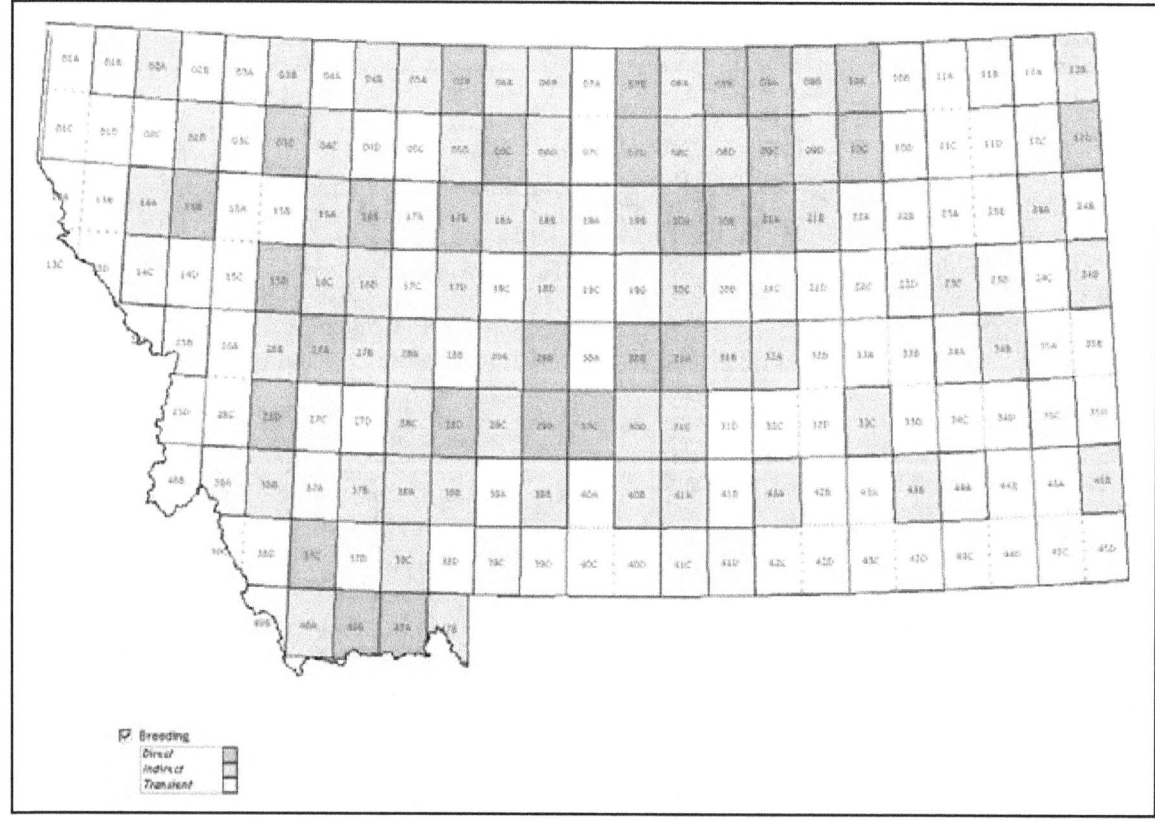

Figure 3.3. Map of Montana QLL (quarter-latilong) for Long-billed Curlews. Records are displayed by latilongs or mapping units formed by successive lines of latitude and longitude, marked at one-degree intervals. Latilongs are numbered, their quarter-latilongs are divided into A, B, C, D (Lenard et al. 2003).

billed Curlews (D. M. Prellwitz, S. J. Dinsmore, and V. Fields, pers. comm.).

Numbers, particularly high counts: Data collected for WHSRN designation at Bowdoin NWR indicate a group of 380 in August 2000 (D. M. Prellwitz, pers. comm.). Migrating Long-billed Curlews in groups of more than 50 individuals in Phillips County are also recorded (S. J. Dinsmore, pers. comm.). In late July and early August 1998 at Nelson Reservoir, numbers ranged from over 500 to a high of 768. Approximately 500 were recorded there the following year as well. Incidental records for migration at Benton Lake NWR consistently show high fall counts in the hundreds including a record of 334 in late July 1999 (V. Fields, pers. comm.).

ABUNDANCE AND POPULATION: Breeding population is estimated at 1500-5000 individuals (SLJ).

HABITAT: Putnam and Kennedy (2005) identify shortgrass prairie, mid-grass prairie, sage-steppe, and prairie potholes as preferred breeding habitats in the state. Long-billed Curlews prefer expansive, open, level to gently sloping or rolling grasslands with short vegetation, such as shortgrass or recently grazed mixed-grass prairie. They commonly nest in hayland, cropland, fallow or stubble fields (D. Casey, pers. comm.). During migration, birds use agricultural fields, grazed pastures, wetlands, and mudflats (Putnam and Kennedy 2005).

MONITORING: There are no current Long-billed Curlew specific monitoring efforts in Montana. However, there are surveys conducted through state wildlife grants to monitor waterbirds and grassland bird surveys. The American Bird Conservancy conducted an Avian Inventory along the Rocky Mountain Front in 2005. This inventory included point counts, landowner outreach, supplemented with Long-billed Curlew specific surveys (following USFWS survey protocol; Jones et al. 2008). Landowner outreach included having inventories conducted by local landowners (D. Casey, pers. comm.).

RESEARCH: There is no current research specifically on Long-billed Curlews. Montana Fish Wildlife and Parks has not issued any permits for banding or collecting specifically for Long-billed Curlews. Juvenile curlew banding has been ongoing since 1999; with one record of a juvenile banded that returned as an adult to Nelson Reservoir (D. M. Prellwitz, pers. comm.).

CONSERVATION ACTIVITIES (ONGOING): There are no Long-billed Curlew specific conservation activities currently ongoing in Montana.

THREATS: Conservation concerns include habitat loss (e.g. sodbusting, weed invasion, general conversion of prairie land to other uses), breeding habitat within the state that is either fragmented, unprotected, or mismanaged, and/or human-directed disturbance to grassland habitats (e.g. impacts of cattle grazing, roads, and adjacent land activities, pesticide

application, and draining of wetlands; Montana Fish Wildlife and Parks 2005).

MANAGEMENT: Proposed management strategies include providing large blocks of suitable habitat by preventing sodbusting, subdivision, and conversion of prairie lands to other land uses; delaying habitat management activities and grazing until after the breeding season (approximately 15 July); and striving to maintain vertical structure through appropriate management techniques such as light grazing, haying, and occasional prescribed burning during the non-breeding season.

Submitted by Allison J. Puchniak
Reviewed by Stephanie L. Jones

Nebraska

SUMMARY: A sizable portion of Long-billed Curlew range covers Nebraska, but the number of birds in the state and their range are poorly known. Furthermore, virtually no information exists on what habitat and other variables are important in sustaining Nebraska numbers, or which threats, potential or realized, are most critical.

STATUS:
State: Long-billed Curlews are a Natural Legacy Plan Tier I "At Risk" Species (Schneider et al. 2005). *Natural Heritage Rank:* Nebraska rank: S5 (Secure); *National rank:* N5N, N5B (Secure Nonbreeding, Breeding); *Global rank:* G5 (Secure; NatureServe 2006).

TRENDS:
North American Breeding Bird Survey (BBS) trends and abundance data: Long-billed Curlews have been recorded on 18 routes within Nebraska. Relative abundance equals 2.02 birds per route. There is a non-significant negative trend from 1966-2007 (-5.2; $P = 0.28$). Credibility of the BBS is marginal, with a BBS Credibility Indicator equal to Yellow (data have a deficiency such as low abundance, low sample size, or significantly different sub-interval trends; Sauer et al. 2008).

Christmas Bird Count (CBC): Long-billed Curlews do not winter in Nebraska.

RANGE:
Breeding: Historic Long-billed Curlew range in Nebraska is not well documented; however, they were probably found throughout the state although more commonly in the west (Ducey 2000). They were known from the eastern edge of the sandhills region (Bruner et al. 1904), Madison County until the 1900s (Sessions 1901), near Fort Kearney, along the Missouri River in northeast Nebraska, and between the Little Blue and Platte Rivers in south-central Nebraska (Ducey 2000). They were extirpated from eastern and most southern areas by the late 1800s. Since 1900, their range has generally been stable with highest densities in the central

and western sandhills and shortgrass prairie of northwestern Nebraska (Sharpe et al. 2001, Mollhoff 2001, Rosche 1982, Sauer et al. 2008). Eastern range limits roughly correspond with the eastern edge of continuous sandhills, with breeding apparently occurring in low densities at least as far east as Rock and Loup counties (Sauer et al. 2008, Mollhoff 2001, Sharpe et al. 2001, Ducey 1988).

Approximate timing: Nesting may be well underway by mid-April; fledged or nearly-fledged young have been observed by mid- and late June (Sharpe et al. 2001).

Breeding atlas or lat-long locations: The highest curlew densities are from central Cherry south to McPherson and west to Garden and Sheridan counties (Sauer et al. 2008, Wells et al. 2005). Eastern range limits roughly correspond with the eastern edge of continuous sandhills. Breeding birds apparently occur in low densities at least as far east as Rock and Loup counties (Sauer et al. 2008, Mollhoff 2001, Sharpe et al. 2001, Ducey 1988). Hypothetical current distribution and relative abundance of Long-billed Curlews in Nebraska are shown in Fig. 3.4.

Migration:

Approximate timing: Spring migration occurs in Nebraska with arrival at breeding areas during late March and early April (Sharpe et al. 2001). Sixty-one percent (61%; $n = 233$) of all spring reports, occur from 1-23 April (Sharpe et al. 2001).

Location of staging areas: Based on the few available reports during spring migration from non-breeding areas, birds may fly directly from areas out of the state to local breeding sites. Sharpe et al. (2001) cited only 9 spring reports prior to 2001 from non-breeding areas south of the Platte River and east of the Sandhills of north-central Nebraska. There are no modern records for extreme eastern Nebraska (Sharpe et al. 2001). Use of spring stopover sites in the west appears limited as well (Jorgensen 2006). Post-breeding and pre-migratory flocking in Nebraska is poorly understood. It is not known whether certain sites are used yearly as staging areas or whether birds favor specific conditions and opportunistically use suitable sites (Jorgensen 2006).

Numbers, particularly high counts: There are very few records of flocks of spring migrating Long-billed Curlews. High counts include 13 curlews in an alfalfa field 1.6 km west of Stratton on 30 March 2004 (T. J. Walker, pers. comm.) and 13 on 18-19 April (year not given) in the Lake McConaughy area (Rosche 1994). Long-billed Curlews generally attempt only one nesting each year (Dugger and Dugger 2002) and birds, perhaps failed breeders, may begin flocking as early as June (Sharpe et al. 2001, Brown et al. 1996). Flocking and migration continues from late June through July with numbers decreasing through August; there are only four records of birds in September (Sharpe et al. 2001). Birds remaining into late August and September may all be juveniles (Jorgensen 2006). Fall flocks can sometimes be large, such as the 67 reported from North Platte NWR on 24 July 1997 (Silcock and Jorgensen 1997), 170 at Box Butte,

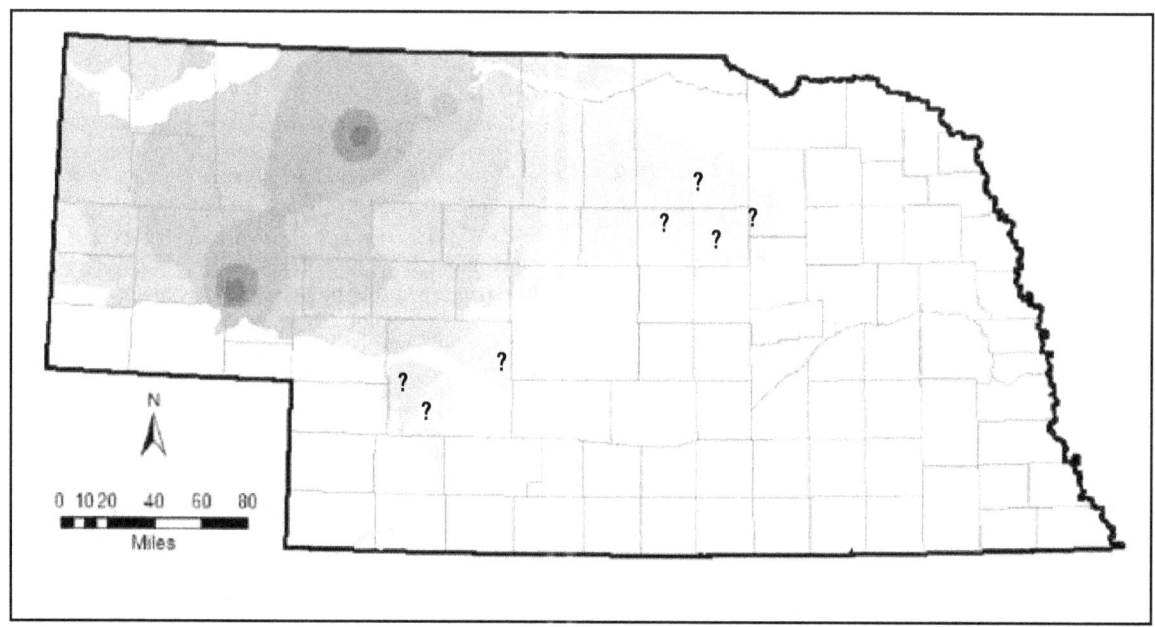

Figure 3.4. Hypothetical current breeding distribution and relative abundance of Long-billed Curlews in Nebraska using interpolated (inverse-distance weighted) BBS data. Range limits were determined using known occurrences from previously-mentioned sources and the boundaries of ecoregions where large tracts of suitable habitat remain and where Long-billed Curlews have been observed. Relative abundance was determined by interpolating (inverse-distance weighted) BBS data to produce a continuous spatial layer. The interpolated layer was then clipped to the ecoregions considered suitable. Darker shades indicate areas of greater abundance. Question marks indicate areas where occurrence is problematic (Jorgensen 2006).

Sheridan County (Skagen et al. 1999), and 200 in Garden County on 12 July 2004 (Silcock 2004). An earlier high count is 75 near Scottsbluff late August 1929 (Jorgensen 2006).

Winter: Long-billed Curlews do not winter in Nebraska. However, a bird banded near Antioch was later recovered on the Texas Coast at Palacios (Jorgensen 2006). This leads to conjecture that Nebraska birds winter in Texas and along the Gulf Coast rather than the Pacific Coast (Jorgensen 2006).

ABUNDANCE AND POPULATION: There are no current abundance or population estimates for Nebraska.

HABITAT: There is limited information available on specific habitats used for nesting and brood-rearing in Nebraska. Long-billed Curlews generally use short- and mixed-grass prairie with flat or gently rolling topography (Dugger and Dugger 2002) for breeding. Large, suitable tracts of native prairie habitat may be necessary (Sauer et al. 2008, Sharpe et al. 2001, Mollhoff 2001). Nests are located on upland areas (Sharpe et al. 2001) and Bicak (1977) found that proximity to meadows was important in determining nest location. This may explain why densities are higher in the Sandhills Alkaline Lakes region of Sheridan and Garden counties where moist, flat meadows are extensive. Bicak (1977) concluded vegetative characteristics were not a critical parameter in nest location. Closer examination of habitats used by curlews, particularly irrigated alfalfa or winter wheat fields, in southwest Nebraska may produce additional, noteworthy observations (T. J. Walker, pers. comm.). All modern spring migration observations in the Eastern Rainwater Basin have been of birds inhabiting sparsely vegetated areas near wetlands (J. G. Jorgensen, pers. comm.). Rosche (1994) noted that summer and early fall birds frequent bare, sandy flats near water, but also use recently cut hay meadows and other areas of short grass such as golf courses.

MONITORING: Outside of the single-season surveys conducted and summarized by Wells et al. (2005), there are no species specific monitoring plans in effect. There is an obvious absence of basic information about overall numbers and range limits in the state. Determining Long-billed Curlew status in Nebraska should be an initial priority, and a broad survey could be employed to determine distribution and abundance. Evidence indicates that the species has been extirpated from a large portion of its former range in Nebraska and data suggest declines are continuing. Surveys will not uncover the source of any such declines and thus should be a supplemental or corollary activity in addition to more focused research.

RESEARCH: Formal research in Nebraska is limited. Bicak (1977) was the only relevant dissertation or thesis located. Cole and Sharpe (1976) provide additional, albeit limited, information. A current project is studying movements and survival of chicks (C. J. Gregory, pers.comm.).

CONSERVATION ACTIVITIES (ONGOING): Even though Long-billed Curlews are of considerable conservation concern, there are currently no ongoing conservation activities within the state of Nebraska focused on the species. Areas occupied by higher densities of curlews and that have higher rates of production should be the focus of conservation efforts.

THREATS: Habitat loss is identified as the single greatest threat to the species (Dugger and Dugger 2002). This is relevant in Nebraska where conversion of native prairie habitat to agriculture is of particular concern in species conservation (Schneider et al. 2005).

MANAGEMENT: There are no Long-billed Curlew specific management recommendations for Nebraska.

Submitted by Joel G. Jorgensen
Revised by Suzanne D. Fellows

Nevada

SUMMARY: The breeding population of Long-billed Curlews in Nevada is estimated at 1150 individuals, with the majority in Ruby Valley. Curlews winter in Nevada in very small numbers, occasionally in the Lahanton Valley. They are uncommon spring and fall migrants. Long-billed Curlews generally prefer short-stature vegetation for nesting; however, they can be relatively flexible in their nest-site selection and are successful in habitats containing tall, relatively homogeneous vegetation. There is an ongoing breeding study in the Ruby Valley. Through the use of satellite telemetry, migration and wintering areas used by Long-billed Curlews which breed in Nevada are being discovered.

STATUS:
State: Long-billed Curlew is identified as a Species of Conservation Priority in Nevada's Wildlife Action Plan (Nevada Department of Wildlife 2005). *Natural Heritage Rank:* Nevada rank: S2 (Imperiled), S3B (Vulnerable Breeding); *National status:* N5N, N5B (Secure Nonbreeding, Breeding); *Global rank:* G5 (Secure; NatureServe 2006).

TRENDS:
North American Breeding Bird Survey (BBS) trends and abundance data: Trends and relative abundance are analyzed using data from 8 routes. Relative abundance was 1.45 and there was a non-significant negative trend from 1966-2007 (-3.1; $P = 0.75$; Sauer et al. 2008). Credibility of the BBS data are poor, with a BBS Credibility Indicator equal to Red (data have important deficiencies such as low abundance and low sample size; Sauer et al. 2008).

Christmas Bird Count (CBC): Long-billed Curlews have been reported in the same count circle of the CBC beginning in 1991 and in four of the last 16 years at Carson Lake south of Fallon. The highest count for these surveys was six individuals (National Audubon Society 2006).

RANGE:
Breeding:
Breeding atlas or lat-long locations: The Nevada Breeding Bird Atlas confirms breeding in Churchill, Humboldt, Elko, Lander, Nye, and White Pine counties (or within 1.3% of the blocks surveyed, 10 blocks). Probable breeding was reported for Douglas and Eureka counties (12 blocks, 1.5% of the total) and possible breeding was reported for Washoe and Lincoln counties (21 blocks, 2.7%; Floyd et al. 2007). The most southerly possible breeding record is in Lincoln County (likely at Pahranagat NWR; L. A. Neel, pers. comm.).

Migration: Uncommon spring and fall migrant. Important staging areas include Lahontan Valley, northern Washoe County, Paradise Valley, and Ruby Valley (L. A. Neel, pers. comm.).
Approximate timing: Spring migration generally runs from 15 March-15 May. Long-billed Curlews typically occur in early April in the Lahontan Valley with the earliest spring record of 7 February 1966 (Chisholm and Neel 2002). Primary fall migration is from 1 August to 15 September (eBird 2008).
Numbers, particularly high counts: Peak numbers are seen in fall migration, 1-15 August (eBird 2008). The high count in Lahontan Valley of a post breeding flock was 240 individuals on 3 July 1995 (Chisholm and Neel 2002). Typical flock size in this area is approximately 100 (L. A. Neel, pers. comm.).

Winter: Chisholm and Neel (2002) report early winter records for Carson Lake of 16 December 1990 and 19 December 1993, 1994, and 1997. There are winter records from 1 January-15 January (eBird 2008).

ABUNDANCE AND POPULATION: Breeding population is estimated at 1150 individuals (range: 1000-2500; SLJ). Ruby Valley has one of the densest breeding assemblages of Long-billed Curlews ever reported: 5 pairs/km² and a total population of 400-500 individuals (Oring and Hartman 2006).

HABITAT:
Breeding: While Long-billed Curlews generally prefer short-stature vegetation for nesting, they can be relatively plastic in their nest-site selection and are successful in habitats containing tall, relatively homogeneous vegetation (Hartman and Oring 2006a).

In Nevada, natural grasslands are scarce and highly degraded. Approximately 4000 km² of irrigated pastures and hayfields are suitable Long-billed Curlew habitat; both hayfields and rangeland are used by nesting curlews (Oring and Hartman 2006). In April, these habitats have similar vegetation structure and by mid-May, hayfield vegetation is taller and denser than rangelands due to irrigation and cessation of cattle grazing (Hartman and Oring 2006a). In Ruby Valley, hayfields were preferred over arid rangeland for both nesting and brood-rearing (Oring and Hartman 2006). Hayfield nests, both early and late-season, had denser surrounding vegetation then rangeland nests (Hartman and Oring 2006a). Nest survival was greater for early-initiated nests, nests with more uniform surrounding vegetation height, and nests located further from water (Hartman and Oring 2006a).

Migration: Long-billed Curlews tend to become habitat generalists during migration through Nevada. Staging areas typically consist of open, shallow water areas (e.g. wet playas, high elevation meadows). Habitats used on migration also include open, shallow water bodies such as wet meadows, flooded saltgrass, and mudflats (L. A. Neel, pers. comm.).

Winter: During the CBC, Long-billed Curlews have been observed using emergent marshes and flooded saltgrass or mudflats (L. A. Neel, pers. comm.).

MONITORING: None specific to Long-billed Curlews.

RESEARCH: An ongoing study on the population ecology of Long-billed Curlews breeding in hayfields and adjacent rangeland habitat was conducted in northern Nevada from 2003-2005 (Oring and Hartman 2006, Hartman and Oring 2006a, b). A preliminary analysis of three years of data showed that absolute nest success was consistently low among years and averaged 25%. Re-nesting occurred in 85% of marked curlews losing first clutches (n = 20; Hartman and Oring 2006a), and resulted in a per female nest success rate of 41 percent (Oring and Hartman 2006). Chick survival varied among years, with the greatest fledging success recorded during the wet year of 2005. On average, females fledged 0.16 female chick per year, which coupled with high juvenile and adult annual survival rates, corresponds to a slightly declining to stable population. However, high levels of egg and chick depredation, due primarily to mammalian predators, were seen (Oring and Hartman 2006). Additionally, egg sterility reduced the number of young hatched from successful clutches (Hartman and Oring 2006b). The success of Ruby Valley curlews was dependent on exploitation of a superabundant earthworm resource (Oring and Hartman 2006).

Using satellite telemetry, Long-billed Curlews were tracked from Ruby Valley to the Central Valley of California; Ensenada, Baja California; and south of Guerrero Negro, Baja California Sur (C. A. Hartman and L. W. Oring, pers. comm.). Information from this study can be used to begin to address several needs outlined in the Conservation Action Plan.

CONSERVATION ACTIVITIES (ONGOING): None specific to Long-billed Curlews.

THREATS: Potential threats include loss of habitat, including agricultural land to urbanization, pesticide and herbicide contamination, and excessive grazing. The primary threat is the plowing of native prairie rangeland for row crop production, causing declines in both population size and breeding distribution of curlews (Oring and Hartman 2006). Exposure to contaminants on the wintering grounds is likely impacting Long-billed Curlew breeding success by reducing hatching success. Among successful (at least one egg hatched) Long-billed Curlew nests, 20% and 24% of eggs failed to hatch in northeastern Nevada and western South Dakota, respectively (L. W. Oring, pers. comm.). This had the direct effect of lowering chick production and the indirect effect of lowering the fledging probability of chicks from smaller broods. An analysis of eggshells for the northeastern Nevada population showed that eggshell thickness was significantly thinner than pre-DDT specimens (L. W. Oring, pers. comm.).

Submitted by Stephanie L. Jones
Reviewed by C. Alex Hartman, Larry A. Neel, Lewis W. Oring, and Susan M. Thomas

---

New Mexico

SUMMARY: Long-billed Curlews are rare to fairly common but local in summer in grasslands in the eastern plains, and occasional in summer west of that area (Hubbard 1978). Breeding has been documented in 13 counties and suspected in two others. They are uncommon to fairly common migrants in the eastern two-thirds of the state and in the southwestern corner (which lies just north of an important wintering area in northwestern Chihuahua, México). They are generally rare elsewhere west of the Rio Grande Valley. Fall migrants continue into early December in some years, which may be incorrectly assumed to be wintering birds. Long-billed Curlews are irregular in mid-winter in the southern tier of counties.

STATUS:
State: Long-billed Curlews have been identified as a Species of Greatest Conservation Need in the state Comprehensive Wildlife Conservation Strategy (New Mexico Department of Game and Fish 2006). *Natural Heritage Rank:* New Mexico rank S3B (Vulnerable Breeding), S4N (Apparently Secure Nonbreeding); National rank: N5N, N5B (Secure Nonbreeding, Breeding); *Global rank:* G5 (Secure; NatureServe 2006).

TRENDS:
North American Breeding Bird Survey (BBS) trends and abundance data: Long-billed Curlews were detected on 17 routes. Relative abundance equals 0.68 individual per route. There is a non-significant increasing trend from 1966-2007 (5.3%/yr; $P = 0.38$). Credibility of the BBS is poor, with a BBS Credibility Indicator equal to Red (data have important deficiencies such as low abundance and low sample size; Sauer et al. 2008).

Christmas Bird Count (CBC): Long-billed Curlews have been recorded in 11 years on CBC circles in New Mexico since the winter of 1956/57. They were reported on only one count per year, with 6 or fewer total curlews counted in all but four of those years. Detected in 6 years over the most recent 14-year span from 1992/93-2005/06, which may represent an increase in regularity of the species in winter (or late fall), or it may reflect an increase in observers. All CBC records have been in the lower Pecos River Valley in Chaves and (primarily) Eddy counties, with the exception of a single occurrence in the eastern plains at Portales, Roosevelt County. The latter may have originated from a known wintering area in the southern Texas panhandle (Seyffert 2001a).

RANGE:
Breeding:
Approximate timing: Territory establishment and courtship: early to mid-April; nest initiation: late April; incubation: May to mid-June; early hatchlings: late May; adults with young of various ages: June to early July; adults with large young: mid-July; begin to leave breeding areas: mid-to late July (S.O. Williams III, pers. comm.).
Breeding atlas or lat-long locations: Although primarily found in the northeast quadrant of counties, Long-billed Curlews are also occasional, but probably regular, west of the Rio Grande Valley in the San Agustin Plains. Breeding has been documented in Colfax, Union, Mora, Harding, Santa Fe, San Miguel, Quay, Bernalillo, Guadalupe, DeBaca, Roosevelt, Chaves, and Socorro counties, and suspected in Torrance and Curry counties (S. O. Williams III, pers. comm.).

Migration:
Approximate timing: Spring migration runs generally from mid-March (occasionally as early as late February) through May, with a peak from late March to mid-April (eBird 2008). Fall migration occurs primarily from late July through October, continuing irregularly into early December, especially in the Pecos River Valley (W. H. Howe, pers. comm.); peak migration is from mid-August to mid-September (eBird 2008).
Location of staging areas: None known in New Mexico with any reasonable degree of predictability.
Numbers, particularly high counts: Few reports exceed 500 birds; however, there are spring accounts of 600 near Arch, Roosevelt County on 29 March 1999 and 400 near Anthony, Doña Ana County on 28 March 1984. Fall high counts include 500 near Loving on 26 September 1992, 1000 east of Roswell on 29 September 1972, and 2000 and 1000 at Grulla NWR on 8 and 11 October 2005, respectively.

Winter:
Approximate timing: Few mid-winter (January) records. December records and mid-late February records likely represent late fall/early spring migrants, respectively.
Locations: Virtually all winter locations are from Lower Pecos River Valley, southeastern

New Mexico, and Luna County, southwestern New Mexico.

Numbers, particularly high counts: Numbers are generally less than 50; however, high counts include 79 at Loving 19 December 2004 (Williams 2005), 125 in southern Luna County 6 December 2004, 177 on Loving CBC on 21 December 1995, and 51 on Portales CBC in Roosevelt County on 1 January 1983 (Williams 2005).

ABUNDANCE AND POPULATION: Population is roughly estimated to be at least 500 nesting pairs but probably fewer than 1000 pairs (S.O. Williams III, pers. comm.)

HABITAT: Primarily found at elevations of 1250-1980 m, occasionally to 2134 m, in the Plains-Mesa grassland and rarely Chihuahuan desert grassland (using classification of Dick-Peddie (1993)), particularly in grasslands with rolling topography containing swales with taller grasses. Breeds also in grasslands interspersed with scattered junipers (Juniper Savannah) or moderate densities of cholla (W. H. Howe, pers. comm.). Not found breeding in flat shortgrass prairie (e.g. Mountain Plover habitat; W. H. Howe, pers. comm.). Grasslands, harvested alfalfa fields and other harvested agricultural fields are used during migration. Desert Grasslands and agricultural fields are used during the winter.

MONITORING: There are currently no Long-billed Curlew specific monitoring programs in New Mexico.

RESEARCH: There are no Long-billed Curlew specific research projects in New Mexico.

CONSERVATION ACTIVITIES (ONGOING): Long-billed Curlews are a target species listed in the National Resource Conservation Services' proposed guidelines for the Environmental Quality Incentives Program in eastern New Mexico and should receive at least indirect benefits from habitat conservation. Currently a pamphlet is under development by the New Mexico Department of Game and Fish designed to familiarize ranchers with the species, add to knowledge of their breeding range, and help address future habitat conservation efforts.

THREATS: Breeding threats include loss of grasslands through conversion to agriculture or urbanization and excessive grazing.

MANAGEMENT: There are currently no Long-billed Curlew-specific management recommendations for New Mexico.

Submitted by William H. Howe
Reviewed by Sartor O. Williams III

North Dakota

SUMMARY: Long-billed Curlews were once more widely distributed and North Dakota probably sustained fairly large populations. Theodore Roosevelt and John James Audubon both observed and wrote about experiences with curlews in North Dakota. In the late 1800s, curlews were recorded several times as nesting on the prairie in Pembina County (Stewart 1975). Long-billed Curlews are much less common now compared to pre-settlement times, but nonetheless are an important piece of North Dakota's avifauna.

STATUS:
State: The North Dakota Natural Heritage Inventory lists the curlew as an Imperiled species (Dirk 2003). The North Dakota Game and Fish Department (NDGFD) designated the curlew as a Level I Species of Conservation Priority in the North Dakota State Wildlife Action Plan (Hagen et al. 2005).

Natural Heritage Rank: North Dakota rank: S2B (Imperiled Breeding); *National rank:* N5N, N5B (Secure Nonbreeding, Breeding); *Global rank:* G5 (Secure; NatureServe 2006).

TRENDS:
North American Breeding Bird Survey (BBS) trends and abundance data: Although Long-billed Curlews have been reported on a few routes, there are no trend data available for North Dakota (Sauer et al. 2008).

Christmas Bird Count (CBC): Long-billed Curlews do not winter in North Dakota.

RANGE:
Breeding:
Approximate timing: Long-billed Curlews arrive on breeding grounds from the last week of March through the third week of April. Nest initiation begins shortly after arrival (20 April to 20 May; Ackerman 2007). Chicks hatch from mid-May through mid-June (Ackerman 2007). Chicks fledge approximately 32 days after hatching.
Breeding atlas or lat-long locations: Township-Range (North to South, and East to West) include: 153-95-97; 148-86; 142-91, 100, and 103; 141-102 and 103; 140-88; 139-77, 102, and 103; 138-100-104; 137-100, 102-104; 136-100, 101, and 104; 135-100, 101, 103, and 104; 134-101 and 106; 133-81 and 106; 131-105 and 106; 130-105-107; and 129-82. Recent sightings come primarily from Slope, Bowman, Billings, Golden Valley, Stark, Morton, Dunn, Burleigh, Sioux, McKenzie, and McLean counties (Fig. 3.5).

Migration:
Approximate timing: Spring migration occurs in late March through mid-May. They leave the breeding grounds from mid-July through early August (Ackerman 2007).

Location of staging areas: The following townships and ranges have been used by staging Long-billed Curlews during migration: T135N R101W Sec. 18 N 1/2, T135N R100W Sections 24 SE ¼ and section 25 NE ¼.

Numbers, particularly high counts: On 26 April 2006, 25 curlews were observed feeding and performing mating displays near Amidon, Slope County. Thirty-four curlews were seen staging as late as 6 August near Amidon (D. S. Ackerman, unpubl. data).

ABUNDANCE AND POPULATION: Conservative statewide breeding population estimates were 518 and 2074 individuals in 2005 and 2006, respectively (Ackerman 2007).

HABITAT: Ackerman's (2007) analysis of vegetative composition and structural measurements at three nests, suggested Long-billed Curlews in North Dakota may prefer habitats which consist predominantly of native grass/forb cover. Nest sites were not placed in areas with shrubs, noxious weeds, bare ground, or on active agricultural land. Placement of nests was within 400 m of wetlands. Long-billed Curlews foraged in grasslands, low shrubs, and on prairie dog colonies. Numerous observations were made of foraging Long-billed Curlews in fallow fields. Curlews tend to move their broods for protection to slightly taller vegetation after hatching (Ackerman 2007).

Habitat used by migrating Long-billed Curlews included fallow agricultural fields, grazed shortgrass and mixed-grass prairie, and mechanically cut alfalfa and sweet clover fields (Ackerman 2007).

MONITORING: NDGFD is developing a Long-billed Curlew monitoring program and will continue to monitor curlews in accordance with the requirements of the State Wildlife Action Plan (S. H. Johnson, pers. comm.).

RESEARCH: Ackerman (2007) conducted a study to determine the distribution and abundance of Long-billed Curlews in southwestern North

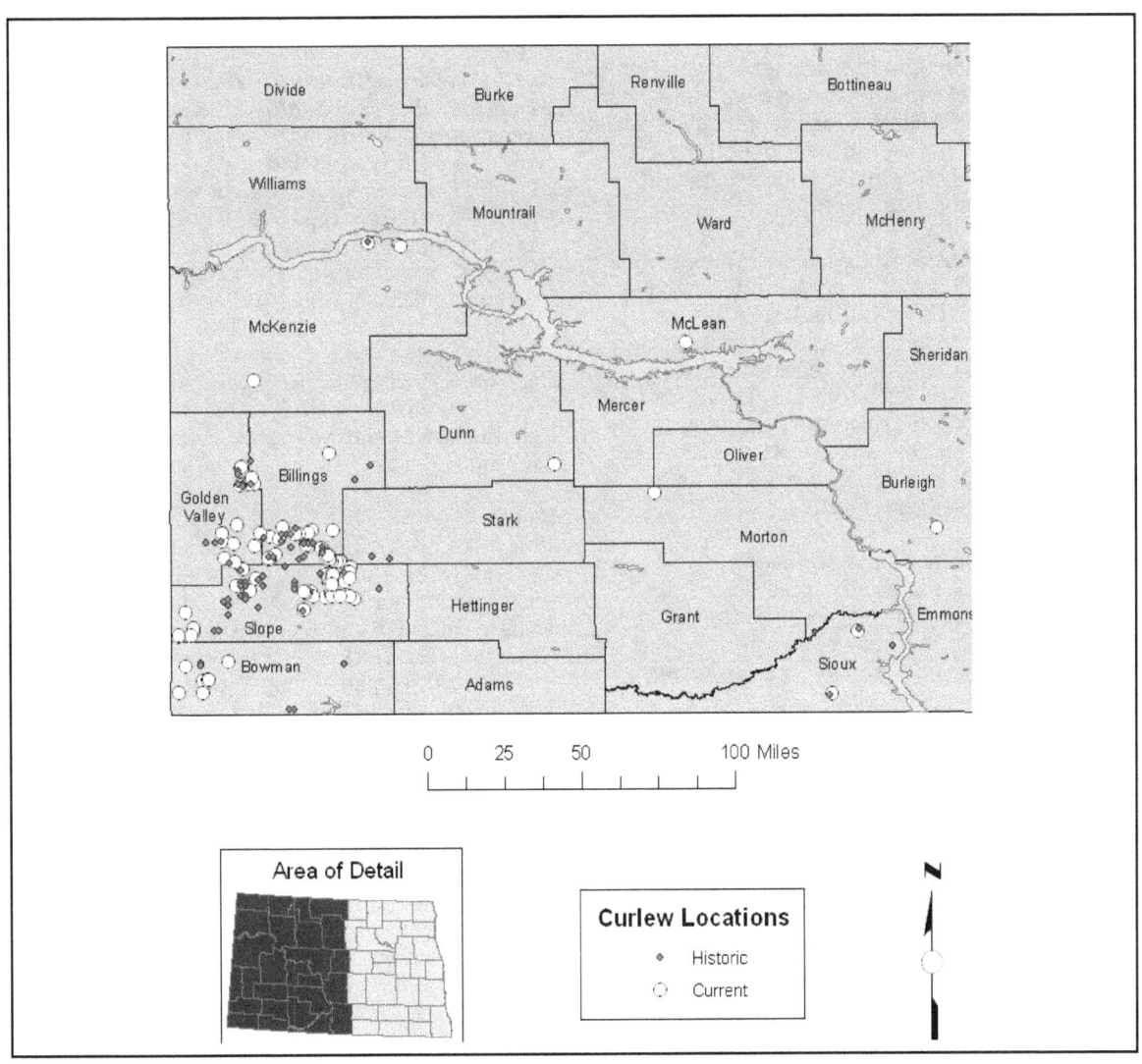

Figure 3.5. Historic (prior to 2005) and current (2005-2006) Long-billed Curlew locations in North Dakota (Ackerman 2007).

Dakota. Objectives included participation in the USFWS-USGS rangewide curlew survey, testing assumptions of the survey protocol by conducting double sampling intensive surveys in selected plots, obtaining an estimate of the population of breeding curlews in southwestern North Dakota, investigating habitat use, and development of a statewide monitoring protocol for North Dakota. Throughout the 2005 and 2006 field seasons, a total of 221 adults, 31 chicks, and 4 nests of Long-billed Curlews were observed in 11 counties. Survey routes run in 2005 and 2006 yielded 11 and 29 curlew observations, respectively.

Curlews were observed performing territorial displays (i.e., encounters between two or more curlews, mate advertisement), nesting behavior (i.e., incubation, brooding young), distraction displays (aerial or ground displays associated with nesting or defense of chicks), feeding (actively pursuing food), flying overhead (passing over area, not involved in territorial displays and other behaviors), and roosting (actively roosting, eyes closed, one leg up, head under wing, etc.), and actively mobbing observers, Northern Harriers, American Crows (*Corvus brachyrhynchos*), Red-tailed Hawks (*Buteo jamaicensis*), and Swainson's Hawks (*Buteo swainsoni*). Chicks were observed near adults and actively pursuing food. Most chicks were observed at a distance of < 5 m while adults actively performed distraction displays (primarily wing dragging; D. S. Ackerman, unpubl. data).

CONSERVATION ACTIVITIES (ONGOING): There are no Long-billed Curlew specific conservation activities ongoing in North Dakota at this time. However, several state and federal agencies, as well as the Northern Great Plains Joint Venture, are working on grassland conservation projects in southwestern North Dakota. NDGFD has published several popular articles on Long-billed Curlews (Bry 1986, Kreil 1987) and televised a feature on the Long-billed Curlew research project.

THREATS: Destruction and degradation of grasslands, particularly native prairies, are the greatest threat. Raptors, coyotes, grazing cattle during incubation, and humans can also be direct threats to curlews (Clarke 2006; D. S. Ackerman, pers. comm.).

MANAGEMENT: Based on preliminary vegetative analysis, habitat restoration of native prairie grasses and forbs are presumed necessary for breeding curlews. Grazing regimes should be manipulated to put cattle on pastures only after curlew nests have hatched (Clarke 2006; D. S. Ackerman, pers. comm.).

Submitted by Sandra H. Johnson
Reviewed by Daniel S. Ackerman

Oklahoma

SUMMARY: Local breeders occur in the shortgrass High Plains region of the Oklahoma Panhandle (primarily in Cimarron and Texas counties). They are uncommon to locally common, and an irregularly common migrant, primarily in the spring, throughout western and central Oklahoma. The distribution of Long-billed Curlews is fairly well documented within the state; however, much more could be learned about specific habitat needs and the most effective state-specific conservation actions.

STATUS:
State: Long-billed Curlews are a State Species of Conservation Concern and classified as a Species of Greatest Conservation Need in the Oklahoma Comprehensive Wildlife Conservation Strategy (M. D. Howery, pers. comm.).

Natural Heritage Rank: Oklahoma rank: S2B (Imperiled Breeding); *National rank:* N5N, N5B (Secure Nonbreeding, Breeding); *Global rank:* G5 (Secure; NatureServe 2006).

TRENDS:
North American Breeding Bird Survey (BBS) trends and abundance data: Although reported on three routes, only two of these routes regularly have Long-billed Curlews. Relative abundance equals 2.98 birds per route. There is a non-significant negative trend from 1966-2007 (-12.4%/yr; $P = 0.23$). Credibility of the BBS is poor, with a BBS Credibility Indicator equal to Red (data have important deficiencies such as low abundance and low sample size; Sauer et al. 2008).

Christmas Bird Count (CBC): This species has not been recorded on any CBC within Oklahoma for at least the past twenty years, and there is only one doubtful mid-winter record for the state.

RANGE:
Breeding: Long-billed Curlews occur in low densities within the middle panhandle counties. They are fairly common on private land and in agricultural areas to the north and east of Rita Blanca National Grasslands (M. D. Howery, pers. comm.).
    Approximate timing: Nesting occurs from May through June. Long-billed Curlews are single-brooded in Oklahoma.
    Breeding atlas or lat-long locations: Breeding was documented or listed as possible in four counties within Oklahoma (Cimarron, Texas, Beaver, and Cotton). Of the 12 sites located on the Oklahoma Breeding Bird Atlas, 6 were confirmed, 5 were probable, and one was possible. Fig. 3.6 shows the location of these sites; most confirmed sites are in the westernmost counties of the Panhandle (Smith 2004).

Migration:

    Approximate timing: In western Oklahoma, migrating Long-billed Curlews have been recorded from 22 March to 22 May and again from 1 July to 26 October. It has been noted that numbers are much higher in spring migration than in fall (Sutton 1967).

    Location of staging areas: Occurs statewide in appropriate habitats but most numerous in central and western Oklahoma (Sutton 1967). Long-billed Curlews are short-distance migrants, with a large proportion of the population wintering in the southern U.S. and northern México, thus regularly passing through western Oklahoma (Sutton 1967, Smith 2004). Some east-west migration occurs, resulting in a wintering population in southern Florida. They may gather in large feeding or migratory flocks in suitable habitat within the main body of the state.

    Numbers, particularly high counts: Historical accounts mention Long-billed Curlews being more common than at present. There are only a few recent reports of flocks totaling more than 500 birds. "Several hundred" were noted in the Panhandle on 8 June 1956 (Baumgartner and Baumgartner 1992).

Winter: There is only one "doubtful" winter record for the state but the date was not noted (Sutton 1967).

ABUNDANCE AND POPULATION: Dugger and Dugger (2002) referenced an older source of between 350-550 pairs breeding in the state, but noted that this estimate is dated. Smith (2004) estimated a total of 6 confirmed nests for the Oklahoma Breeding Birds Atlas, with an additional 6 probable or possible nests. Preliminary population estimates from systematic surveys estimate 100-150 pairs of curlews breed in Oklahoma (M. Howery, pers. comm.).

HABITAT: Long-billed Curlews primarily use a wide range of habitats during migration including dry shortgrass prairie, wetlands associated with alkali lakes, playa lakes, wet pastures, alfalfa fields, barley fields, fallow agricultural lands and harvested rice fields. In the Playa Lakes region of western and northern Texas, and presumably into Oklahoma, most of the flocks use sparsely vegetated wetlands, and use of shallowly flooded habitats was common (Dugger and Dugger 2002). Open grasslands, sagebrush prairie, and wet meadow were used during the breeding season. Long-billed Curlews

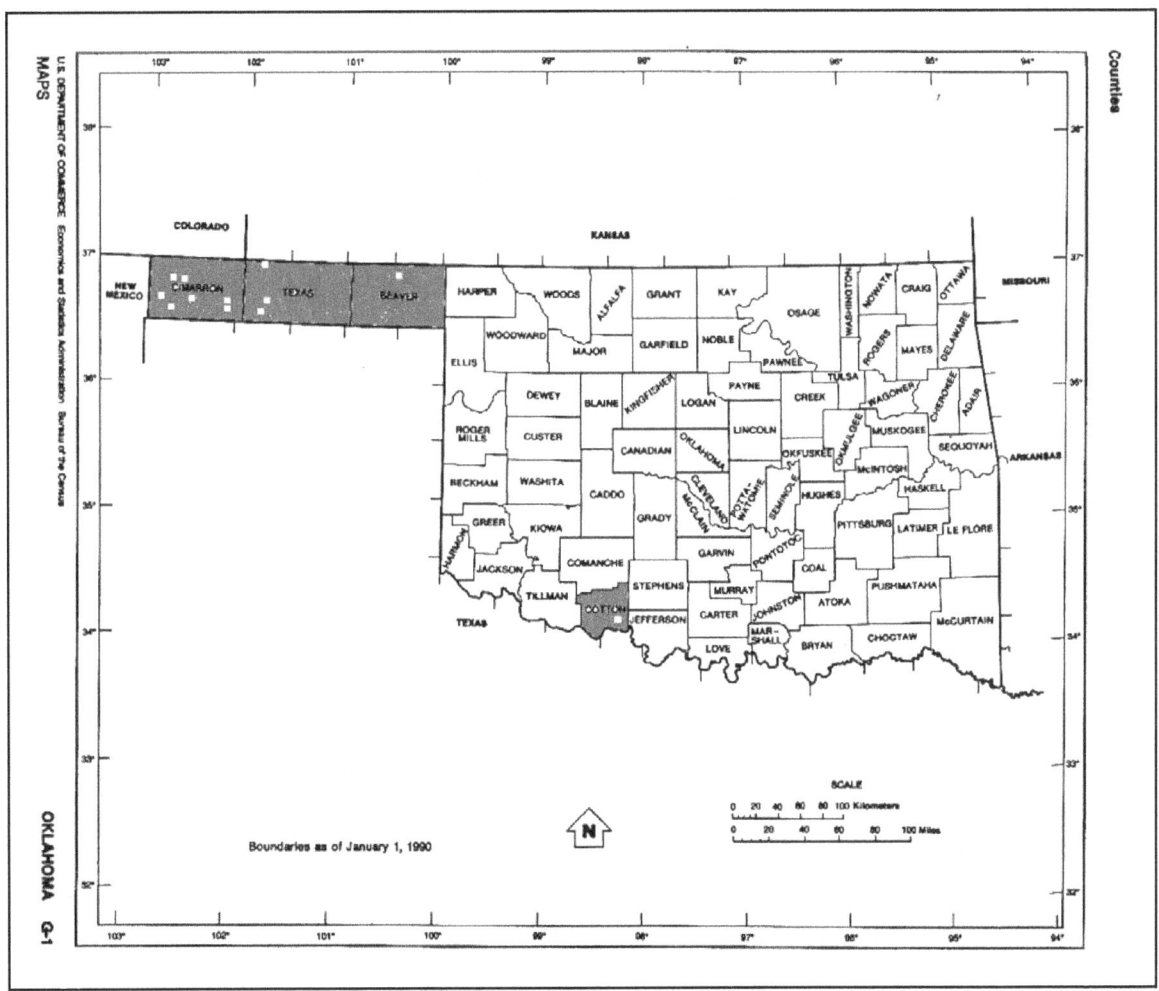

Figure 3.6. Locations of Long-billed Curlews reported during the Oklahoma Breeding Bird Atlas (Smith 2004).

occasionally nest on agricultural fields, usually near the edge, close to cover. Native shortgrass prairie, planted winter wheat fields, fallow wheat and milo fields, ungrazed CRP fields, and around hog farm lagoons are also used. They are often observed near damp low spots, such as un-cropped playas, which may be important as feeding areas for chicks (M. D. Howery, pers. comm.). They seem to occur less commonly in areas with rolling or rough topography; most records are of birds in relatively flat, playa lakes areas (M. D. Howery, pers. comm.).

MONITORING: Location information was collected for Long-billed Curlews as part of a State Wildlife Grant surveying for Mountain Plovers; if a curlew monitoring plan is developed for Oklahoma, information gathered during this study will be used (M. D. Howery, pers. comm.).

RESEARCH: No known Long-billed Curlew specific research projects.

CONSERVATION ACTIVITIES (ONGOING): None specific to Long-billed Curlews.

THREATS:
Breeding: As with most grassland and prairie species, the continued loss of grasslands through conversion to agriculture or urbanization is the primary threat.

MANAGEMENT: Although the distribution of Long-billed Curlews is fairly well documented within the state, more needs to be learned about specific habitat needs and the most effective conservation actions (M. D. Howery, pers. comm.).

Submitted by David J. Krueper
Reviewed by Mark D. Howery and William H. Howe

Oregon

SUMMARY: Long-billed Curlews are locally common east of the Cascade Range during the breeding season, particularly in the Columbia Basin and Northern Basin and Range. Curlews are considered rare along the coast in winter, with limited sightings in Coos Bay and Tillamook Bay. Concern for this species stems from loss of habitat, population declines in some areas, and human disturbance during nesting. The Oregon Conservation Strategy (OCS) identifies the Columbia Plateau and Northern Basin and Range as the highest priority ecoregions in the state to implement conservation actions, particularly conservation of short grass habitats and sub-irrigated meadows. There is historic information of curlew distribution in the state and the Willamette Valley.

STATUS:
State: Long-billed Curlews are listed as a "Vulnerable" sensitive species in the OCS (Oregon Department of Fish and Wildlife 2005).

Natural Heritage Rank: Oregon rank: S3B (Vulnerable Breeding); *National rank:* N5N, N5B (Secure Nonbreeding, Breeding); *Global rank:* G5 (Secure; NatureServe 2006).

TRENDS:
North American Breeding Bird Survey (BBS) trends and abundance data: Long-billed Curlews are reported on 26 routes. Relative abundance equals 2.34 birds per route. There is a significant positive trend from 1966-2007 (8.2%/yr; P = 0.05). Credibility of the BBS is moderate, with a BBS Credibility Indicator equal to Yellow (data have a deficiency; Sauer et al. 2008).

Christmas Bird Count (CBC): Curlews have been reported on 5 count circles on the coast in small numbers (0-9 birds) for the past 13 of 39 years (National Audubon Society 2006). The highest recorded CBC (9 individuals) was reported for Coos County in 1995 (National Audubon Society 2006).

RANGE:
Breeding: Curlews mainly breed in the Columbia Plateau and Northern Basin and Range ecoregions of eastern Oregon.
    Approximate timing: Curlews typically arrive on the breeding grounds in late March, eggs are laid during the last two weeks of April and hatching generally occurs during May and early June. Birds arrive as early as 14 March on the breeding grounds at Malheur NWR (Paulson 1993). Transients to the area move on by 1 May and nesting typically occurs in May with most eggs hatching during the last week of May (Littlefield 1990). Nesting occurs through late June in the Harney Basin, which encompasses Malheur NWR, however most young fledge by mid-July (G. L. Ivey, C. Foster, and D. G. Paullin, pers. comm.). Further north, the earliest reported curlew was 16 March; hatching dates ranged from 1 May to 4 June.
    Breeding atlas or lat-long locations: The Oregon Breeding Bird Atlas (Adamus et al. 2001) shows confirmed breeding of Long-billed Curlews in Baker, Crook, Gilliam, Grant, Harney, Jefferson, Lake, Malheur, Morrow, Umatilla, and Union counties (26% of all hexagons surveyed). Probable breeding was reported for Baker, Benton, Crook, Grant, Harney, Klamath, Lake, Malheur, Morrow, Umatilla, Union, Wheeler, and Wallowa counties (31% of all hexagons surveyed). Possible breeding was reported for Baker, Crook, Gilliam, Grant, Harney, Klamath, Lake, Malheur, Morrow, Polk, Umatilla, Union, Wheeler, and Wallowa counties (43% of hexagons surveyed).

Migration: Long-billed Curlews are one of the first shorebirds to be seen in Oregon each spring.
    Approximate timing: The earliest the species has been reported in spring is 14 March at Malheur NWR (Paulson 1993). Paulson (1993) notes that later spring records along the coast and in the Willamette Valley are probably restricted northward movements of subadults after adults have set up territories on the breeding range. Females

leave breeding areas first, departing by mid-June (Pampush 1980a). Most adults have left the breeding range by late July/early August; juveniles depart from mid-August to mid-September (Nehls 1994). Gullion (1951) and Nehls (1994) note individual records in interior western Oregon from early July to mid-September; the latest fall sighting at Malheur NWR is mid-October (Paulson 1993).

Location of staging areas: Inland curlews typically stage in the same agricultural foraging habitats used during brood rearing; along the coast they use estuaries and wet pastures. The majority of curlews fly directly between Oregon breeding grounds and wintering grounds in California and México (Paulson 1993).

Numbers, particularly high counts: During spring migration, flocks of 10-50 are common; sometimes 100 can be seen (Dugger and Dugger 2003). A peak number of 1327 curlews were observed on 24 April 1975 in the Harney Basin (G. L. Ivey, C. D. Littlefield, and D. G. Paullin, pers. comm.). The highest post-breeding concentration was reported near Boardman with 600 curlews on 8 July 1980 (Paulson 1993).

Winter: Most of Oregon's breeding birds winter in California (Nehls 1994), thus the species is rare in Oregon during the winter.

Approximate timing: A few birds have been reported on the coast as early as late June (Dugger and Dugger 2003).

Location: Notable sites include Coos, Tillamook, and Yaquina bays (Contreras 1998). There are no records of the species east of the Cascades or interior western Oregon in winter (H. B. Nehls, pers. comm.).

Numbers, particularly high counts: Very few records are available for this species in the winter. The largest 'flock' to be reported in winter totaled 36 birds at the north spit of Coos Bay (Contreras 1998).

ABUNDANCE AND POPULATION: Pampush's study of curlew distribution and abundance throughout the Columbia and Northern Great Basin combined with questionnaires to local area/species experts in 1980 provides the most recent comprehensive curlew estimates for Oregon (see Table 3.1). Jewett (1929)

noted that the species was reported as a common summer resident in the Grande Ronde Valley, Union County, in the early 1900's, yet by 1929 they were absent. No other range shifts have been noted in the state. An estimate for southern Lake and Klamath counties could not be separated from the total of 200 pairs given for the entire 'Upper Klamath Lake Drainage' in Oregon and California (Pampush 1980b). The counties in the California portion of the drainage supported the majority of the pairs at the time. We estimated a statewide total of at least 3500 pairs of breeding curlews in 1980. However, the data have limitations due to time and logistical constraints on the total survey area. Further, the data are approximately 25-years old and agricultural conversion has continued within curlew habitat.

HABITAT: Throughout the state, curlews prefer nesting habitats that are composed of low, sparse vegetation with an open ground component. Flat to rolling topography is preferred, and nests are often found near a partially concealing object such as a rock or cow pie. Breeding habitats consists of mixed-grass meadows or annual grassland (e.g. cheatgrass, medusahead (*Taeniatherum asperum*)) associations, particularly in northeastern Oregon. Structural characteristics, specifically low vertical profile and low vertical density, appear to influence curlew habitat selection during the breeding period. In a 2-year study of habitat use and nest site selection in the Columbia Basin (Morrow and Umatilla counties), researchers found that the greatest density of curlews nested in annual grasslands. Annual grasslands in this area were composed mainly of cheatgrass and supported nest densities of up to 9 nests/40 ha (average 3.6 nest/40 ha). Bunchgrass habitat, primarily consisting of bluebunch wheatgrass (*Pseudoroegneria spicata*), needle-and-thread grass, and Sandberg's bluegrass, supported the second largest densities with an average nest density of 1.4 nests/40 ha, followed by dense forb at 1.3 nests/40 ha, open low shrub at 1.0 nest/40 ha and bitterbrush at 0.5 nest/40 ha (Pampush and Anthony 1993). An earlier report by Pampush (1980b) indicates curlew use of saltgrass/greasewood (*Distichlis spicata/Sarcobatus vermiculatus*) associations in the southeastern portion of the state (near Lake Abert and Summer Lake) in low

Table 3.1. Location and number of Long-billed Curlew pairs found in Oregon.

Oregon Sub-basin	Number (pairs)	Oregon Counties
Mid-Columbia	2500	Wasco, Jefferson, Deschutes, northern Klamath, Sherman, Gilliam, Wheeler, Crook, Morrow, Umatilla, and northern Grant
Oregon Closed	750	Harney, Lake, southern Grant, and southern Crook
Central Snake	200	Malheur, Baker, southeastern Harney
Upper Klamath Lake Drainage	~50	Lake and Klamath
Total	3500	

densities (0.5 pairs/40 ha), however these habitats were not thoroughly surveyed due to logistical constraints. Pampush and Anthony (1993) also found that adults with and without broods generally used similar habitats. Those with broods used cheatgrass habitats significantly more than the proportion available ($P < 0.05$) and adults without broods tended to prefer this habitat as well. Cropland (mainly wheat, potato, and alfalfa) were used by both adults with and without broods until vegetation height reached > 30 cm tall, particularly on Umatilla NWR. Breeding densities tend to increase from south to north, east of the Cascade crest. Curlews are not known to breed west of the Cascade crest, although a small number of nonbreeding individuals summer on the coast (Nehls 1994). Inland curlews typically stage in the same agricultural foraging habitats used during brood rearing; along the coast they use estuaries and wet pastures. Preferred wintering habitat includes tidal estuaries, wet pastures, and occasionally sandy beaches.

MONITORING: Current monitoring programs include breeding surveys using point count techniques on Umatilla NWR in spring 2005 and 2006 and are planned for 2007. The data will be used to help guide habitat management for the benefit of nesting curlews. Each year, curlews are reported along various BBS routes in eastern Oregon (see above). Several status documents have been produced in the recent past for this species in Oregon (Pampush 1980a, Nehls 1994). They provide strong baseline data from numerous historic monitoring efforts during the breeding season and on migration. Oregon Department of Fish and Wildlife recorded opportunistic sightings of this species during annual breeding shorebird surveys in the 1980's along Summer Lake; however, no organized surveys have been conducted in the area.

RESEARCH: Few significant studies have been conducted in Oregon for this species in the past 20 years; however a cooperative research project between USGS and the USFWS was initiated in 2007 on Umatilla NWR as part of an overall study on nesting habitat use (S. M. Thomas, pers. comm.). Pampush (1980b) and Pampush and Anthony (1993) provide information on nest success, habitat utilization and nest-site selection of curlews in the Columbia Basin. In addition, Blus et al. (1985) provides information on the impact of contaminants on curlews in the Columbia Basin.

CONSERVATION ACTIVITIES (ONGOING): Long-billed Curlews are listed as a high priority species in the OCS with specific recommendations to minimize human disturbance at known nesting areas from 15 March through July (Oregon Department of Fish and Wildlife 2005). The OCS identifies restoration of large patches of short grass habitat as a key conservation action for this species (Oregon Department of Fish and Wildlife 2005). Curlews are abundant on parts of Umatilla NWR and adjacent private lands. The Intermountain West Shorebird Conservation Plan (Oring et al. 1999) specifically

identifies Harney Basin as an important breeding area. It identifies several measures to increase water availability during key brood rearing periods such as the development of impoundments, securing water rights on public and private lands, and the development of incentives for private land managers to use more compatible water management practices. Maintaining and increasing curlew nesting and foraging habitat are listed as objectives in the Umatilla NWR Comprehensive Conservation Plan (U.S. Fish and Wildlife Service 2007). Outreach efforts to private land managers, particularly on range lands, is identified in the OCS as a conservation action that will benefit curlews (Oregon Department of Fish and Wildlife 2005).

THREATS: One of the most pervasive threats to curlews is loss of breeding habitat in Oregon. Specifically, urbanization of preferred habitats and conversion of cropland to unsuitable crop types such as cottonwood or grapes. Large ranching operations (cattle and hay) support curlew breeding and brood rearing habitat. If economics no longer support large ranches, urban development of the area will limit curlew breeding habitat. To counter this threat, a comprehensive inventory of breeding distribution and abundance is needed. This inventory, when compared to data collected by Pampush (1980a), and an assessment of habitat changes since then, will provide a framework from which to direct conservation actions in breeding areas with the highest impact from habitat loss.

Little is known about basic reproductive success in different habitats, response to habitat improvements, minimum habitat requirements, or response to human disturbance or predation. This information, combined with current information on distribution and abundance, will assist land managers in habitat conservation and long-term planning for curlew conservation.

Agriculture can play a large role in fledgling success given the amount of time spent in agriculture during brood rearing. Research is needed to determine nest and/or fledgling success in short grass croplands throughout the state. Traditionally, the use of flood irrigation provided a good source of forage from wet soils and dense vegetation in agricultural fields used as thermal cover for broods. To conserve water and because of increasing costs of irrigation, land managers are adopting more conservative measures, such as sprinkler irrigation. This switch results in a loss of suitable brood rearing habitat.

Limited data show pesticide use during the breeding season can impact curlews (Blus et al. 1985). Dieldrin and chlordane poisoning appear to have caused the deaths of two male curlews and likely was an indirect cause of death in one female collected in Morrow and Umatilla counties during the early 1980s (Blus et al. 1985). Seven eggs collected from the same area and tested for pesticide residues during the same period showed DDE residues, but egg shells were not detectably thinner than uncontaminated eggs

(Blus et al. 1985). Other pesticides were detected irregularly and at low levels which lead researchers to believe that contaminants had little influence on reproductive success of curlews in this area (Blus et al. 1985). These samples were of limited number and scope, however.

MANAGEMENT: No Long-billed Curlew specific management recommendations for Oregon exist. However, land managers are restoring native grasslands in cheatgrass-dominated habitats.

Submitted by Susan M. Thomas
Reviewed by Peg Boulay, Howard Browers, and Gary L. Ivey

South Dakota

SUMMARY: Uncommon breeder, although common in local areas. Historically, the range in South Dakota has contracted, and Long-billed Curlews are no longer found east of the Missouri River.

STATUS: Uncommon migrant and summer resident west; causal migrant east, formally breeding east (Tallman et al. 2002).

State: Long-billed Curlews are listed as a Species of Greatest Conservation Need in South Dakota due to a significant portion of their breeding range occurring here (South Dakota Department of Wildlife 2006).

Natural Heritage Rank: South Dakota rank: S3B (Vulnerable Breeding); *National rank:* N5N, N5B (Secure Nonbreeding, Breeding);

Global rank: G5 (Secure; NatureServe 2006).

TRENDS:
North American Breeding Bird Survey (BBS) trends and abundance data: Thirteen routes have recorded Long-billed Curlews. Relative abundance equals 1.59 birds per route. There is a nonsignificant decreasing trend from 1966-2007 (-2.6%/yr; $P = 0.07$), a nonsignificant negative trend from 1966-1979 ($n = 8$), and again in 1980-2007 ($n = 11$; Sauer et al. 2008). Credibility of the BBS is moderate, with a BBS credibility indicator equal to Yellow (data with a deficiency; Sauer et al. 2008).

Christmas Bird Count (CBC): Long-billed Curlews do not winter in South Dakota.

RANGE:
Breeding: Long-billed Curlews currently breed west of the Missouri River in South Dakota, with limited early records in the eastern portion of the state (South Dakota Ornithologists' Union 1991, Smith et al. 2002, Tallman et al. 2002).
Approximate timing: Long-billed Curlews arrive from late March to early April (Clarke 2006). Breeding commences as birds arrive; nesting is primarily from May and June, with earliest dates

(eggs) 1-3 May and latest dates (young) 11-15 July (South Dakota Ornithologists' Union 1991, Tallman et al. 2002). Nesting dates were reported as 19-23 May during the Breeding Bird Atlas project (Peterson 1995).
Breeding atlas or lat-long locations: Over the two years of the Breeding Bird Atlas project, there were 18 confirmed, 42 probable, and 38 possible breeding records, all west of the Missouri River (Peterson 1995).
Counties recorded: Long-billed Curlews have been recorded breeding in Stanley (Clarke and Jensen 2006), Bennett, Butte, Custer, Harding, Jackson, Meade, Pennington, Todd, Tripp (NatureServe 2006), and Perkins counties (South Dakota Ornithologists' Union 1991).

Migration: Uncommon migrant west of the Missouri River (Tallman et al. 2002), and formally abundant migrant in the southeast portion of the state (South Dakota Ornithologists' Union 1991). Recent records east river: 11 April 1982 in McCook County and 3 June 1996 in Miner County (Tallman et al. 2002).
Approximate timing: Spring migration during third and fourth week of April, with earliest arrival dates in Meade County of 16 March and 28 March (D. Backlund, pers. comm.). Curlews depart breeding grounds from early June to mid-August depending on age, sex and breeding status. Most birds (83-93%) had departed prior to 1 July in a two year study in Stanley County (Clarke 2006). Successful male breeders and their young were generally the last individuals to depart, while unsuccessful female breeders departed the earliest (J. N. Clarke and K. C. Jensen, pers. comm.). The latest date for fall migration is reported as 25 October (South Dakota Ornithologists' Union 1991).
Location of staging areas: Jackson and Meade counties (Tallman et al. 2002). Dates of late summer concentrations: 12-28 July (South Dakota Ornithologists' Union 1991). Most post-breeding flocks number only 30-50 birds (South Dakota Ornithologists' Union 1991) and are composed primarily of males and junveniles (Clarke 2006).
Numbers, particularly high counts: High counts 15 June but no numbers reported (eBird 2008).

Winter: Not known to occur in South Dakota during the winter. There are currently no data linking curlews breeding in South Dakota to a specific wintering area (J. N. Clarke and K. C. Jensen, pers. comm.).

ABUNDANCE AND POPULATION: Breeding population estimated 1000-3000 individuals (SLJ); populations appear to be decreasing (Tallman et al. 2002). Surveys conducted in Stanley County estimated a density of approximately 3.2 curlews/km² within a 40 km² core area of the Triple U Buffalo Ranch study site (Clarke 2006).

HABITAT: Long-billed Curlews usually nest on hilly

mixed-grass prairies, including mowed wet meadows (Peterson 1995). They used idle and grazed cattle pastures, but not sheep pastures (Timken 1969). In central South Dakota, chicks were reported in grass that was 18 cm tall (Spomer 1981). Field work in Stanley County, during 2006, a drought year, demonstrated that curlews selected nest sites with more forb cover and less shrub cover than points randomly selected throughout the study area. Brood-rearing areas had less grass cover and more bare ground than random points. Both nest sites and brood rearing areas also had shorter and less dense vegetation than random points. In both 2005 and 2006, curlews selected nest sites located on gently sloping hills near piles of manure (Clarke 2006).

MONITORING: There is no monitoring specific to Long-billed Curlews.

RESEARCH: Clarke (2006) is the only major Long-billed Curlew study undertaken in South Dakota. It was initiated to investigate nesting success, brood survival, and habitat use from 2005-2006 on the Triple U Buffalo Ranch in Stanley County (Clarke and Jensen 2006). Total nest success estimates dropped from 0.39 in 2005 to 0.15 during the drought in 2006 when vegetation cover was significantly reduced and nest predation increased greatly (Clarke 2006). In 2005, 50% of broods had at least one viable chick one week after hatching and 30% of the broods were known to produce fledglings. In 2006, 40% of broods had at least one viable chick one week after hatching and all of these broods produced fledglings. Egg inviability was frequent in 2005 when 24% of eggs present at hatch time did not hatch. After losing their first nests, six pairs renested; two pairs even attempted a third nest. In 2005, the single renest attempt was placed 331.5 m from the original nest; in 2006 the mean distance was 1.03 km (range 0.85 km – 5.85 km; Clarke 2006).

This study indicated that the main threats to nests on the ranch were trampling by livestock and predation. During this study bison and cattle trampled 20-30% of the nests. Chick mortality may have largely been due to avian predators such as Northern Harriers and Short-eared Owls (*Asio flammeus*), which were in high densities on the ranch, especially in 2005 (Clarke 2006). Some chicks apparently also died of hyperthermia (Clarke and Jensen 2006) or heat prostration (Clarke 2006).

A minimum of 54% of the adult Long-billed Curlews radio-marked in 2005 returned to the ranch to breed in 2006 (Clarke 2006). They placed their nests a mean distance of 608.6 m (range 0.089 km – 1.1 km) from their previous nest sites (Clarke 2006). Three years of intense observation on the Ft. Pierre NG (mostly restored, nonnative praire) indicated an absense of Long-billed Curlews. The abundance of birds on the unbroken native prairie grasslands of the Triple U study site may indicate that native prairie conservation is paramount to the sustainability of curlew populations in South Dakota (J. N. Clarke and K. C. Jensen, pers. comm.). Location of breeding

South Dakota birds during the winter is unknown, although work on this is ongoing (K. C. Jensen, pers. comm.).

Behavioral observations from other studies lead to interesting anecdotal information about the species. A male was observed tending 6 young of three different sizes, apparently from three different broods (Peterson 1995). In 2003, Long-billed Curlews were observed feeding on wolf spiders (*Lycosa aspersa*), a large (2.3 g) burrowing spider (D. Backlund, pers. comm.)

CONSERVATION ACTIVITIES (ONGOING): There are no ongoing conservation activities specific to Long-billed Curlews.

THREATS:
Breeding. Loss of breeding habitat to agriculture is the primary threat (Tallman et al. 2002). In 2005, 75% of nest failure was attributed to trampling by bison or cattle, and the other 25% failed due to abandonment after a disturbance (Clarke and Jensen 2006). However, grazing prior to the nesting period is important to help provide the short vegetation structure preferred for nesting. Thus, grazing livestock in habitat used by curlews may help increase use of an area and is a much preferred alternative to the conversion of grasslands for agricultural crops and development (J. N. Clarke and K. C. Jensen, pers. comm.). The production of inviable eggs, as observed in Stanley County, may also pose a threat to the fitness of Long-billed Curlew populations.

MANAGEMENT: There are no Long-billed Curlew specific management activities ongoing in South Dakota. However, any habitat management aimed directly at conserving native short- and mixed-grass prairies will benefit this species. The high level of breeding site fidelity displayed by Long-billed Curlews in Stanley County underscore the importance of conserving habitat in traditional breeding areas (J. N. Clarke and K. C. Jensen, pers. comm.).

Submitted by J. Nan Clarke, Kent C. Jensen, and Stephanie L. Jones
Reviewed by Robert P. Russell and Doug Backlund

Texas

SUMMARY: Locally numerous summer resident and breeder in the northwestern counties of the Panhandle. Nesting has also occurred historically on the Upper Coast, once recently on the mid-Coast, at least once in the trans-Pecos, and twice (1 historical, 1 recent) in the lower Rio Grande Valley (Lockwood and Freeman 2004, Brush 2005). Nonbreeders regularly summer on the coast (Lockwood and Freeman 2004) and occasionally in western grasslands (Peterson and Zimmer 1998). Uncommon migrant through the western two-thirds of the state but essentially absent as a migrant in the forested eastern third. In winter, locally common on the coast; generally rare to uncommon inland in the southern part of the state north and west to Bell County (Lockwood and Freeman 2004), Kerr County (Lockwood 2001), Midland County (Texas Ornithological Society 1995), the southwest Panhandle (Seyffert 2001a), and various parts of the trans-Pecos (Lockwood and Freeman 2004).

STATUS:
State: Long-billed Curlews are a State Species of Concern (Texas Parks and Wildlife Department 2005).

Natural Heritage Rank: Texas rank: S3B (Vulnerable Breeding), S5N (Secure Nonbreeding); *National rank:* N5N, N5B (Secure Nonbreeding, Breeding); *Global rank:* G5 (Secure; NatureServe 2006).

TRENDS:
North American Breeding Bird Survey (BBS) trends and abundance data: Trend and abundance data are analyzed from seven routes in the northwestern Panhandle, southern High Plains, and lower Rio Grande Valley. Relative abundance equals 0.69 birds per route. There is a significant negative trend from 1966-2007 (-3.7; $P = 0.02$). However, credibility of the BBS is poor, with a BBS Credibility Indicator equal to Red (data have important deficiencies such as low abundance and low sample size; Sauer et al. 2008).

Christmas Bird Count (CBC): Although the number of curlews recorded on CBC in Texas has increased over the past 50 or so years, this is likely due to an increase in number of observers, number of counts, and improved knowledge of where birds are in count circles during that time. When corrected for party-hours, a far different pattern emerges, one showing a possible decline through the mid-80's and a potential slight increase since then. No statistical analyses have been performed on these data, and analyses are probably not warranted due to the inconsistent manner with which CBC counts are conducted (W. H. Howe, pers. comm.).

RANGE:
Breeding:
Approximate timing: Few data are available on timing of breeding in Texas. In the Panhandle, breeders arrive by late March or early April, and breeding activities extend from mid-April to early July (Seyffert 2001b). Oology collection records indicate incubation during the first two weeks of May in coastal breeding sites (Pemberton 1922). By back-counting, one could estimate adults arrive at their breeding site by the end of March, nest initiation could begin in early April, chicks could be hatched between early May and early June, with fledging occurring by early to mid-June (SDF).
Breeding atlas or lat-long locations: Fig. 3.7 is copied from Seyffert (2001b). The rare historic breeding records in Jeff Davis, Harris, and Cameron counties are not depicted on the map. Although the

map indicates confirmed breeding in Matagorda County, this was considered only a probable nesting attempt (Seyffert 2001b).
Locations: Currently known to nest only in the northwestern Panhandle counties of Dallam, Hartley, Moore, Oldham, and Sherman (Seyffert 2001a) and very rarely on the mid- and lower coasts. Historic nesting has been documented in 1936 in Jeff Davis County of the trans-Pecos (Oberholser 1974, Peterson and Zimmer 1998), and near the coast in Harris County in 1910 (Oberholser 1974) and Cameron County in 1877 (Oberholser 1974). Long-billed Curlews purportedly nested in Aransas County (Oberholser 1974), has recently been documented as nesting in Cameron County in 1990 (Seyffert 2001b, Brush 2005), and nesting is probable in Matagorda, Willacy, and Hidalgo counties (Seyffert 2001b).

Migration: Long-billed Curlews are found throughout the Southern Great Plains region of Texas during both fall and spring migration. They show highly seasonal variation in abundances through the Playa Lakes Region, being more abundant during the fall than in spring. Skagen and Knopf (1993) described migration as broadly to moderately dispersed, which is defined as 60% of the individuals occurring at ten or greater sites annually. The high seasonal variation may be due primarily to a longer occupancy in the area during the fall (Davis and Smith 1998). Within the Southern Great Plains, Long-billed Curlews were one of the more abundant shorebird species found on playas, representing 22.2% of fall sightings during surveys in 1994, but were much less common during spring migration through the area (Davis and Smith 1998).
Approximate timing: Spring migration runs primarily from mid-March to mid-May; fall migration from mid-July to early November (Oberholser 1974, Lockwood and Freeman 2004). During fall migration Long-billed Curlews move through the Playa Lakes Region of the Southern Great Plains into late October (Davis and Smith 1998) although they reach their peak numbers during August (Andrei et al. 2006). Spring migrants have departed the Southern Great Plains by mid-April (Andrei et al. 2006).
Location of staging areas: Major staging areas within Texas are unknown or unrecorded at this time.
Numbers, particularly high counts: At Hereford, Deaf Smith County, 19 July 1981, 500 individuals were reported; 3000 were reported on 9 October 1981 in Castro County (Seyffert 2001a).

Winter: Igl and Ballard (1999) classified Long-billed Curlews as a migrant and winter resident in Texas with a contiguous or slight overlap between wintering and breeding ranges during their wintering grassland temperate breeding bird study in Brooks, Jim Wells, Kenedy, and Kleberg counties.
Location of wintering areas: Common to abundant winter resident on the coast (Lockwood and Freeman 2004). Long-billed Curlews are known to winter in the Playa Lakes Region of the Southern

Great Plains of Texas (Davis and Smith 1998). A large winter roost occurs in some years in the saline lakes of the Lower Rio Grande NWR (D. S. Stolley, pers. comm.).

Numbers, particularly high counts: High winter numbers include 300 in Castro County 21 December 1983 (Seyffert 2001a); 2261 at East Lake and La Sal del Rey, Cameron County, 11 February 2004 (D. S. Stolley, pers. comm.).

ABUNDANCE AND POPULATION: There are no abundance or population estimates for Texas.

HABITAT: Long-billed Curlews use many habitats in Texas. Within the Pineywoods, Gulf Coast Prairies and Marshes, Post Oak Savannah, Blackland Prairie, Cross Timbers and Prairies, Rolling Plains, and South Texas Plains ecosystems they are found in native and introduced grasses; in the Gulf Coast Prairies and Marshes, High Plains, and South Texas Plains ecosystems croplands are used; within the Edwards Plateau Ecosystem they use parkland; and within the Gulf Coast Prairies and Marshes, Blackland Prairie, Cross Timbers and Prairies, High Plains, and Trans Pecos ecosystems they are recorded using grasslands (Texas Parks and Wildlife Department 2005).

During the breeding season, Long-billed Curlews use shortgrass to mid-grass prairies in the Panhandle and moist meadowlands and mowed areas (e.g. golf courses) along the coast (Seyffert 2001b). Pemberton (1922) noted that when searching for nests in the Rio Grande Delta area he concentrated on the grassy meadows adjoining the sloughs and salt-water covered areas. Occasionally they place their nests in fallow agricultural land (Seyffert 2001b). The presence of fresh water within a certain distance (e.g. 400 m) may be important (Seyffert 2001b). Migratory staging areas included shortgrass prairies, meadows, airports, golf courses, prairie ponds and sloughs, fresh and salt marshes. Along the Gulf Coast flats and shores are used (Oberholser 1974). Migrating curlews used playas and, to a lesser extent, saline lakes within the Southern Great Plains region (Davis and Smith 1998, Andrei et al. 2006). Although not specific to Long-billed Curlews, most playas selected by shorebirds in the Southern Great Plains contained < 25% vegetation cover, 10-15% mudflat, 10-20% water habitat which was < 4 cm deep water, and playas with higher invertebrate populations (Davis and Smith 1998). Igl and Ballard (1999) found them using grasslands and brushlands during nonbreeding seasons in southern Texas.

MONITORING: Although no current, statewide monitoring program for Long-billed Curlews exists, Texas Parks and Wildlife Department (2005) identified several monitoring, survey, and evaluation needs. These include: 1) surveys to document and monitor high priority habitats and to test survey protocols; 2) monitoring programs to evaluate habitat (natural and artificial, as well as high priority areas, and in relation to species range); 3) evaluation and monitoring the effects of various management practices; and 4) evaluation and monitoring population characteristics such as season fluctuations, long-term trends, incidental take, and

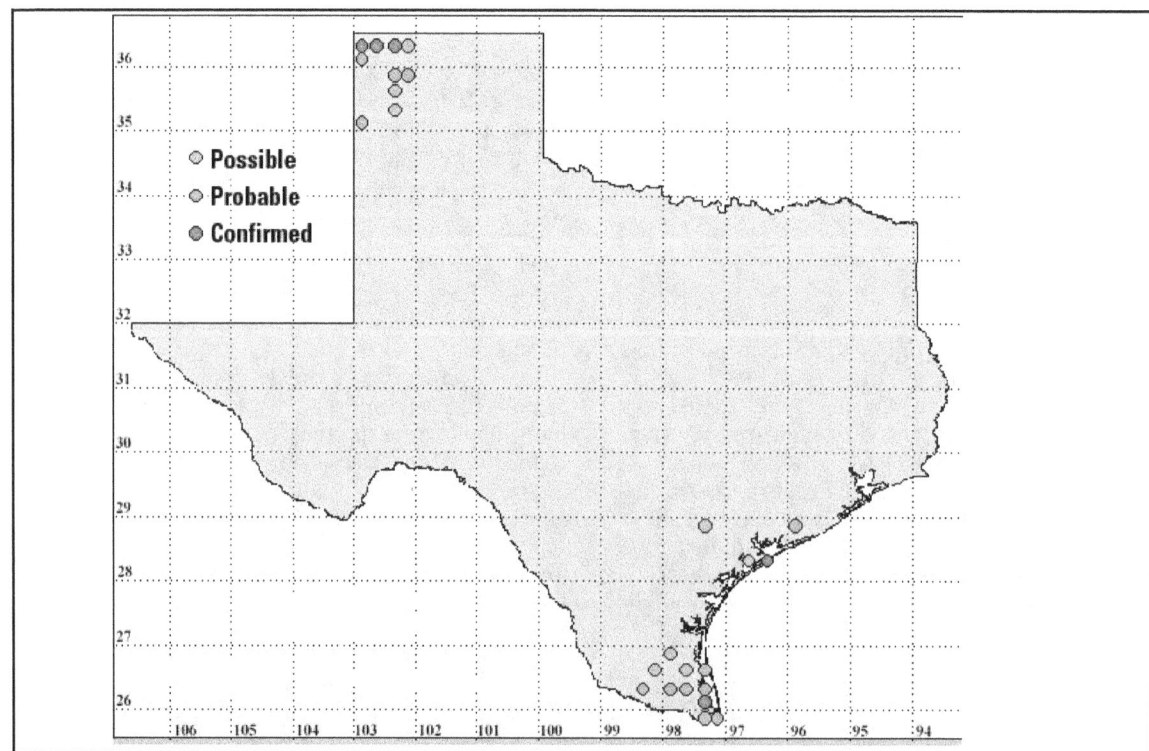

Figure 3.7. Location of breeding Long-billed Curlews in Texas (Seyffert 2001b).

life history parameters (Texas Parks and Wildlife Department 2005).

RESEARCH: There are several recent studies of shorebird habitat use within the Southern Great Plains which included data on Long-billed Curlew. Davis and Smith (1998) documented relative abundance, chronology, species composition, and habitat selection during migration, evaluated habitat characteristics and invertebrate availabilities at used and unused playa locations, and investigated the effects of shorebird foraging activities on invertebrate populations. Andrei et al. (2006) looked at similar questions surrounding use of saline lakes in the same region. Dronen and Badley (1979) investigated parasite loads of Long-billed Curlews collected in the Galveston area. They confirmed use by several species of trematodes in Long-billed Curlews and documented two new trematode species using curlews as a host. Igl and Ballard (1999) included Long-billed Curlews in their study of the ecology and habitat requirements of nonbreeding season temperate nesting grassland birds (Igl and Ballard 1999).

CONSERVATION ACTIVITIES (ONGOING): Texas Parks and Wildlife Department (2005) identified many actions necessary for Long-billed Curlew conservation. These recommendations involve developing and implementing compatible grazing practices; working with Farm Bill programs to promote compatible habitat programs; proper planning of site placement for wind power, and other energy development, and urbanization to reduce wildlife impacts; reduction of erosion especially around wetlands; working with partners to reduce habitat fragmentation; control of invasive species; and education and outreach to various groups and law makers to improve understanding of wildlife needs and threats.

THREATS: Texas Parks and Wildlife Department (2005) identified several potential threats which currently or potentially could affect Long-billed Curlews within the state. These included development of habitat into intensive cropland, destructive grazing practices, urbanization, siltation of wetlands, beach erosion, habitat fragmentation and alteration, and invasive species encroachment. It was noted that the original vegetation of southern Texas has undergone a dramatic alteration since settlement (Igl and Ballard 1999). This has probably had an important negative impact on Long-billed Curlews during the nonbreeding season.

MANAGEMENT: Brusati et al. (2001) found no clear differences in behavior of Long-billed Curlews on natural vs. created sites with natural hydrology and tidal circulation. Although this should be investigated at greater depth and monitored more stringently, created sites may be a management option for restoring Long-billed Curlew habitat. Although there are no specific management guidelines for Long-billed Curlews in Texas, management for fall migrant shorebirds across the

Southern Great Plains includes recommendations for creating and maintaining playas with sparse vegetation cover, at least 10-15% exposed mudflats, and at least 10-20% shallow water (< 4 cm deep) habitats. Gradual drawdowns of deep water playas and flooding of dry playas would enhance invertebrate populations. Providing a detrital food base for invertebrates can be achieved by mowing and shallow disking of wetlands. Timing of these and other management actions should coincide with the period of use by shorebirds; in the case of Long-billed Curlew, at least July through October (Davis and Smith 1998).

Submitted by William H. Howe, Suzanne D. Fellows, and David J. Krueper

---

Utah

SUMMARY: Long-billed Curlews occur most often in the northern and central valleys of Utah (Utah Division of Wildlife Resources 1999). Great Salt Lake is the major breeding site in the state and is an important breeding and staging site for the species throughout its range. Long-billed Curlews occur as a migrant throughout most of Utah. Loss of breeding habitat and habitat modification are the greatest threats to the species. Large portions of Long-billed Curlew breeding habitat on the east side of the Great Salt Lake have been lost because of urban encroachment.

STATUS:
State: This species is included on the Utah Division of Wildlife Resources Sensitive Species List (Utah Division of Wildlife Resources 2003). Utah Partners in Flight identifies it as a Priority Species (Parrish et al. 2002). Long-billed Curlews are also a Tier II species in the State Wildlife Action Plan (Gorrell et al. 2005).

Natural Heritage Rank: Utah rank: S2 (Imperiled), S3B (Vulnerable Breeding); *National rank:* N5N, N5B (Secure Nonbreeding, Breeding); *Global rank:* G5 (Secure; NatureServe 2006).

TRENDS:
North American Breeding Bird Survey (BBS) trends and abundance data: Trends and relative abundance are analyzed using data from 19 routes. Relative abundance equals 2.31 individuals per route. There is a non-significant negative trend from 1966-2007 (-0.4%/yr; $P = 0.87$; Sauer et al. 2008). Credibility of the BBS is poor, with a BBS Credibility Indicator equal to Red (data with an important deficiency; Sauer et al. 2008).

Christmas Bird Count (CBC): Long-billed Curlews have only been recorded twice in Utah during the winter; both reports were from the Salt Lake City CBC, the first in December 1962 and the second in December 1964 (National Audubon Society 2006).

RANGE:

Breeding: Long-billed Curlews are fairly common summer residents and migrants in Utah, especially through the central and more northern valleys. They are less common in the Colorado River drainage. Long-billed Curlews breed in scattered localities throughout the state, primarily in northern Utah, but also in the west, southwest (Behle 1985, Behle et al. 1985), and northeast (K. A. Hersey, pers. comm.). Nesting elevations range from 1280 m at the Great Salt Lake to over 2130 m in high elevation valleys in the northeast and south-central parts of Utah (K. A. Hersey, pers. comm.).

    Approximate Timing: In Utah, Long-billed Curlews start to arrive around the Great Salt Lake during the last week in March, and establish territories by mid-April. Birds arrive later in northern Utah and remain longer than curlews in other parts of the range. Clutch initiation dates in northern Utah were from mid-April to mid-May (Paton and Dalton 1994).

    Counties recorded: Beaver, Box Elder, Cache, Carbon, Daggett, Davis, Duchesne, Iron, Juab, Millard, Piute, Salt Lake, San Juan, Sanpete, Sevier, Tooele, Uintah, Utah, Washington, Wayne, Weber (NatureServe 2006; K. A. Hersey, pers. comm.).

Migration:

    Approximate timing: Spring migration runs generally from 15 March through 15 April (Paton and Dalton 1994). Peak numbers are seen in the post dispersal period, 15 May through 5 June. Satellite tracking in neighboring eastern Nevada has shown that southern movements begin as early as mid-June (K. A. Hersey, pers. comm.). Fall migration occurs primarily from 1 August through 15 October; birds in northern Utah generally depart by mid-August (Paton and Dalton 1994), although as many as 26 individuals have been seen as late as 20 November (eBird 2008).

    Location of staging areas: Primary staging areas occur around the Great Salt Lake and large wetland complexes.

    Numbers, particularly high counts: A group of 68 individuals, primarily young of the year fledglings, were observed in sagebrush flats around Locomotive Springs at the north end of Great Salt Lake in June 1991 (SDF). Over 80 individuals were observed feeding in an agricultural field on 14 April 2005 (K. A. Hersey, pers. comm.).

ABUNDANCE AND POPULATION: Populations are thought to have declined from historical levels (Hayward et al. 1976, Behle et al. 1985, Paton and Dalton 1994, Parrish et al. 2002), but little quantitative data are available to estimate the size of the historical population. Historically Long-billed Curlews were considered a fairly common summer resident and migrant (Hayward et al. 1976) and a common summer resident in localized areas (Behle et al. 1985). Loss of nesting habitat and disturbance to nest sites are suspected factors leading to population declines (Hayward et al. 1976, Parrish et al. 2002). In 2003, the Utah breeding population

was estimated at 200-1000 individuals based on expert opinion, although most surveys upon which this estimate was based were considered to be of poor or unreliable accuracy (SLJ). The 2004-2005 Rangewide Long-billed Curlew Breeding Survey included routes in Utah; results from this survey demonstrated that there are more Long-billed Curlews rangewide than previously estimated (Stanley and Skagen 2007, Jones et al. 2008). Preliminary results from a current study conducted by the Utah Division of Wildlife Resources indicated that there were 8064 (2994-15, 460; 95% CI) individuals in the Central Region of the state. This translates to a mean density of 0.20 (0.07-0.38; 95% CI) Long-billed Curlew/km^2 in that portion of Utah (K. A. Hersey, pers. comm.).

HABITAT: This species lives and breeds in higher and drier meadowlands than many other shorebird species (Hayward et al. 1976; see Fig. 3.8). Long-billed Curlew habitat includes arid grasslands, grassy shorelines, and agricultural areas (Walters and Sorensen 1983). At the Great Salt Lake, they nested near the edges of barren alkali flats (Paton and Dalton 1994, Wolfe 1931). Nests in Box Elder and Cache counties were typically a grass-lined depression located in a clump of grass (Forsythe 1972).

MONITORING: The Utah Division of Wildlife Resources has established a monitoring protocol for Long-billed Curlew. A GIS based habitat model was created to help identify areas of suitable habitat. Random survey points were placed on the landscape stratified by a model-based probability distribution. Each survey consists of a 5-point transect with 400 m radius, fixed-distance point counts spaced 800 m apart occurring during the pre-incubation period. Double sampling is used to correct for detection probability. In 2006 and 2007 surveys were restricted to the central portion of the state; in 2008 survey effort was extended statewide. Surveys will be repeated every three years to determine distribution, population, and occupancy trends (K. A. Hersey, pers. comm.).

RESEARCH: Paton and Dalton (1994) quantified nest site characteristics, breeding densities, and migratory chronology of Long-billed Curlews at Great Salt Lake. The species is apparently declining in Utah and little is known about their breeding ecology in the eastern Great Basin Desert. Their study was designed to provide baseline data that could be used to successfully manage this species. Nest densities at Great Salt Lake ranged from 0.64- 2.36 males/km^2. The habitat at curlew nest sites consisted of significantly shorter vegetation than nearby random locations (5.7 versus 9.0 cm respectively; $P < 0.01$). Nests tended to be located in small patches of vegetation near barren ground. Maintenance of relatively short vegetation appears to be important in managing curlew habitat. In addition, only 2 of 10 nests monitored in 1992 were successful, with most lost to mammalian predators. They recommended that further research be conducted to determine the impact of mammalian predators on curlew populations (Paton and Dalton 1994).

In 2007 and 2008 digital cameras were placed on nearly 30 Long-billed Curlew nests at Great Salt Lake. One nest was depredated in 2007 by a Common Raven (*Corvus corax*); no nests were depredated in 2008 (J. Cavitt, unpubl. data). In conjunction with this study incubation rhythms are also being investigated (J. Cavitt, pers. comm.).

CONSERVATION ACTIVITIES (ONGOING): Long-billed Curlews have not been specific targets of land protection and habitat restoration and acquisition; however, wetland and upland habitats along the Great Salt Lake and Utah Lake serve as important nesting and staging habitat. The Utah Division of Wildlife Resources is completing a status assessment to document the distribution and abundance of Long-billed Curlews in the state (K. A. Hersey, pers. comm.). A GIS model has been built that predicts the likelihood of curlew occurance on a site; the model has been used in impact assessments and to identify core conservation areas (K. A. Hersey, pers. comm.).

THREATS:

Breeding: Loss of grassland breeding habitat and habitat modification are among the greatest threats to Long-billed Curlews in Utah. Large portions of their primary breeding areas on the east side of the Great Salt Lake have been lost due to housing development (Utah Division of Wildlife Resources 2003). Predation by red foxes (*Vulpes vulpes*) could also represent a significant threat to Long-billed Curlews (Utah Division of Wildlife Resources 2003). Habitat fragmentation may provide predators with increased travel corridors (Utah Division of Wildlife Resources 2003).

Migration: As above, particularly development around the Great Salt Lake.

MANAGEMENT: Currently there are neither Long-billed Curlew specific management recommendations for Utah nor are there species specific activities occuring within the state (K. A. Hersey, pers. comm.).

Submitted by Stephanie L. Jones
Reviewed by Kimberly A. Hersey

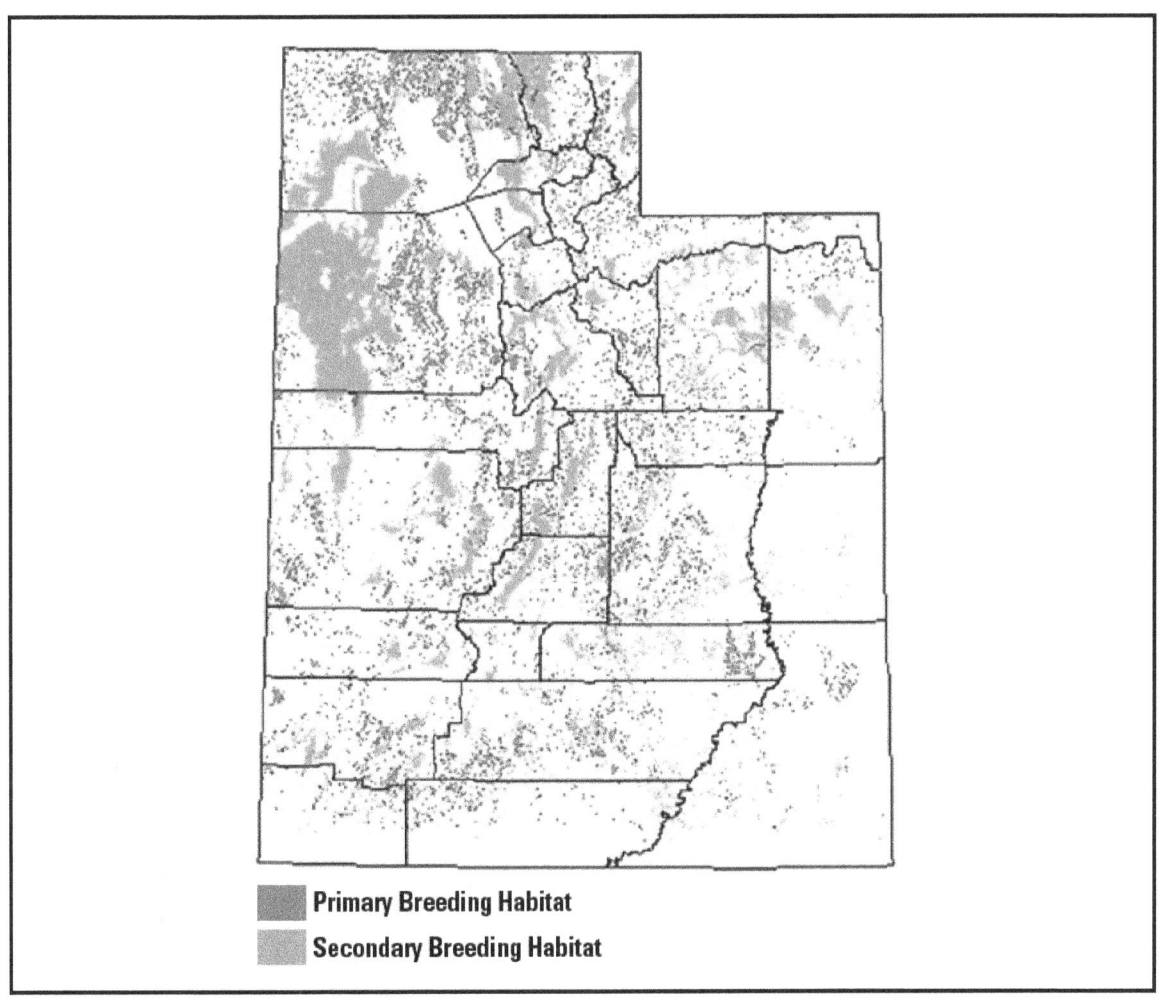

Primary Breeding Habitat
Secondary Breeding Habitat

Figure 3.8. Utah Long-billed Curlew breeding habitat (Utah Division of Wildlife Resources 1999).

Washington

SUMMARY: Long-billed Curlews breed primarily in the Columbia Basin. Wintering flocks can occasionally be found at Grays Harbor, Willapa Bay, and, to a lesser extent, Puget Sound. There are few large-scale conservation or management actions currently ongoing; however, there are several examples of local conservation actions found throughout the state. NWRs in the Columbia Basin have recently initiated local monitoring and research activities and local monitoring of Long-billed Curlews occurs at several other locations throughout the state. A number of potential threats have been identified, and current research and monitoring efforts should evaluate their significance to curlew populations.

STATUS:
State: Long-billed Curlews are a protected wildlife species in Washington.

Natural Heritage Rank: Washington rank: S2S3B (Imperiled/Vulnerable Breeding), S2N (Imperiled Nonbreeding); *National rank:* N5N, N5B (Secure Nonbreeding, Breeding); *Global rank:* G5 (Secure; NatureServe 2006).

TRENDS:
North American Breeding Bird Survey (BBS) trends and abundance data: Long-billed Curlew data were analyzed from 13 routes. Relative abundance equals 0.77 individuals per route. There is a non-significant negative trend from 1966-2007 (-3.6; $P = 0.68$). Credibility of the BBS is poor, with a BBS Credibility Indicator equal to Red (data have important deficiencies such as low abundance and low sample size; Sauer et al. 2008).

Christmas Bird Count (CBC): Long-billed Curlews in Washington do not regularly winter in areas covered by the CBC. With the exception of unusually high CBC totals in 1992 (100), 1994 (55), and 1999 (35) at Grays Harbor (this area includes Ocean Shores), the species was seen there in only 5 of 20 additional counts (median number of birds present = 1) between 1980 and 2004 (National Audubon Society 2006).

RANGE:
Breeding: The breeding distribution of Long-billed Curlews in Washington is primarily within the Columbia Basin.

Approximate timing: Most birds arrive in breeding areas between 15 and 28 March (Hand and Cadwell 1994, Stepniewski 1999). Data from seasonal reports indicate early arrival dates between 7 and 10 March from 1997 to 2005. A record of 2 March 1983 was reported from Grant County (J. B. Buchanan, pers. comm.). Eggs are typically laid in the first two weeks of April and hatching occurs in mid- to late-May (Pampush and Anthony 1993). A late nest was reported from 28 August 1999 at Columbia NWR (J. B. Buchanan, pers. comm.).

Breeding atlas or lat-long locations: The known or predicted range includes Adams, Benton, Douglas (although few records), Franklin, Grant, and Lincoln counties, the eastern half of Kittitas County, eastern and southern Klickitat County, Okanogan Valley portions of Okanogan County, western Whitman County, and the eastern half of Yakima County (Smith et al. 1997). In addition, numerous pairs have been documented in western Walla Walla County (M. Denny, pers. comm.). Despite the presence of a substantial amount of suitable habitat, there are no records of breeding Long-billed Curlews in Columbia County (M. Denny, pers. comm.). Several hundred additional breeding season records of Long-billed Curlews are known from eastern Washington (J. B. Buchanan, pers. comm.); a substantial proportion of them occur outside the modeled distribution of the species presented by Smith et al. (1997).

Locations: For unknown reasons, but likely due to habitat loss, a slight range contraction has occurred in the northeastern part of the state. Long-billed Curlews were collected in Kettle Falls (northwestern Stevens County) and at the confluence of the Spokane and Columbia rivers (the vicinity of extreme southwestern Stevens County) in 1826 and 1827, respectively (Hall 1934). In 1884, Long-billed Curlews were "a noticeably common spring nesting visitor" east of Spokane Falls (Spokane County; Cheney Cowles Museum, Spokane; Merrill 1897). Long-billed Curlews no longer nest or occur in these areas. Large aggregations have been reported: about 300 at the U.S. Department of Energy Hanford site and adjacent Wahluke Slope (Allen 1980), about 150 on 30 May 1968 at McNary NWR, 50 pairs in 1968 at Columbia NWR, and 60 on 10 May 1972 at Umatilla NWR (J. B. Buchanan, pers. comm.).

Migration: Long-billed Curlews are one of the earliest arriving spring migrant shorebirds in Washington. Some spring migrants observed in Washington likely continue northward to breeding areas in interior British Columbia (Campbell et al. 1990). Observation of Long-billed Curlews in the Cascade Mountains in mid- to late-June (Paulson 1993) suggests that at least some Washington breeders may migrate to the Washington coastal wintering area.

Approximate timing: Long-billed Curlews leave the breeding grounds in early summer. Adult females begin to depart by the third week in June. Adult males and juveniles usually begin to depart by the end of June. Long-billed Curlews have been documented at coastal locations by 16-24 June (Paulson 1993), indicating a rapid movement of some birds from breeding areas to migratory and wintering sites. A record at Ocean Shores on 6 June 2004 (J. B. Buchanan, pers. comm.) was either an early migrant or a bird that spent the summer on the coast. Few birds linger to late autumn; the late record for eastern Washington was 7 November 2002 at Columbia NWR (J. B. Buchanan, pers. comm.).

Location of staging areas: Autumn aggregations in eastern Washington are not well documented although flocks of 100-250 have been observed along the Columbia River adjacent to the U.S. Department of Energy Hanford site in mid-June (Allen 1980, J. B. Buchanan, pers. comm.). A group of 32 at Cow Lake, Adams County, on 22 July 2001 (J. B. Buchanan, pers. comm.), was likely staging prior to departure from the breeding grounds.

Numbers, particularly high counts: Large aggregations of migrants in spring are only occasionally reported (e.g. 36 individuals on 23 March 2003, south of Moxee, Yakima County; J. B. Buchanan, pers. comm.).

Winter: The winter range of Long-billed Curlews in Washington is extremely limited. It is unknown what proportion of winter birds are breeders from Washington or elsewhere (e.g. British Columbia), or are non-reproductive members of the regional population.

Location: It is believed coastal birds in autumn and winter move back and forth between Grays Harbor and Willapa Bay, the latter site being the primary use area and location of the now-traditional roost (Paulson 1993, Buchanan 2005). Winter records date back only to 1970 (Buchanan 2005), indicating recent colonization by Long-billed Curlews. There are few records from elsewhere in western Washington, primarily in Puget Sound (Buchanan 2005).

Numbers, particularly high counts: High counts include 80 on 26 December 1995 and 78 on 6 February 1983 at North River, Willapa Bay (Buchanan 2005).

ABUNDANCE AND POPULATION: Although long-term data for this species are generally lacking, a general accounting of changes in this species' status in Washington is possible. Accounts from the early twentieth century indicate Long-billed Curlew abundance had declined in parts of eastern Washington (Dice 1918) which coincided with regional population changes likely influenced by loss or degradation of nesting habitat (Page and Gill 1994). By the mid-twentieth century, Yocom (1956) reported Long-billed Curlew abundance had increased in eastern Washington, likely in response to abandonment of agricultural practices at failed homesteads and the increase of irrigated croplands in the northern Columbia Basin, which may have enhanced insect prey populations.

The current number of Long-billed Curlews present during the breeding season in Washington is unknown. The abundance and density varies substantially throughout the state; estimates of breeding season pair density in various areas are presented in Table 3.2. Given the broad distribution of the species it is not unreasonable to estimate a breeding population of at least several hundred pairs in Washington.

Because Long-billed Curlews in Washington are scarce in areas covered by CBC, winter trends have only been derived from incidental and anecdotal data in seasonal reports from Willapa Bay and Grays Harbor (J. B. Buchanan, pers. comm.). Analysis of seasonal high counts indicates strong positive relationships between abundance and year (autumn:

Table 3.2. Density of Long-billed Curlew territories in different breeding areas in Washington. Note that the two sites with highest densities are on small islands.

Location	Size of area (km²)	Number of territories	Density (pairs/km²)	Reference
Hanford Reach Nat. Mon. Benton Co.	419.24	Not specified	0.02 – 0.03	K. Goldie and H. Newsome, pers. comm.
Southwestern Walla Walla Co.	93.24	12	0.13	M. Denny, pers. comm.
Juniper Dunes Wilderness, Franklin Co.	≈ 69	20	0.29	WDFW database
Hanford Reach Nat. Mon. ("100-F" area), Benton Co.	5.18	3	0.58	Allen (1980)
Hanford Reach Nat. Mon. ("100-H/100-D area"), Benton Co.	15.48	10	0.65	Allen (1980)
Hanford Reach Nat. Mon. ("300 Area"), Benton Co.	10.36	15	1.45	Allen (1980)
Western Walla Walla Co.	2.59	4	1.54	M. Denny, pers. comm.
Washburn Island, Okanogan Co.	≈ 0.8	2	2.6	WDFW database
Gaileys Island, Grant Co.	≈ 0.4	5	12.3	WDFW database

n = 23 years between 1965 and 2004, F-ratio = 14.77, r^2 = 0.41, P = 0.0009; winter: n = 22 years between 1970 and 2003, F-ratio = 8.07, r^2 = 0.29, P = 0.01; J. B. Buchanan, pers. comm.).

HABITAT: Breeding Long-billed Curlews use a variety of native and nonnative grasslands and irrigated pastures and croplands for nesting (Allen 1980, Stepniewski 1999). In particular, they use areas with cover of Idaho fescue (*Festuca idahoensis*), Sandberg's bluegrass, broom snakeweed (*Gutierrezia sarothrae*), and rabbit brush (*Chrysothamnus* spp.). CRP fields older than approximately five years will be used by Long-billed Curlews if native bunchgrasses have begun to replace planted crested wheatgrass. Long-billed Curlews have successfully fledged young from areas where a mix of crested wheatgrass and other vegetation (e.g. shrub-steppe) was present (J. B. Buchanan, pers. comm.). These areas occasionally include heavily grazed sites (J. B. Buchanan, pers. comm.). Nesting areas are generally on flat or very gently sloping terrain (Allen 1980), although in some areas slopes of up to 20 degrees may be used (M. Denny, pers. comm.).

Long-billed Curlews forage extensively, but do not nest, in actively irrigated or recently plowed alfalfa fields and other croplands (Campbell et al. 1990). Birds are probably attracted to easily accessible, highly concentrated insects and worms found on these sites (M. Denny, pers. comm.). Croplands (including recently burned sites) occasionally attract individuals from multiple territories. There are several breeding season records of greater than 20 individuals and one record of 107 individual Long-billed Curlews feeding together on alfalfa fields (J. B. Buchanan, pers. comm.). A long-time rancher in Yakima County reported Long-billed Curlews nested on his property after he began irrigating in the early 1980s (J. B. Buchanan, pers. comm.).

Information on productivity of Long-billed Curlews in different types of habitats is not available. Curlews forage, bathe and rest in wetlands and exposed mudflats associated with ponds and rivers (J. B. Buchanan, pers. comm.); however, the distance between nesting areas, upland foraging areas (i.e., croplands) and water sources has not been quantified.

The location and description of habitats used by migrant Long-billed Curlews in Washington is not well documented. However, curlews are known to regularly use grasslands and the shorelines of lakes and rivers during migration (Allen 1980; Paulson 1993; J. B. Buchanan, pers. comm.). There are observations of curlews using wet meadows in the Cascade Mountains (Paulson 1993). Curlews at Ocean Shores and Willapa Bay use sandy beaches and mud flats (Paulson 1993, Buchanan 2005).

MONITORING: Several local efforts to monitor Long-billed Curlews are underway in the state. Consultants have initiated a 30-year grassland bird monitoring efforts in the vicinity of wind turbines in Walla Walla County (M. Denny, pers. comm.). Data collected from a Long-billed Curlew survey in the Walla Walla Valley, suggest population stability there for the past 26 years (M. Denny, pers. comm.). Breeding surveys, using point count techniques adapted from the 2004-2005 rangewide survey, have been conducted at Hanford Reach National Monument (NM), and Umatilla, McNary and Columbia NWRs (Goldie 2005; H. Browers, pers. comm.; R. Hill, pers. comm.). While initially developed to provide current abundance information, these survey routes can be used for long-term monitoring.

RESEARCH: There has been little research conducted on Long-billed Curlew ecology, behavior or habitat use in Washington in the last 25 years. Allen (1980; Washington) and Pampush and Anthony (1993; Oregon portion of the Columbia Basin) are the only published studies of this species in Washington or the Columbia Basin. Aspects of the breeding ecology of Long-billed Curlews have been investigated in several studies from the Pacific Northwest (e.g. Allen 1980, Redmond and Jenni 1986, Pampush and Anthony 1993). A two year study of nesting habitat use was initiated on Hanford Reach NM and Columbia, McNary, and Umatilla NWRs in 2007 (H. Browers, pers. comm.).

CONSERVATION ACTIVITIES (ONGOING): Active Long-billed Curlew habitat conservation in the state consists of specific management actions undertaken on public lands or is incidental to private efforts. Hanford Reach NM and Saddle Mountain NWR have engaged in integrated pest management and post-fire restoration efforts targeting priority native grassland communities and species such as the Long-billed Curlew (U.S. Fish and Wildlife Service 2006). Maintaining and increasing nesting and foraging habitats are objectives in the McNary and Umatilla NWRs' Comprehensive Conservation Plan (U.S. Fish and Wildlife Service 2007). Given that Long-billed Curlews occur in low densities in Washington, and their distribution, abundance, and productivity on lands of differing conservation status (i.e., refuges, private lands) is unknown, it appears that private lands may contribute significantly to the species' persistence. Private lands at risk of being converted should be identified and protected through purchase or negotiation of conservation easements. Steps can then be taken to assist private landowners in providing highly productive Long-billed Curlew breeding sites.

Incidental and voluntary actions by ranchers have directly benefited curlews during the nesting season. For example, several ranchers have reported curlew nests to Washington Department of Fish and Wildlife biologists, and a rancher in Yakima County intentionally retained a buffer around three active nests in his agricultural fields at harvest (J. B. Buchanan, pers. comm.).

CRP lands benefit Long-billed Curlews, but as this is not a target species of the program, it does not strongly influence CRP efforts. Habitat conservation value may occur with implementation of mitigation associated with wind turbine placement and operation, although specific details of such efforts have not been developed. As Long-billed Curlews forage in alfalfa fields and other irrigated croplands, improved irrigation throughout the Columbia Basin following construction of major hydroelectric facilities (Muckleston and Highsmith 1978) has likely been beneficial to this species.

There are a few education and outreach activities which specifically relate to Long-billed Curlews in Washington. The Blue Mountain Audubon Society chapter hosts an annual Long-billed Curlew field day which includes site visits and presentations on a variety of subjects including species ecology and conservation (M. Denny, pers. comm.). Hanford Reach NM recently began a program to monitor curlews using local volunteers which increases public awareness and community support. Articles are published in the newsletter of the Lower Columbia Basin Audubon Society ("The Curlew") to recruit volunteers and provide information about project activities (H. Newsome, pers. comm.). Breeding Long-billed Curlews are a highlight on field trips during the annual Sandhill Crane Festival held in the Columbia Basin (R. Hill, pers. comm.).

THREATS: A number of potential threats have been identified which may impact Long-billed Curlews in Washington. The significance of these potential threats has not been evaluated. They are organized into four general categories and described below: 1) invasive species, 2) crop management techniques, 3) habitat conversion, and 4) various factors associated with development of wind power.

The invasion of exotic plants may reduce the area suitable for foraging and nesting Long-billed Curlews. Tumbling mustard (*Sisymbrium altissimum*) has rapidly invaded disturbed areas associated with wind turbines and roads in southeastern Washington (M. Denny, pers. comm.); Long-billed Curlews do not nest or forage in areas dominated by this species (Dechant et al. 2003). Grasslands dominated by cheatgrass and lacking other grasses are not used for nesting (Allen 1980; M. Denny, pers. comm.). Purple loosestrife (*Lythrum salicaria*) and the common reed (*Phragmites australis*), two invasive species, have become established at the Walla Walla River Delta (M. Denny, pers. comm.) and have the potential to eliminate exposed shoreline areas used by foraging Long-billed Curlews. Other invasive plants may also alter the functional value of areas currently used by curlews.

Long-billed Curlews appear to have adapted to certain agricultural practices, although some practices may be harmful to them. For example, the potential value of CRP lands is sometimes not realized when registered lands are plowed in the spring, when curlews are present, rather than in the fall, when curlews are absent (Pampush 1980b). Also, chemicals used in agriculture, primarily insecticides, but also rodenticides, may directly impact Long-billed Curlew health or indirectly their food sources. In the Columbia Basin, pesticide use during the breeding season has been known to impact Long-billed Curlews (Blus et al. 1985).

Conversion of native or disturbed grasslands to purposes incompatible with curlew use is a potentially significant problem in some areas in eastern Washington. Agricultural conversion to unsuitable crop types (e.g. cottonwood plantations grown for pulp production, apple orchards, and vineyards) and urban development continue in and around Franklin and Walla Walla counties, an area which supports a sizable portion of the state's curlew population (H. Newsome, pers. comm.). Rock-mining in south-central Klickitat County (and perhaps elsewhere) has resulted in local loss of suitable curlew nesting habitat (D. Anderson, pers. comm.).

The population-level significance of wind turbine effects is currently unknown; however, there may be significant impacts on individual Long-billed Curlews or local populations. Although there are no records of Long-billed Curlews colliding with wind turbines in Washington, several aspects of wind turbine placement may impact these birds. First, wind turbine placement, related road construction, and subsequent operation of wind turbines may be responsible for abandonment of known nesting areas in southeastern Washington (M. Denny, pers. comm.). Second, construction activities have resulted in damage to macrobiotic soil crust, areas of locally abundant insect prey used by Long-billed Curlews (M. Denny, pers. comm.). Third, Common Raven abundance has increased around these sites and ravens regularly scavenge carcasses of other birds killed by turbine blades (M. Denny, pers. comm.). The increased abundance of Common Ravens may increase their interactions with nesting Long-billed Curlews; indeed, groups of ravens have been observed actively seeking, finding, and removing eggs in Walla Walla County (M. Denny, pers. comm.). Installation of wind turbines on Rattlesnake Mountain near Hanford Reach NM was recently proposed but has not moved forward.

MANAGEMENT: Several NWRs and one NM have identified specific management actions for Long-billed Curlews in their long-term planning documents (U.S. Fish and Wildlife Service 2006, 2007). Land managers are actively restoring native grasses to recently burned or weed-infested areas. However, little is known of curlew response to habitat improvements, minimum habitat requirements, or the best management options for restoration so future evaluation of Long-billed Curlew response will be critical (H. Newsome, pers. comm.).

In addition, many information needs are evident. The population of Long-billed Curlews appears stable within Washington; however, its possible vulnerability to changes in the Columbia Basin warrants attention. A high priority should be to devise a method to reliably evaluate population trends. Other relevant research or monitoring needs include aspects of habitat use (e.g. the value and timing of use of croplands, patch size, or spatial arrangement of nest areas, especially with respect to foraging areas), the effectiveness of CRP activities, sensitivity to environmental contaminants, and the influence of increased irrigation efficiency on habitat use. It may be useful as a management tool to model projected losses of habitat to conversion and assess projected future population distribution and performance under a number of varying management scenarios. Other research needs include the evaluation of depredation and other factors that may influence reproductive success or survival.

Submitted by Joseph B. Buchanan
Reviewed by Howard Browers, Randy Hill, Neil Holcomb, Heidi Newsome, and Susan M. Thomas

---

Wyoming

SUMMARY: Breeds in scattered locations throughout but generally is uncommon. Local monitoring and surveys target Long-billed Curlews.

STATUS:
State: This species is included in the Wyoming Game and Fish Department's Comprehensive Wildlife Conservation Strategy (Wyoming Game and Fish Department 2005) as a Species of Greatest Conservation Need, with a Native Species Status 3 classification: populations that are restricted in distribution and habitat is vulnerable but no on-going significant loss (Wyoming Game and Fish Department 2006). Wyoming Partners in Flight identifies Long-billed Curlews as a Level I Priority Species (Nicholoff 2003).

Natural Heritage Rank: Wyoming: S3B (Vulnerable Breeding); *National rank:* N5N, N5B (Secure Nonbreeding, Breeding); *Global rank:* G5 (Secure; NatureServe 2006).

TRENDS:
North American Breeding Bird Survey (BBS) trends and abundance data: Trends and relative abundance analyzed using data from 11 routes. Relative abundance equals 0.15 individuals per route. Non-significant positive trend from 1966-2007 (7.9%/yr; $P = 0.20$; Sauer et al. 2008). Credibility of the BBS data are poor, with a BBS Credibility Indicator equal to Red (data have important deficiencies such as low abundance and low sample size; Sauer et al. 2008).

Christmas Bird Count (CBC): Long-billed Curlews do not winter in Wyoming.

RANGE:
Breeding: Long-billed Curlews breed throughout the state (Cerovski et al. 2004). Most sightings occur in the western portion of the state (Nicholoff 2003). It is considered an uncommon summer resident in Wyoming. Only populations near Pinedale, Cody, and Lusk are locally common.
Approximate timing: Primary breeding occurs in May-July.
Counties recorded: Park, Teton, Sublette, Lincoln, Uinta, Big Horn, Fremont, Sweetwater, Sheridan, Campbell, Crook, Niobrara, Weston, Goshen, Platte, Carbon (Cerovski et al. 2004).

Migration: Uncommon spring and fall migrant.
Approximate timing: Spring migration runs generally from 15 April-30 May. Primary fall migration is from 1 August to 15 September (eBird 2008).
Numbers, particularly high counts: Peak numbers are seen in fall migration, 1-15 August, and during spring migration (eBird 2008).

ABUNDANCE AND POPULATION: Breeding population estimated 200-1000 individuals (SLJ).

HABITAT: Habitat is a variety of grassland types ranging from moist meadow grasslands to agricultural areas to dry prairie uplands, usually near water. Prefers a complex of shortgrass prairies, agricultural fields, wet and dry meadows and prairies, and grazed mixed-grass and scrub communities. Adequate shortgrass prairie nesting habitat may be the most important factor in sustaining populations (Nicholoff 2003).

MONITORING: Cochrane (1983) conducted roadside curlew surveys from 8 May to 19 July 1982, modifying the BBS. In 1987, Cochrane's (1983) survey routes and methods were replicated. Since 1991, the routes have been modified to include the number of curlews both seen and heard (A. O. Cerovski pers. comm.). Long-billed Curlew populations in eastern Wyoming may be declining significantly.

RESEARCH: The only significant study is Cochrane (1983). Habitat and land-uses were compared between relatively high-density (HC) and low-density (NF) Long-billed Curlew breeding grounds in western Wyoming. One-third as many Long-billed Curlews were seen on the NF site during roadside surveys from May through July 1981 as compared to the HC site. Further, local residents claimed that curlew numbers have declined since 1960 on the NF site. Habitat measures included vegetation height measured as visual obstruction, ground cover by major plant forms, microtopography, amount of open terrain, and vegetation types. Visual obstruction remained short uniformly through mid-incubation and below 2.5 cm on summer pastures. Tame hays grew significantly taller and denser than native hays. Microtopography, soil moisture, and forb cover did not vary significantly between field types. One-quarter of the HC was summer grazed, not hayed.

This site had more wet soil as well. The NF site received most of the dragging, fertilizing, and minor seeding plus dense spring grazing. Curlew nests ($n = 21$) were on significantly higher ground with more dense grass cover than occurred randomly. Nest survival was 38.6% and human disturbance or flooding preceded or caused all nest failures. Feeding curlews selected for significantly wetter than average ground. Detrimental disturbances were greater at the NF site. In contrast, summer grazing provided preferred vegetation profiles and less intensive hay production provided disturbance refugia at the HC site. Direct disturbances, not the availability of suitably structured habitat, correlated most strongly with both nest failures and observed population differences.

CONSERVATION ACTIVITIES (ONGOING): There are no conservation activities specific to Long-billed Curlews occurring in Wyoming.

THREATS
Breeding. Long-billed Curlew populations were impacted by uncontrolled hunting in the late 1800s and early 1900s, conversion of native shortgrass prairie to agricultural fields, and organochlorine pesticides. The loss of grasslands through conversion to agriculture or urbanization, excessive grazing, and oil and gas development are considered the primary threats in Wyoming. Current agricultural practices, livestock grazing, urban expansion, and particularly oil and gas development may have prevented recovery in many areas.

MANAGEMENT: Intensive grazing and fires can be effective management tools when used at the proper time to create preferred short vegetation for nesting areas (Clark and Harvey 1989). Other recommendations include creating and maintaining vegetative diversity within grasslands, meadows, and prairies by conducting rotational burning, mowing, and grazing; use livestock grazing as a tool to maintain areas of short grass and open ground. Pre-nesting grazing, rotational grazing, and rest rotational grazing may be beneficial to create these conditions (Nicholoff 2003). Prescribed burns should be conducted in late summer or early fall to promote vegetation and habitat characteristics preferred by Long-billed Curlews (i.e. reduced shrub cover and increased habitat openness; Nicholoff 2003). Grasslands should be mowed rotationally in strips 6 to 15 m wide depending on the field's size once or twice in early spring before nesting has begun, and/or in the fall after nesting activities have ended (Nicholoff 2003). Oil and gas development and recreational activities should be restricted near Long-billed Curlew habitat during the peak breeding and migration season (April through July; Nicholoff 2003).

Submitted by Stephanie L. Jones
Reviewed by Andrea Orabona

Alabama, Florida, Georgia, Louisiana, Mississippi, North Carolina, and South Carolina

SUMMARY: Long-billed Curlews are rare and irregular winter and fall migrants in Alabama, Mississippi, North Carolina and South Carolina. Florida: Long-billed Curlews are uncommon, but are regularly found during the nonbreeding season along the coasts. Georgia: Long-billed Curlews are uncommon, but regularly winter on the Georgia coast near the Altamaha River. Louisiana: Long-billed Curlews are regular winter and fall migrants.

STATUS:
State: Long-billed Curlews do not have a state designated status in Alabama, Florida, Mississippi, North Carolina, or Louisiana. Georgia: Long-billed Curlews are identified as a Species of Concern in the Comprehensive Wildlife Conservation Strategy (Georgia Department of Natural Resources Wildlife Resources Division 2005). South Carolina: Long-billed Curlews are listed as a Species of Highest Priority in the Comprehensive Wildlife Conservation Strategy (South Carolina Department of Natural Resources 2006).

Natural Heritage Ranks: Alabama: S2N (Imperiled Nonbreeding); Georgia: S3 (Vulnerable); Louisiana: S5N (Secure Nonbreeding); Florida, Mississippi, North Carolina and South Carolina: SNA (Not Applicable). *National rank:* N5N, N5B (Secure Nonbreeding, Breeding); Global rank G5 (Secure; NatureServe 2006).

TRENDS: There are no trends reported for Long-billed Curlews in these states.

Christmas Bird Count (CBC):
Alabama: Since the 1980's Long-billed Curlews have been recorded irregularly on CBC routes in Alabama. A high count of three individuals was recorded on the 1987-1988 count in the Mobile – Tensaw River Delta area (National Audubon Society 2006).
Florida: Single Long-billed Curlews have been recorded annually on CBC routes in Florida since 1953. Numbers are relatively few; counts range from 1-5 individuals. Birds have been seen on routes in the Tampa Bay, Waccasassa, Florida Bay, St. Francis-Apalachicola Bay, and Jacksonville areas (National Audubon Society 2006).
Georgia: Single individuals have been recorded irregularly (National Audubon Society 2006).
Louisiana: Long-billed Curlews have been recorded on CBC routes with numbers fluctuating dramatically between years. Areas of concentration include the Sabine NWR. Numbers are estimated to be over 25 individuals in several years (National Audubon Society 2006).
Mississippi: Only twice have individual Long-billed Curlews been reported on routes. A single bird was seen during the 1962-1963 count and

another sighting reported in 2005-2006 (National Audubon Society 2006).

North Carolina: Long-billed Curlews have been recorded semi-regularly on CBC routes. Counts number between 2-5 individuals in the Cape Fear, Cape Hatteras, and Beaufort areas (National Audubon Society 2006).

South Carolina: Long-billed Curlews were recorded irregularly on CBC routes until the 1988-1989 count. At this time they began to be regularly reported. Yearly high counts are of 5-10 individuals primarily in the Santee River delta area (National Audubon Society 2006).

RANGE:

ALABAMA:

Migration: Birds have been present during fall migration during the second week of October through the last week of November. Observations of up to a total of two birds have been made in the Mobile-Tensaw River Delta area. Sightings are not recorded for all years (eBird 2008). There are no recorded spring migration sightings (eBird 2008).

Winter: High counts for Alabama are less than five individuals total during the winter (S. L. Melvin, pers. comm.).

FLORIDA:

Migration: Long-billed Curlews have been recorded throughout the year in Florida but are most often observed between September and May (Kale and Maehr 1990). Spring and fall observations may represent individuals migrating to and from unknown breeding locations or they may represent nonbreeding birds.

Winter: They were reportedly less common early in the 1900s and have recently become more regular (Kale and Maehr 1990) however high counts for Florida are still estimated at less than ten individuals total during the winter (S. L. Melvin, pers. comm.).

GEORGIA:

Migration: Small numbers (up to four individuals at a time) have been reported during both the fall and spring migration periods. All reports have come from coastal areas (eBird 2008).

Winter:

Approximate timing: Long-billed Curlews are documented and regularly present during all months between August and April.

Location of wintering areas: Primary wintering locations include Wolf, Little St. Simons, St. Catherine's, and Ossabaw islands and Little Egg Island Bar.

Numbers, particularly high counts: The number of individuals ranges from 0-6 annually during the midwinter survey which is conducted in late January or early February.

LOUISIANA:

Migration: Long-billed Curlews are present between August and April (eBird 2008). A high of 75 individuals have been reported during spring and fall migrations, February and November, respectively (eBird 2008).

Winter: High counts for Louisiana are estimated to be less than 30 individuals total during the winter (eBird 2008).

MISSISSIPPI:

Migration: Birds have been irregularly reported during fall migration during the third and fourth week of November. There are recorded irregular spring sightings of single birds in the April and May. Observations of single birds have been made along the Mississippi Sound at the Mississippi-Alabama border (eBird 2008).

Winter: There are no reported wintering populations in Mississippi.

NORTH CAROLINA:

Migration: There are no recorded spring migration sightings. During fall migration, single birds were reported on the Outer Banks in July, August, and September (eBird 2008).

Winter: High winter counts for North Carolina are less than five individuals.

SOUTH CAROLINA:

Migration: Long-billed Curlews are probably present from mid-October through mid-November during fall migration. There is only one fall (October) record on eBird (2008). Three indivdiduals were observed at this time (eBird 2008). Seven birds were observed in February (eBird 2008).

Winter: High counts for South Carolina are less than ten individuals total during the winter.

ABUNDANCE AND POPULATION: Populations of migrating and wintering Long-billed Curlews in Alabama, Florida, Georgia, Mississippi, North Carolina, and South Carolina are small and irregular, probably numbering less than 5-10 individuals in any one year in each state. Louisiana: populations of migrating and wintering Long-billed Curlews are small but regular, probably numbering between 25 and 50 individuals wintering in any one year.

HABITAT: Long-billed Curlews use mudflats and coastal beaches during the migration and the wintering period. Specific habitat characteristics used by curlews in all of these states are unknown.

MONITORING: No Long-billed Curlew specific monitoring occurs.

RESEARCH: No Long-billed Curlew research projects are available or ongoing in these states; in Georgia, attempts have been made in the past few winters to color band individuals for re-sighting purposes, but due to the small population size no birds have been captured.

CONSERVATION ACTIVITIES (ONGOING): No Long-billed Curlew specific conservation effects are currently under way in most of these states. Conservation activities directed at other high priority beach shorebirds such as Piping and Snowy plovers or American Oystercatchers could benefit Long-billed Curlews.

Georgia: Most of the barrier islands used by Long-billed Curlews are owned by either the state of Georgia or the federal government. Bird islands in Georgia are protected by the Bird Island Rule (state rule OCGA 391-4-7-.03), which prohibits or limits public access to the five islands/sandbars that are important shorebird nesting, stopover, and wintering sites. Little Egg Island Bar and St. Catherine's Bar are both used by Long-billed Curlews and public access is prohibited year-round at both of these sites. Ongoing efforts to increase public awareness about all shorebirds are underway including the Georgia Colonial Coast Birding and Nature Festival, which occurs annually in October.

South Carolina: Cape Romain NWR is a designated International Site of Importance by WHSRN. Long-billed Curlews and other shorebird species benefit from the management and public attention drawn by this designation (Western Hemisphere Shorebird Reserve Network 2006).

THREATS: Long-billed Curlews face the same threats as many of the migratory and wintering shorebird species. Beach erosion, beach re-nourishment projects, development, and disturbance are threats shared by all migratory shorebirds. Loss of food resources due to changes in water quality or quantity from upstream may also be a consideration.

South Carolina: Cape Romain NWR also faces threats from recreational shrimp baiting as well as the possibility of a major oil spill or other contamination from Charleston Harbor (Western Hemisphere Shorebird Reserve Network 2006).

MANAGEMENT: No Long-billed Curlew specific management activities are currently under way.

Alabama, Florida, Louisiana, Mississippi, North Carolina, and South Carolina:
Submitted by Stefani L. Melvin
Revised by Suzanne D. Fellows and Stephanie L. Jones

Georgia:
Submitted by Brad Winn
Reviewed by Stefani Melvin
Revised by Suzanne D. Fellows and Stephanie L. Jones

Illinois, Indiana, Iowa, Michigan, Minnesota, and Wisconsin

SUMMARY: Long-billed Curlews were formerly thought to breed in these states, but their historical breeding ranges are poorly documented. Currently, Long-billed Curlews are occasional to rare migrants here. Illinois: Historically bred in the northeastern section of the state; currently, the species is a very rare migrant in the northern half. Indiana: Formerly a regular visitor and possibly a former breeding species in the northwestern section of the state, Long-billed Curlews are now very rare migrant. Iowa: Currently very rare migrant, Long-billed Curlews formerly bred in the north and west and perhaps elsewhere in the state. Michigan: No historical breeding season reports from the small tallgrass prairie region of southwestern Michigan; currently, the species is known only as an extremely rare migrant. Minnesota: currently classified as casual migrants, Long-billed Curlews formerly bred on the prairies but their range was not well documented. Wisconsin: No longer breeders, they are now extremely rare migrants.

STATUS:
State: Long-billed Curlews do not have a state designated status in any of these states.

Natural Heritage Ranks: Illinois, Iowa, Minnesota, and Wisconsin: SXB (Presumed Extirpated Breeding). Indiana and Michigan: No State Natural Heritage rank. *National rank:* N5N, N5B (Secure Nonbreeding, Breeding); *Global rank:* G5 (Secure; NatureServe 2006).

TRENDS:
North American Breeding Bird Survey (BBS) trends and abundance data: No modern breeding records.

Christmas Bird Count (CBC): No winter records.

HISTORICAL RANGE:
ILLINOIS:
Breeding: Kennicott (1854) noted that the species nested in Cook County and Nelson (1876) found a pair nesting on the Calumet marshes in 1873. Kennicott (1854) noted that curlews were abundant on the large prairies in the middle of the state. Aitkin, a collector in the late 1800s, recorded the species in the Chicago region (Ford 1956). Little information exists on the rapid decline of the Illinois breeding population, but by 1900 the species was no longer recorded in the state except as a very rare migrant (R. P. Russell, pers. comm.).

INDIANA:
Breeding: No breeding records, but there are many reports from counties dominated by wet prairie habitat. Birds were known to breed just over the border at Lake Calumet, Illinois which would strongly hint at possible past breeding in

counties such as Lake, Newton, Benton, Jasper, and Starke. Butler (1898) considered it a rare migrant and a possible nester in the northern part of the state. Mumford and Keller (1984) note that the presettlement prairies of Indiana were mostly quite wet. For example, in 1830, Benton County, with prevalent tallgrass prairie, was 69 percent wetlands with about 4860 ha permanently ponded. Nearly 55 percent (43,700 ha) of Starke County where Long-billed Curlews were recorded was permanently ponded at this same time as were more than 20 percent of Kosciusko, Lake, LaPorte, Newton, Porter, St. Joseph, and White counties.

Migration: Records from southwestern Indiana in the 1800s were likely migrants occurring on isolated wet prairie outliers amid the largely forested landscape. This landscape was traversed by bison trekking to salt licks in southern Indiana (French Lick) and northern Kentucky which may have created ideal conditions for stopover birds moving northwest from the southeast Atlantic coast amid an otherwise hostile environment (B. McCoy, pers. comm.).

IOWA:
Breeding: Early ornithologists suggested that curlews were a fairly common breeder and that habitat loss probably led to their disappearance. The last mentioned nesting date was about 1885 (Kent and Dinsmore 1996). The extent of the breeding range is unknown, but likely extended at least as far east as the lake country of northwestern Iowa and perhaps throughout the entire Des Moines Lobe region.

Migration: Currently very rare migrant in the west and north of Iowa.

MICHIGAN:
Breeding: There are no documented records of Long-billed Curlews using Michigan grasslands for breeding. Granlund et al. (1994) does not mention the species within the state.

Migration: Currently they are only seen as extremely rare migrants within the state (R. P. Russell, pers. comm.).

MINNESOTA:
Breeding: Roberts (1932) noted Long-billed Curlews were extirpated from Minnesota about the turn of the twentieth century. He noted that, curlews were formerly a summer resident, numerous on the western prairies north of the Iowa line, and breeding south and west of the heavy timber. The account by Hatch (1892) indicated that curlews bred primarily in the western part of the state. Roberts (1932) did not find curlews in Grant or Traverse counties in 1879, nor did he find them at Heron Lake after 1893. At least as late as 1883, Long-billed Curlews were still breeding in southern Jackson County. Local observers told Roberts (1932) that a few years prior to 1893, curlews had been very abundant on prairies near Jackson, Jackson County and nests and eggs

had been collected by local farmers. It appears that sometime between 1883 and 1893 Long-billed Curlews disappeared as a breeding species from this region (Roberts 1932). Farther north a bird near Euclid, Polk County, was probably breeding on 10 June 1897, but no additional breeding records came from that northwestern area (Roberts 1932). Coues (1874) found curlews breeding with Marbled Godwits and Upland Sandpipers on Minnesota and eastern Dakota prairies in 1873. The last documented Minnesota breeding report appears to be that of a female shot in Lac Qui Parle County on 24 April 1891 (Roberts 1932).

Migration: Hatch (1892) indicated curlews were only common in the eastern part of the state in migration, primarily during fall. A handful of records appear from the 1890s. In 50 years of travel around the state, Roberts (1932) observed Long-billed Curlews only once, a probable migrant seen in Sherburne County east of the Mississippi River, on 10 August 1880.

WISCONSIN:
Breeding: Formerly a common breeding species on prairies in the southern counties from Kenosha County west to Stoughton and north to the vicinity of the Wisconsin River and northeast to Fond du Lac County. Hoy (1853) noted it as an abundant breeder in Columbia and Fond du Lac counties and common on large tracts of sparsely settled prairies. Kumlein and Hollister (1903) noted that although it bred in suitable localities in different parts of the state between the 1840s and 1860s, it decreased rapidly between the 1860s and 1890s, and when found at all during this later period it was as a migrant only. The last definite date for nesting in Wisconsin was 1859 (Robbins 1991).

Migration: Currently the species is an extremely rare migrant.

ABUNDANCE AND POPULATION: There are no historical estimates for Long-billed Curlew abundance or populations in <u>Illinois</u>, <u>Indiana</u>, <u>Iowa</u>, <u>Michigan</u>, or <u>Minnesota</u>. In <u>Wisconsin</u>, as an indication of their former abundance, at least locally, in Kenosha County in the 1850s, farmers plowing virgin prairie sod were able to gather curlew eggs for consumption (Kumlein and Hollister 1903).

HABITAT: Historically Long-billed Curlews nested in native prairie. Specific habitat characteristics used are undocumented in <u>Illinois</u>, <u>Indiana</u>, <u>Iowa</u>, <u>Michigan</u>, and <u>Wisconsin.</u> In <u>Minnesota</u>, historically Long-billed Curlews nested in native grasslands in the western prairies of Minnesota. There was a reported preference for the sandy ridges and old beaches around the Red River Valley area (Roberts 1932).

CONSERVATION ACTIVITIES (ONGOING): There are no ongoing Long-billed Curlew specific conservation activities. <u>Minnesota</u>: Grassland restoration at Glacial Ridge NWR, Polk County, in the center of the historic state range, can potentially provide over 10,110 ha of breeding habitat for potential reintroduction site (R. P. Russell, pers comm.).

THREATS: Like many prairie nesting birds, habitat loss is thought to be the primary reason for extirpation in Wisconsin. Kumlein and Hollister (1903) attributed the disappearance of the birds to the breakup of the original prairie sod.

Submitted by Robert P. Russell
Revised by Suzanne D. Fellows and Stephanie L. Jones

Long-billed Curlew, High Island. Bob Gress©.

CANADA

Alberta

SUMMARY: Long-billed Curlews are primarily found in the southern Grassland Natural Region of the province. A long-term monitoring program which includes Long-billed Curlews has been instituted within the province. Several conservation actions have been undertaken to protect grassland nesting birds within the province; however, there are very few curlew specific activities or management actions ongoing.

STATUS:
Province: Long-billed Curlews are currently on the 'Blue List' indicating that this species may be at risk in the province. It was down-listed from the 'Red List' in 1996 due to better information on provincial numbers (Hill 1998).

Natural Heritage Rank: Alberta rank: S3 (Vulnerable); National rank: N4B (Apparently Secure Breeding); Global rank G5 (Secure; NatureServe 2006).

TRENDS:
North American Breeding Bird Survey (BBS) trends and abundance data: Long-billed Curlews are reported on 39 routes. Relative abundance equals 3.02 individuals per route. There is a slight non-significant negative trend from 1966-2007 (-0.2%/yr; $P = 0.79$). Credibility of the BBS is good, with a BBS Credibility Indicator equal to Blue (Sauer et al. 2008).

Christmas Bird Count (CBC): Long-billed Curlews do not winter in Alberta.

RANGE:
Breeding:
    Approximate timing: In Alberta, Long-billed Curlews begin nesting in May (Hill 1998).
    Locations: They primarily breed in the southern Grassland Natural Region (GNR) of Alberta. The breeding distribution is bound by the southern foothills, Calgary, Stettler, and Provost with high densities in the grasslands south of the Red Deer River between Gem and Empress, and at Canadian Forces Base (CFB) Suffield (De Smet 1992, Semenchuk 1992, Hill 1998).

Migration:
    Approximate timing: In spring migration, Long-billed Curlews arrive in southern Alberta between 13 and 24 April (Renaud 1980, Hill 1998). During fall migration, adult and juvenile Long-billed Curlews form post-breeding flocks in July and August. Long-billed Curlews leave Alberta by the end of August; the latest observation in Alberta was 2 September (Hill 1998).
    Location of staging areas: Long-billed Curlews may be observed beyond their breeding

limits during migration in the following areas: Waterton Lakes National Park, east and north of Edmonton at Beaverhill Lake, Belvedere, west of Calgary at Glenbow Lake, and in Banff (Sadler and Myres 1976, Salt and Salt 1976, Hill 1998).

ABUNDANCE AND POPULATION: The Alberta population estimate for Long-billed Curlews is 23,884 (95% confidence interval of 19,122 - 28,646) based on a population estimate study conducted in the Grasslands Natural Region (Saunders 2001).

HABITAT: The breeding habitat of Long-billed Curlews generally consists of open, expansive shortgrass or mixed-grass native prairie and grassy meadows (De Smet 1992, Hill 1998). Nevertheless, there appears to be some flexibility in their breeding habitat preferences. Long-billed Curlews do not nest in areas with extensive cultivation however they will occasionally nest in fallow or stubble fields or in tame pastures (Renaud 1980, Hill 1998). Within the GNR in Alberta, Long-billed Curlews are often found nesting in fescue grasslands, native mixed grasslands, and sandhills (Hill 1998). A limited number of surveys have indicated that maximum breeding densities of curlews occur in moderately-grazed mixed grasslands with sandy loam soil (De Smet 1992). Once chicks hatch, broods will often be moved to areas with greater vegetative cover, if available (Renaud 1980). Use of cultivated land may be associated primarily with adults tending broods that were hatched in native grassland rather than nesting (Renaud 1980, Foster-Willfong 2003). The effects of habitat fragmentation on the habitat selection and reproductive success of Long-billed Curlews is currently unknown, however their current distribution in southeastern Alberta suggests a preference for large tracts of habitat (Hill 1998). Within Alberta, habitat requirements during migration are less critical than breeding habitat requirements. During spring migration, Long-billed Curlews are predominately observed in upland prairie, stubble, and fallow fields and they also spend time in sloughs and runoff ponds (Renaud 1980). During fall migration and staging, Long-billed Curlews are often observed near bodies of water, such as lakeshores and river valleys (Renaud 1980).

MONITORING: In 2000 a stratified random sample survey was used to estimate the numbers of Long-billed Curlews within the GNR of Alberta. A portion of the survey routes are rerun every year to monitor changes in population trend throughout the province (Saunders 2001; R. Quinlan, pers. comm.).

RESEARCH: Gratto-Trevor (2006) conducted a study on managed wetlands in southern Alberta to determine their effects on upland nesting shorebirds. Effects were determined by comparing numbers of breeding species (Long-billed Curlews, Willets, and Marbled Godwits) among areas of managed wetlands, natural wetland basins, and no wetland basins, between 1995 and 2000. Long-billed Curlews had pre-incubation surveys averages of 0.1, 0.2, and 0.1 birds/km², and 0, 0.2, and 0 nests/km² in each of the three habitat types respectively. Nest success appeared to be similar in all areas. Shallow managed wetlands were not necessarily beneficial to Long-billed Curlews.

CONSERVATION ACTIVITIES (ONGOING): Currently, there are no Long-billed Curlew specific conservation activities. The main programs and management plans currently in effect are designed to protect native grasslands for the species that rely upon it. Some of these programs include Operation Grassland Community, a public awareness program operated by the Alberta Fish and Game Association. The Prairie Conservation Action Plan is working towards increasing awareness and protecting remaining native prairie as well as implementing protective strategies and land use management practices that sustain diverse ecosystems across the prairie landscape (Prairie Conservation Forum 2006). The Grassland Bird Monitoring program, initiated by the Canadian Wildlife Service (CWS), has been designed to supplement data from the BBS by improving coverage of "at risk" endemic grassland birds. The program's pilot study illustrates that it has the potential to improve monitoring and provide a better understanding of population changes of many grassland species (Dale et al. 2005). Subsequently, this information can contribute to the planning and implementing of conservation efforts. Recommendations have been made for the Grassland Bird Monitoring program to be upgraded to operational status and be included as part of regular monitoring activities in addition to the BBS (Dale et al. 2005). In addition, the northwest portion of CFB Suffield, which is located within the Long-billed Curlews breeding range in Alberta, was designated a National Wildlife Area (Hill 1998). Dinosaur Provincial Park Resource Management Plan adopted the use of Long-billed Curlews as a representative species of native prairie habitat for public awareness and education programs within the park (Hill 1998).

THREATS: Long-billed Curlews were heavily hunted in the late 1800s and early 1900s which resulted in initial significant declines in their populations throughout North America (De Smet 1992). Although they are no longer a game or commercial species, Long-billed Curlews may be at risk of being shot illegally due to their large size, prominent mobbing and tenacious incubation behaviour (Redmond and Jenni 1996, Hill 1998). Habitat loss due to cultivation of native prairie and urban development has been identified as the single greatest cause of past declines in curlew populations (Hill 1998). In Alberta, over two-thirds of the native prairie has been converted to cropland and the remaining grasslands are threatened by cultivation and overgrazing (De Smet 1992). Habitat heterogeneity required for successful nesting and brood-rearing is most likely provided by moderate grazing regimes. However, intense grazing may contribute to the loss of brood-rearing areas and increase egg loss due to trampling by livestock (Hill 1998). Although the effects of pesticide residues on

Long-billed Curlews have rarely been studied, it has been noted that pesticide residues sometimes contribute to eggshell-thinning, direct mortality of adults and chicks, and/or reduce prey important in their diet (De Smet 1992). Limited availability of nesting and brood-rearing habitat likely restricts the distribution and abundance of Long-billed Curlews in Alberta (Hill 1998). Curlews have a conservative breeding strategy — they are a late-maturing, long-lived species with low reproductive output and do not, or rarely, renest after a failed nesting (De Smet 1992, Hill 1998). Therefore, loss of breeding adults or nests can potentially have a negative impact on population levels. Long-billed Curlews are also faced with high rates of predation by mammalian and avian predators (De Smet 1992). Drought conditions may also threaten the breeding success of Long-billed Curlews by reducing the abundance of dense vegetation areas needed for brood-rearing (Hill 1998). Exploration and development of renewable and non-renewable resources (e.g. road and pipeline construction) can cause habitat loss and degradation (Driver 1992, Hill 1998) and human disturbance can result in nest desertion (Redmond and Jenni 1986, Hill 1998). Furthermore, Long-billed Curlews are also at risk of nest, adult and/or chick predation by domestic dogs and cats (Hill 1998).

MANAGEMENT: There are no Long-billed Curlew specific management recommendations for Alberta.

Submitted by Cheri L. Gratto-Trevor

British Columbia

SUMMARY: Long-billed Curlews are found breeding in several disjunct regions within British Columbia. The Fraser River Delta supports the only regularly observed wintering population. As elsewhere throughout their range, the disappearance of shortgrass prairies has been identified as a major threat. Recent surveys in the Cariboo-Chilcotin Region indicate that province-wide population estimates are probably low and identify the need for a province-wide long-term monitoring effort for this vulnerable species.

STATUS:
Province: Long-billed Curlews are currently on the "Blue List" indicating that this species is vulnerable and may be at risk in the province (Royal British Columbia Museum 2002).

Natural Heritage Rank: British Columbia rank: S3B (Vulnerable Breeding); *National rank:* N4B (Apparently Secure Breeding); *Global rank:* G5 (Secure; NatureServe 2006).

TRENDS:
North American Breeding Bird Survey (BBS) trends and abundance data: Long-billed Curlews are reported on 11 routes. Relative abundance equals 0.21 individuals per route. There is a non-significant positive trend from 1966-2007 (0.8;

$P = 0.80$). Credibility of the BBS is poor, with a BBS Credibility Indicator equal to Red (data have important deficiencies such as low abundance and low sample size; Sauer et al. 2008).

Christmas Bird Count (CBC): Long-billed Curlews do not generally winter in British Columbia.

RANGE:
Breeding:
Approximate timing: Cannings (1999) summarizes timing as adults arrive on breeding grounds in late March to early April; clutches are initiated in April through the first half of May; most young fledge in early July (Cannings 1999).
Locations: Primary breeding locations include Cariboo-Chilcotin grasslands, Thompson Plateau, Okanagan Valley, East Kootenay, near McBride, Quesnel, Creston, Prince George, and Vanderhoof (Royal British Columbia Museum 2002) with the highest concentrations in the Fraser-Chilcotin region (Cannings 1999). The following forest districts have documented nesting: Central Cariboo, Chicotin, Cascades, Headwaters, Kamloops, 100 Mile House, Okanagan Shuswap, Prince George, Quesnel, and the Rocky Mountain Forest District (British Columbia Ministry of Environment 2007).

Migration:
Approximate timing: Cannings (1999) suggests that fall migration starts with adults leaving the breeding grounds for coastal habitats in early July, the young leave beginning in late July and continuing through early August (Cannings 1999)
Location of staging areas: Cannings (1999) surmised that there are no known regularly used staging areas in British Columbia. Dog Creek Plateau and Alkali Creek have reported large flocks (Cannings 1999).
Numbers, particularly high counts: Cannings (1999) summarized sightings of larger flocks.

Winter: Cannings (1999) reported that a single bird was recorded to have wintered between 1990 and 1997 at Blackie Spit in south Surrey. In addition to this individual, there are fewer than 50 records of Long-billed Curlews on the coast between April and October in the period 1982-1995 (Cannings 1999). Single birds are seen every month in the Fraser River estuary (Bird Studies Canada, unpubl. data). This is the only place where Long-billed Curlews are seen in winter on a regular basis in the province (R. W. Butler, pers. comm.).

ABUNDANCE AND POPULATION: Cannings (1999) reported a minimum of 250 pairs breeding in British Columbia. This would be slightly higher than later estimates of 300-500 birds (Royal British Columbia Museum 2002) and a few hundred breeding pairs (British Columbia Ministry of Environment 2001). Volunteer-based Long-billed Curlew surveys were conducted in the Cariboo-Chilcotin Region between 2002 and 2004 (J. Steciw, pers. comm.). Appropriate

habitat was surveyed on a single day along roads. Within the region 232 (34 routes, 2002), 220 (41 routes, 2003), and 211 (40 routes, 2004) Long-billed Curlews were observed (K. VanSpall and J. Steciw, pers. comm.). These are minimum numbers for this region primarily because the protocol did not take into consideration detectability issues and because the surveys were road based and did not cover many interior grassland sites (K. VanSpall and J. Steciw, pers. comm.). These numbers do indicate that the breeding population of Long-billed Curlews in British Columbia would exceed previous estimates (K. VanSpall and J. Steciw, pers. comm.).

HABITAT: Cannings (1999) summarizes breeding habitat as being restricted to the very dry, hot, warm and mild subzones of the Bunchgrass, Ponderosa Pine and Interior Douglas-fir, Interior Cedar-Hemlock (near Creston), and Sub-boreal Spruce (near McBride) biogeoclimatic zones in the Southern Interior, Southern Interior Mountains and Central Interior ecoprovinces of British Columbia (Cannings 1999). Curlews in British Columbia nest between 280-1220 m in elevation in large tracts of open, usually flat grasslands, and on open ridges and hillsides. Vegetative cover is short and they avoid tall thick patches of grasses and shrubs. Broods are reared in relatively moist habitats such as hay fields (Royal British Columbia Museum 2002). They have also bred in the cultivated fields in Southern Columbia Mountains and Fraser Basin ecoregions (Cannings 1999). They are reportedly tolerant of rangeland which has been burned in late summer (Cannings 1999). Long-billed Curlews were observed using agricultural fields, pastures, and native grasslands during the 2002-2004 Cariboo-Chilcotin Region survey (K. VanSpall and J. Steciw, pers. comm.). Greater than 95% of the birds were observed in vegetation less than 30 cm tall and 85% were found in vegetation less than 15 cm. It is unknown if these observations reflect habitat availability or are an indication of true habitat preference (K. VanSpall and J. Steciw, pers. comm.).

During migration they have been known to use alfalfa fields in East Kootenay for foraging (Ohanjanian 1985). Along the British Columbia coast they have used a variety of shoreline habitats but are predominantly found on mudflats (Campbell 1972).

MONITORING: Cannings (1999) recommended an annual monitoring program comprising at least of a relative abundance index from all breeding locations following standards suggested by Ohanjanian (1992). Based on a three-year survey of the Cariboo-Chilcotin Region several recommendations for future province-wide surveys and a long-term monitoring program were developed (K. VanSpall and J. Steciw, pers. comm.). They supported the Cariboo-Chilcotin and Thompson-Okanagan regions coordinating future monitoring and survey programs which they suggested should be run a minimum of three years in a row, every 5-10 years. Approximately 411 observer-hours were required to survey the Cariboo-Chilcotin Region over the three year period. Volunteers for this survey were recruited from government agencies, conservation organizations, and the general public. Approximately $40,000 was donated by in-kind services and represents a substantial savings to the government (K. VanSpall and J. Steciw, pers. comm.). The regional survey was road based with stops every 400 m and a survey period of 4 min at each stop.

RESEARCH: Cannings (1999) proposed that studies of Long-billed Curlew productivity in agricultural habitats as well as in areas under intense development would be beneficial to developing management options and strategies. A more thorough GIS analysis of the 2002-2004 survey results was also recommended (K. VanSpall and J. Steciw, pers. comm.). This would allow for comparisons of habitats and locations with the number of Long-billed Curlew observations and could provide much needed information on habitat characteristics used by curlews in the Cariboo-Chilcotin Region.

CONSERVATION ACTIVITIES (ONGOING): Currently, there are no ongoing conservation activities aimed specifically at curlews. Because much of curlew habitat within British Columbia is on private land, protection must take the form of stewardship agreements. Long-billed Curlews could become an ideal icon for outreach and education efforts promoting grassland conservation in the province (Cannings 1999). To this end there has been a 2-page informational flyer developed for the public through funding by Forest Renewal British Columbia (British Columbia Ministry of Environment, undated).

THREATS: As for most species across North America, loss of habitat remains the primary threat. Natural habitat has been lost through intensive agricultural development and overgrazing by livestock (Royal British Columbia Museum 2002). There is a continued habitat loss due to rapid urban development and corridors for transmission lines and pipelines (World Wildlife Fund 2001). There are very few protected areas which provide nesting habitat for curlews (Cannings 1999). For example, it has been estimated that only 20% of the original Okanagan dry forest ecoregion remains intact. Protection of grassland habitats, long-term restoration, and private stewardship and nature trust activities will assist in conservation in the Okanagan region (World Wildlife Fund 2001). Forest encroachment, due to fire suppression, has also been detrimental to grasslands and reduced the natural habitat available for breeding (Cannings 1999). Stands of invasive species which have dense tall growth are avoided by breeding curlews probably because birds cannot detect predators and it inhibits chick movement (Cannings 1999). Sensitivity to human disturbance and off-road vehicle use around nesting habitats have also been cited as threats (British Columbia Ministry of Environment 2001). Although found to be problematic elsewhere, there are no data from British Columbia to document population level effects of illegal shooting, pesticides or predation on Long-billed Curlews (Cannings 1999).

MANAGEMENT: Management recommendations include maintaining open grasslands with low vegetation height (< 30 cm), protecting from human disturbance, delaying harvest until after mid-June (end of nesting season), fall grazing, seeding with low profile native species (avoiding crested wheatgrass), managing forest encroachment on grasslands, not establishing recreational trails through grasslands, and limiting or avoiding driving off-road through possible nesting locations at least during the breeding season (15 March-15 July; summarized in British Columbia Ministry of Environment 2001, Cannings 1999).

Submitted by Suzanne D. Fellows
Reviewed by Julie Steciw

Saskatchewan

SUMMARY: Approximately 3000 Long-billed Curlews are estimated to nest in Saskatchewan. They are found primarily in the southwestern part of the province.

STATUS:
Province: Long-billed Curlews currently do not have an official designation; however, they are being considered for provincial listing (Hill 1998).

Natural Heritage Rank: Saskatchewan rank: S4B (Apparently Secure Breeding), S4M (Apparently Secure Migration); *National rank:* N4B (Apparently Secure Breeding); *Global rank:* G5 (Secure; NatureServe 2006).

TRENDS:
North American Breeding Bird Survey (BBS) trends and abundance data: Long-billed Curlews are reported on 10 routes. Relative abundance equals 0.80 individuals per route. There is a significant negative trend from 1966-2007 (-9.2; $P = 0.02$). Credibility of the BBS is poor, with a BBS Credibility Indicator equal to Red (data have important deficiencies such as low abundance and low sample size; Sauer et al. 2008).

Christmas Bird Count (CBC): Long-billed Curlews do not winter in Saskatchewan.

RANGE:
Breeding:
    Approximate timing: Long-billed Curlews begin nesting in early May with peak nesting occurring in mid-May to mid-June (Renaud 1980).
    Locations: Long-billed Curlew breeding areas in Saskatchewan are mainly located in the southwestern part of the province south of the South Saskatchewan and Qu'Appelle rivers and west of 106° W (Renaud 1980, Smith 1996). Long-billed Curlews occur southwest of Biggar, along Eagle

Creek, at White Heron Lake, the Missouri Coteau near Elbow, the upper benchlands along the South Saskatchewan River, and along the Qu'Appelle Valley from the Qu'Appelle dam to Buffalo Pound Lake. Also in the east block and "Gap" regions of Cypress Hills, the Frenchman River near Val Marie, and the Boundary and Old Man On His Back plateaus (De Smet 1992). In the southeastern part of the province (east of 106° W), Long-billed Curlews have virtually been extirpated even though apparently suitable habitat still remains in the Weyburn and Quill Lake areas (Smith 1996).

Migration:

Approximate timing: In spring migration, Long-billed Curlews begin to arrive in Saskatchewan in early April. The average arrival time in the extreme southwest of Saskatchewan occurs around 17-18 April (Renaud 1980). During fall migration, in Saskatchewan, small groups of curlews begin to form by mid-July, with most individuals departing from all parts of the breeding range by late-August. Long-billed Curlews are rarely seen in southeastern Saskatchewan, suggesting that few individuals migrate southeast from breeding areas in western Saskatchewan (Dugger and Dugger 2002).

ABUNDANCE AND POPULATION: The Saskatchewan population estimate for Long-billed Curlews is estimated at 2984 ± 658 (range of 2325 to 3642) based on surveys conducted in 1988 (Driver 1992). The latest provincial population estimate is 3000 adult Long-billed Curlews (Smith 1996).

HABITAT: The breeding habitat of Long-billed Curlews generally consists of open, expansive shortgrass or mixed-grass native prairies and grassy meadows (De Smet 1992, Hill 1998). Nevertheless, there appears to be some flexibility in their breeding habitat preferences. In Saskatchewan, Long-billed Curlews have been reported to nest in damp, grassy prairie hollows at Cypress Hills and in dry, open prairie near Matador (De Smet 1992). Although curlews do not nest in areas with extensive cultivation, they will occasionally nest in fallow, stubble, and tame hay pastures (Renaud 1980, Hill 1998). Crested wheatgrass pastures have been identified as important breeding habitats for Long-billed Curlews in Saskatchewan (Hill 1998). However, Foster-Willfong (2003) found that curlews consistently avoided areas of fallow, stubble and tame hay during the breeding season in a study conducted in an 8000 km² area between the South Saskatchewan River and Maple Creek. Once chicks hatch, broods will often be moved to areas with greater cover, if available (Renaud 1980). Use of cultivated land may be associated primarily with adults tending broods that were hatched in native grassland rather than nesting (Renaud 1980, Foster-Willfong 2003). The effects of habitat fragmentation on the habitat selection and reproductive success of Long-billed Curlews is currently unknown, however their current distribution in southwestern Saskatchewan suggests a preference for large tracts of habitat (Hill 1998). In Saskatchewan, Long-billed

Curlews are usually observed in dry upland prairie both near and at some distance from wetlands, in stubble and fallow fields, and also in sloughs and runoff ponds (Renaud 1980). During fall migration and staging, Long-billed Curlews are often observed near bodies of water, such as lakeshores and river valleys (Renaud 1980).

MONITORING: Saskatchewan was part of the efforts by USFWS to establish a rangewide estimate of Long-billed Curlews in 2004-2005 (Jones et al. 2008). Grassland bird surveys conducted between 1988 and 1991 were used to develop estimates of the Long-billed Curlews within the province (Driver 1992). The Grassland Bird Monitoring program, initiated by CWS, has been designed to supplement data from the BBS by improving coverage of "at risk" endemic grassland birds. The program's pilot study illustrates that it has the potential to improve monitoring and provide a better understanding of population changes of many grassland species (Dale et al. 2005). Subsequently, this information can contribute to the planning and implementing of conservation efforts. Recommendations have been made for the Grassland Bird Monitoring program to be upgraded to operational status and be included as part of regular monitoring activities in addition to the BBS (Dale et al. 2005).

RESEARCH: Foster-Willfong (2003) studied census methodology and habitat use by Long-billed Curlews within the province. Results indicated that call response surveys were ineffective at detecting curlews compared to a traditional listening census technique. It also demonstrated that Long-billed Curlews generally preferred native prairie grassland and avoided area of stubble, fallow, and tame hay. A large proportion of curlews were observed in spring/summer cropland during the post-hatch periods.

CONSERVATION ACTIVITIES (ONGOING): Currently, there are no conservation projects that exist specifically for Long-billed Curlews. The main programs currently in effect are designed to protect native grasslands for the species that rely upon it. Some of these programs include the Prairie Habitat Stewardship program operated by the Saskatchewan Watershed Authority which promotes the conservation and management of native grasslands in southern Saskatchewan. The program encourages sustainable land-use practices and activities that contribute to the welfare of species at risk such as habitat enhancement and landowner outreach and education (Canadian Wildlife Service 2007). The Nature Conservancy of Canada operates the Missouri Coteau Habitat Securement and Stewardship Project which focuses on the conservation of migratory birds in the Missouri Coteau region and surrounding grasslands in south-central Saskatchewan by maintaining important habitat for the survival and recovery of species at risk (Canadian Wildlife Service 2007). The Prairie Conservation Action Plan is working towards increasing awareness and understanding of native prairie, conserving remaining native prairie, maintaining its biological diversity, as well as promoting complementary sustainable uses of native prairie (Prairie Conservation Action Plan Partnership 2003).

THREATS: Long-billed Curlews were heavily hunted in the late 1800s and early 1900s which resulted in initial significant declines in their populations throughout North America (De Smet 1992). Although they are no longer a game or commercial species, Long-billed Curlews may be at risk of being shot illegally due to their large size, prominent mobbing, and tenacious incubation behaviour (Redmond and Jenni 1996, Hill 1998). Habitat loss due to cultivation of native prairie and urban development has been identified as the single greatest cause of past declines in curlew populations (Hill 1998). In Alberta, over two-thirds of the native prairie has been converted to cropland and the remaining grasslands are threatened by cultivation and overgrazing (De Smet 1992). The situation in Saskatchewan is as bad if not worse. Habitat heterogeneity required for successful nesting and brood-rearing is most likely provided by moderate grazing regimes. However, intense grazing may contribute to the loss of brood-rearing areas and increase egg loss due to trampling by livestock (Hill 1998). Although the effects of pesticide residues on Long-billed Curlews have rarely been studied, it has been noted that pesticide residues sometimes contribute to eggshell-thinning, direct mortality of adults and chicks, and/or reduced prey important to the curlews diet (De Smet 1992). Limited availability of nesting and brood-rearing habitat may restrict the distribution and abundance of Long-billed Curlews in Saskatchewan, as it is thought to in Alberta (Hill 1998). Curlews have a conservative breeding strategy, i.e., they are a late-maturing, long-lived species with low reproductive output, and do not, or only rarely, renest after a failed nesting attempt (De Smet 1992, Hill 1998). Therefore, loss of breeding adults or nests can potentially have a negative impact on population levels. Long-billed Curlews are also faced with high rates of predation by mammalian and avian predators (De Smet 1992). Drought conditions may also threaten the breeding success of Long-billed Curlews by reducing the abundance of dense vegetation areas needed for brood-rearing (Hill 1998). Exploration and development of renewable and non-renewable resources (e.g. road and pipeline construction) can cause habitat loss and degradation (Driver 1992, Hill 1998) and human disturbance can result in nest desertion (Redmond and Jenni 1986, Hill 1998). Furthermore, Long-billed Curlews are also at risk of nest, adult and/or chick predation by domestic dogs and cats (Hill 1998).

MANAGEMENT: There are no Long-billed Curlew specific management recommendations for Saskatchewan. The primary management recommendations currently available are designed to protect native grasslands for the species that rely upon them.

Submitted by Cheri L. Gratto-Trevor

México

Baja California

SUMMARY: Long-billed Curlews are common winter visitors on the west coast of Baja California from late July to May. There are two critical sites, the Estero de Punta Banda and Bahía San Quintín which support large numbers of Long-billed Curlews. Statewide population estimates and trend data are lacking. Major gaps remain in the understanding of Long-billed Curlew ecology during the non-breeding season, including population structure, survival estimates, migratory connectivity, habitat use at natural and anthropogenic sites, foraging behavior, assessment of farmland habitat use, and evaluation of the impacts of contaminants on Long-billed Curlews. Habitat loss and degradation may be the most important threat to Long-billed Curlews. The Estero de Punta Banda and Bahía San Quintín are bordered by agricultural land where Long-billed Curlews may be exposed to potentially harmful chemicals. There is growing recreational use of estuarine and other shallow water areas by humans, but the effects of these activities on migrating and/or wintering Long-billed Curlews are unknown.

STATUS: Long-billed Curlews do not have a state designated status in Baja California.

TRENDS: Long-billed Curlew trends are not measured in Baja California.

North American Breeding Bird Survey (BBS) trends and abundance data: Long-billed Curlews do not breed in Baja California.

Christmas Bird Count (CBC): There is one CBC circle (Ensenada) established in Baja California. Numbers range from a low of 208 in December 2005 to a high of 580 in January 2002, with an average of 321 for the seven years (2002-2008) the count has been conducted (National Audubon Society 2006; W. H. Howe, pers. comm.). There are too few data available to develop a CBC population trend.

RANGE:
Migration: Migration patterns in Baja California are unknown. It is possible that Long-billed Curlews may use some sites as both staging areas during migration and as wintering areas, at least for portions of the population. A recent satellite telemetry study showed that a male Long-billed Curlew which bred in Ruby Lake, Nevada used wetlands in Ensenada at least during the fall (C. A. Hartman and L. W. Oring, pers. comm.).

Winter:
  Locations: Long-billed Curlews are common winter visitors in coastal wetlands and adjacent habitats in the state (Morrison et al. 1992, Page et al. 1997, Ruiz-Campos et al. 2005). Sites used by at least 100 curlews during the winter are the Estero de Punta Banda (31°42'–31°47'N, 116°37'–116°40'W) and Bahía San Quintín (30°29'–30°30'N, 115° 57'–116°01'W; Palacios et al. 1991, Page et al. 1997). The species is also present at El Ciprés, El Salado, El Rosario, and Laguna Manuela (Page et al. 1997, Ruiz-Campos et al. 2005).
  Approximate timing: Long-billed Curlews are present from late July to May (Howell and Webb 1995).
  High counts: Maximum counts are 179 Long-billed Curlews in Estero de Punta Banda (Palacios et al. 1991), and 1814 in Bahía San Quintín (Page et al. 1997). Bahía San Quintín is a designated Important Bird Area (Arizmendi and Márquez Valdelamar 2000).

ABUNDANCE AND POPULATION: There is no information on Long-billed Curlew abundance in Baja California.

HABITAT: Wintering Long-billed Curlews use tidal estuaries and open parts of salt marshes during low tide, and commonly roost in high-elevation salt marshes during high tide. They also use farmlands and salt ponds (Page et al. 1997, Ruiz-Campos et al. 2005). In the Estero de Punta Banda, birds move between intertidal flats and adjacent farmland areas (G. Fernández, pers. comm.).

MONITORING: There are no current statewide monitoring programs. In 1992 and 1993, aerial surveys were conducted in the region by CWS and PRBO (Morrison et al. 1992, Page et al. 1997).

RESEARCH: No specific research on Long-billed Curlew in Baja California has been done. Estero de Punta Banda has had several shorebird studies (Palacios et al. 1991, Maimone-Celorio and Mellink 2003). Ruiz-Campos et al. (2005) studied avian composition from 13 small coastal wetlands and adjacent habitats in northwestern Baja California.

CONSERVATION ACTIVITIES (ONGOING): There are no current population conservation actions or management efforts directed specifically at Long-billed Curlews in the state. Opportunities for effective habitat conservation for Long-billed Curlews are probably enhanced when important sites in the state, such as the Estero de Punta Banda and Bahía San Quintín, are formally recognized at local, regional and international scales. These two sites may qualify for inclusion as Ramsar and WHSRN sites of Regional Importance because they support at least 1% of the Long-billed Curlew population. The Nature Conservancy is working with a coalition of partners to foster the protection and long-term management of Bahía San Quintín. Furthermore, if appropriate management plans for Estero de Punta Banda and Bahía San Quintín are developed, they should include key terrestrial habitats used by Long-billed Curlews. There is no education program directed specifically at Long-billed Curlews in the state.

THREATS: Habitat loss and degradation may be the most important threats to Long-billed Curlews.

Across the state, coastal wetlands have been drained for urban and agricultural purposes. Estero de Punta Banda and Bahía San Quintín are bordered by agricultural land where Long-billed Curlews may be exposed to potentially harmful chemicals. Chemicals used for agriculture or other purposes, either individually or in combination, have the potential to harm shorebirds on-site or following run-off and it is possible that these chemicals reduce prey available for Long-billed Curlews. Pesticide types and levels in coastal wetlands along the Pacific Coast are unknown. Moreover, changing agricultural practices, from open farm fields to mega-greenhouses, may reduce the "farm habitat" available for Long-billed Curlews. There is growing recreational use of estuarine and other shallow water areas by humans, but the effects of these activities on migrating and/ or wintering Long-billed Curlews are unknown. Disturbance from human activities (e.g. pedestrians, motorized vehicles, water craft, pets, shellfish harvest activities, and hunting) are potential threats to Long-billed Curlews along the coast of Baja California.

MANAGEMENT: There are no Long-billed Curlew specific management recommendations for Baja California.

Submitted by Guillermo Fernández

Baja California Sur

SUMMARY: Long-billed Curlews are common winter visitors in Baja California Sur. The species has been observed over-summering in Ensenada de La Paz, thus the area may be particularly important for younger birds, enabling them to survive and improve their foraging efficiency during summer. Critical sites in the state are Ojo de Liebre-Guerrero Negro, Laguna San Ignacio, Bahía Magdalena, and Ensenada de La Paz. Major gaps remain in understanding Long-billed Curlew ecology during the non-breeding season, including population structure, survival estimates, migratory connectivity, and habitat use. Habitat loss and degradation may be the most important threats to Long-billed Curlews.

STATUS: Long-billed Curlews do not have a state designated status in Baja California Sur.

TRENDS: Long-billed Curlew trends are not measured in Baja California Sur.

North American Breeding Bird Survey (BBS) trends and abundance data: Long-billed Curlews do not breed in Baja California Sur.

Christmas Bird Count (CBC): There is one CBC circle (Ensenada de La Paz) established in Baja California Sur. Numbers range from a low of 36 in December 2006 to a high of 122 in December 2007, with an average of 72 for the three years (2006-2008) that the count has been conducted (National

Audubon Society 2006; W. H. Howe, pers. comm.). There are too few data available to develop a CBC population trend.

RANGE:
Migration: A recent satellite telemetry study tracked two female Long-billed Curlews, which bred in Ruby Lake, Nevada, to Baja California Sur (C. A. Hartman and L. W. Oring, pers. comm.).

Approximate timing: In Ensenada de La Paz, southward migration is between late-May and June and northward migration is from March to early-April (Brabata 1995, Carmona 1995).

Location of staging areas: Long-billed Curlews have been recorded in Ojo de Liebre-Guerrero Negro (27°59'–27°24'N, 114°31'–113° 55'W), Laguna San Ignacio (27°12'–26° 27'N, 113° 16'–112°50'W), Bahía Magdalena (24°00'–25°00'N, 112°W), and Ensenada de La Paz (Morrison et al. 1992, Carmona 1995, Page et al. 1997, Zárate-Ovando et al. 2006). It is possible that Long-billed Curlews use some sites as staging areas during migration and also as wintering areas, at least for a portion of the population.

Numbers, particularly high counts: In Ensenada de La Paz, maximum counts are 40 Long-billed Curlews during northbound migration and 80 curlews during southbound migration (Brabata 1995). Ensenada de La Paz is an Important Bird Area (Arizmendi and Márquez Valdelamar 2000) and a WHSRN Site of Regional Importance.

Winter:
Approximate timing: In Ensenada de La Paz, numbers of Long-billed Curlews are relatively stable from late-June to early-March (Brabata 1995, Carmona 1995).

Locations: During the winter, Long-billed Curlews have been recorded in Ojo de Liebre-Guerrero Negro, Laguna San Ignacio, Bahía Magdalena, Estero de San Jose del Cabo, and Ensenada de La Paz.

Numbers, particularly high counts: Maximum counts are 671 Long-billed Curlews in Ojo de Liebre-Guerrero Negro (Page et al. 1997), 615 in Laguna San Ignacio (Page et al. 1997), 135 in Bahía Magdalena (Zárate-Ovando et al. 2006), and 150 in Ensenada de La Paz (Brabata 1995, Carmona 1995). Besides Ensenada de La Paz, Ojo de Liebre-Guerrero Negro, Laguna San Ignacio, Bahía Magdalena are Important Bird Areas (Arizmendi and Márquez Valdelamar 2000). Ojo de Liebre-Guerrero Negro and Laguna San Ignacio are part of the Biosphere Reserve El Vizcaíno. In Ensenada de La Paz (25°15'N, 110°15'–110°30'W), 25% and 30% of the winter population have been observed between late-April and early-June in Chametla and Conchalito Beaches, respectively (Brabata 1995, Carmona 1995). Long-billed Curlews delay breeding until their second or third year (Redmond and Jenni 1986); thus, it may be that birds remaining at these sites in the summer months are first- or second-year birds. This suggests that the area may be particularly important for younger birds, enabling them to survive and improve their foraging efficiency during summer.

ABUNDANCE AND POPULATION: There are no abundance estimates for Long-billed Curlews in Baja California Sur.

HABITAT: Long-billed Curlews use tidal estuaries and open parts of salt marshes during low tide, and commonly roost in high-elevation salt marshes during high tide; the species also uses farmlands and salt ponds (Brabata 1995, Carmona 1995, Page et al. 1997). In Ensenada de La Paz, birds move between intertidal flats and adjacent farmland areas (G. Fernández, pers. comm.). In Ojo de Liebre-Guerrero Negro, curlews may move between the mudflats of the lagoon and the Guerrero Negro saltworks (Danemann et al. 2002).

MONITORING: There are no current statewide monitoring programs. Aerial surveys were conducted in the region by CWS and PRBO from 1992 to 1994 (Morrison et al. 1992, Page et al. 1997). Most studies are limited in seasonality and the area surveyed.

RESEARCH: Brabata and Carmona (1999) studied the foraging behavior of Long-billed Curlews in relation to tide levels at Ensenada de La Paz. The Universidad Autónoma de Baja California Sur has a shorebird research program in progress at Ensenada de La Paz and Guerrero Negro saltworks and the Centro de Investigaciones Biológicas del Noroeste also has a shorebird project at Bahía Magdalena.

CONSERVATION ACTIVITIES (ONGOING): There are no specific ongoing conservation activities for Long-billed Curlews in Baja California Sur.

THREATS: Habitat loss and degradation may be the most important threats to Long-billed Curlews. Coastal wetlands have been drained for urban development, tourism, and water-use systems, including the construction of channels, dikes, and piers (Arriaga-Cabrera et al. 1998). Additionally, the quality of water entering wetlands from adjacent urban and agricultural areas has declined in Bahía Magdalena and Ensenada de La Paz. Chemicals used for agriculture or other purposes, either individually or in combination, have the potential to harm Long-billed Curlews on-site or following run-off.

MANAGEMENT: There are no curlew specific management recommendations for Baja California Sur.

Submitted by Guillermo Fernández and Daniel Galindo-Espinosa

Chihuahua

SUMMARY: Grasslands in Chihuahua provide important wintering and migration habitat for Long-billed Curlews. Long-term monitoring, research, and management projects have been developed and implemented to learn more about Long-billed Curlews and other grassland species at several sites. Several actions have recently occurred in Chihuahua

which will assist in the conservation of Long-billed Curlews.

STATUS: Long-billed Curlews do not have a state designated status in Chihuahua.

TRENDS:
North American Breeding Bird Survey (BBS) trends and abundance data: Long-billed Curlews are occasionally present in the summer but are not known to breed in Chihuahua.

Christmas Bird Count (CBC): There are two CBC circles in Chihuahua. At Ejido San Pedro near Janos, in northwestern Chihuahua, Long-billed Curlews have been reported regularly since the count was initiated in 1997 (2-296 individuals per CBC, average 99). They have not been reported at Rancho el Palomino in southcentral Chihuahua (National Audubon Society 2006; W. H. Howe, pers. comm.). There are too few data available to estimate a CBC population trend.

RANGE: Manzano-Fischer et al. (2006) considered Long-billed Curlews in the Janos-Nuevo Casas Grandes grassland complex to be year-round residents.

Migration:
    Numbers, particularly high counts: Long-billed Curlews observed in late spring may be spring migrants but more likely represent non-breeding summer holdovers. Breeding Bird Surveys in this area documented 9 individuals at El Cuervo southwest of Janos on 30 May 1999 and a single individual on 27 May 2001 (W. H. Howe and J. S. Dieni, pers. comm.). At Ejido San Pedro 8 individuals were seen on 1 June 2004 and 20 on 29 May 2005. On 28 May 2008, a flock of 48 Long-billed Curlews flew by Laguna Fierro near Nuevo Casas Grandes (eBird 2008; W. H. Howe and J. S. Dieni, pers. comm.). Manzano-Fischer et al. (1999) observed the largest numbers in the early fall in Salto de Ojo and El Cuervo in the Janos-Nuevo Casas Grandes area.

Winter:
    Locations: The semidesert grasslands west of Janos, provide relatively intact grasslands used by large numbers of wintering Long-billed Curlews (Dieni et al. 2003). Laguna de Babicora was also known to support wintering Long-billed Curlews (Drewien et al. 1996).
    High counts: 296 on 30 December 2001 near Janos (Dieni et al. 2003); 1500 at El Uno on 11 November 2005 (eBird 2008); in central Chihuahua, 450 were recorded at Laguna Enns in 2005 and 1900 and 280 at Laguna de Tejanero, in 2005 and 2008, respectively (B. A. Andres, pers. comm.).

ABUNDANCE AND POPULATION: Long-billed Curlews are considered fairly common to uncommon in Chihuahua (Howell and Webb 1995).

HABITAT: Manzano-Fischer et al. (2006) found Long-billed Curlews in the Janos-Nuevo Casas Grandes grassland complex to use habitats characterized by grasses (e.g. grama; treeawn; fescue; and tobosa, *Hilaria mutica*), annual forbs, and scattered low shrubs (e.g. mesquite, *Prosopis* spp.). It has been hypothesized that Long-billed Curlews may be less numerous in areas of the grassland where shrubs have encroached (Desmond 2004). Following a summer rain event in late August, approximately 400 individual Long-billed Curlews were seen using flooded grasslands (Manzano-Fischer et al. 2006).

MONITORING: Increased interest in the Janos region over the past two decades led to the establishment of the Ejido San Pedro CBC circle (Dieni et al. 2003; National Audubon Society 2006; W. H. Howe, pers. comm.) in Chihuahua, which has been conducted annually since 1997 after a pilot year in 1996. Continuation of monitoring efforts will assist in developing long-term winter population trend information for the area. Two BBS routes established in this area in 1998 have been surveyed in 7 years between 1998 and 2008 (W. H. Howe, pers. comm.). These may provide insight into long-term oversummering trends in Long-billed Curlews.

RESEARCH: Manzano-Fischer et al. (1999) studied grassland birds in the Janos-Nuevo Casas Grandes prairie dog complex between 1994 and 1995 to determine avian species composition, spatial and temporal distribution, and abundance. Data they collected provide base line information which can be used to further conservation of grassland bird species, including Long-billed Curlew.

CONSERVATION ACTIVITIES (ONGOING): In addition to the CBC monitoring efforts in the Janos-Nuevo Casas Grandes grasslands, initial studies have been conducted to gather baseline data on avian use by migrating and wintering species (e.g. Manzano-Fischer et al. 1999) and in the breeding season (W. H. Howe, pers. comm.). Pronatura Noreste in a cooperative effort with The Nature Conservancy recently purchased the 18,500 ha Rancho El Uno through their Private Land Conservation Program in Janos and works with land owners to monitor and manage habitat for shorebirds such as Long-billed Curlews (Vega and Cruz 2007).

Laguna de Babícora, which supports the largest number of wintering Sandhill Cranes (*Grus canadensis*) in México as well as other migratory birds including Long-billed Curlews (Wilson and Ryan 1997), was proposed to be drained for agricultural and flood control purposes (Drewien et al. 1996). However, a conservation management plan was developed and implemented to protect this site (Wilson and Ryan 1997) and it was designated as a Ramsar Wetland of International Importance in February 2008 (Ramsar Convention on Wetlands 2008).

North American Wetlands Conservation Act and Neotropical Migratory Bird Conservation Act grants have also been awarded to several entities working on monitoring and conservation issues in Chihuahua which are designed to benefit Long-billed Curlews and their habitats (Wilson and Ryan 1997, U.S. Fish and Wildlife Service 2008d).

THREATS: Currently less than 2% of the Chihuahuan Desert is protected throughout México and livestock grazing is permitted on most protected areas (Askins et al. 2007). The Janos-Nuevo Casas Grandes grasslands are among the most intact grassland complex remaining in North America and are used by many species of migrating and wintering birds that breed in the U.S. and Canada (Manzano-Fischer et al. 1999). Grasslands in the Chihuahuan Desert are being converted to croplands and cattle ranches, have experienced a decline in native herbivores, and are being encroached upon by native shrubs; these forces all have the potential to alter the habitat and affect the avian composition in the region (Manzano-Fischer et al. 1999, Desmond and Montoya 2006, Askins et al. 2007). Establishment of cotton fields by Mennonite farmers is a current primary threat to Long-billed Curlew habitat in the region (W. H. Howe, pers. comm.). The use of flowable carbofuran and collision with and electrocution from power lines have also been suggested as possible threats to Long-billed Curlews and other species using the Janos-Nuevo Casas Grandes grasslands (Manzano-Fischer et al. 2006; W. H. Howe, pers. comm.).

MANAGEMENT: Currently only 15% of the land is held as *ejidos* [rural lands designated as communal properties and used primarily for domestic livestock grazing] in Chihuahua (Askins et al. 2007); privately owned land does not generally tend to be as intensively grazed as *ejidos* (Desmond and Montoya 2006). Manzano-Fischer et al. (1999) suggest five measures for management of the Janos-Nuevo Casas Grandes grasslands which would help protect this area for Long-billed Curlews and other wintering and migrating grassland bird species: establishment of a biosphere reserve, cessation of prairie dog elimination activities, an increase in technical information and support to improve grazing management, increasing local awareness of the importance of the grassland ecosystem, and further research on the habitat requirements, abundance, and distribution of species using the grasslands. Shrub management through use of prescribed burning may be necessary to maintain grasslands in some parts of the Chihuahuan Desert (Askins et al. 2007). The current government programs that provide incentives for the conversion of habitat only marginally suited for crops may need to be reevaluated for their effectiveness and balanced against the need for conservation of wintering grassland bird habitat (Askins et al. 2007).

Submitted by Suzanne D. Fellows and William H. Howe

Coahuila

SUMMARY: Grasslands in Coahuila provide important wintering and migration habitat for avian species. Currently there are not any Long-billed Curlew specific monitoring, research, or management projects in Coahuila. However, an increased interest in the native and endemic wildlife of Coahuila could provide future opportunities. Several actions have recently occurred in Coahuila and the neighboring states which will assist in the conservation of Long-billed Curlew habitat.

STATUS: Long-billed Curlews do not have a state designated status in Coahuila.

TRENDS:
North American Breeding Bird Survey (BBS) trends and abundance data: Long-billed Curlews are not known to breed in Coahuila.

Christmas Bird Count (CBC): There is one CBC circle in Coahuila, Colonias de Perritos Llaneros de Coahuila. It was established in 2005 and has been run for three of the past four years. Long-billed Curlews were first observed in the 2007-2008 count; 114 were reported on 14 December 2007 (National Audubon Society 2006; W. H. Howe, pers. comm.). There are too few data available to develop a CBC population trend at this time.

RANGE:
Migration: Reports of 3000-6000 Long-billed Curlews have come from the area of El Tokio, near Saltillo, during October and November (M. A. Cruz, pers. comm.). On 1 July 2007, a flock of 124 were observed west of El Cercado at a water tank (R. Clay, pers. comm.). Contreras-Balderas et al. (2004) reported 40 individuals on 17 May 1997 in the Cuatro Ciénegas Basin.

Winter: Part of the southeast edge of the Chihuahuan Desert, the Altiplano Mexicano Nordoriental, is located in Coahuila. It provides wintering and migrating habitat to Long-billed Curlews and other grassland species (Desmond and Montoya 2006).

ABUNDANCE AND POPULATION: Long-billed Curlews are considered fairly common to uncommon in Coahuila (Howell and Webb 1995). Contreras-Balderas et al. (2004) considered Long-billed Curlews winter visitors in the Cuatro Ciénegas Basin based on observations from November 1996 to November 1997.

HABITAT: Long-billed Curlews were documented using three habitat types in Coahuila: pasture lands, agricultural areas, and aquatic and subaquatic areas (Garza de León et al. 2007). In the Cuatro Ciénegas Basin, migrant and wintering Long-billed Curlews used disturbed areas (Contreras-Balderas et al. 2004).

MONITORING: There are no Long-billed Curlew specific monitoring projects in Coahuila. Monitoring projects developed for other grassland species, such as Worthen's Sparrows (*Spizella wortheni,* Scott-Morales 2008) and Mountain Plovers, and on those areas enrolled in Private Land Conservation projects (Vega and Cruz 2007), may include anedotal information on Long-billed Curlews.

RESEARCH: There are no Long-billed Curlew specific research projects in Coahuila. However, research on Mexican prairie dogs (*Cynomys mexicanus*) and other grassland obligate species may provide information on Long-billed Curlews using the area.

CONSERVATION ACTIVITIES (ONGOING): In combination with the state of San Luis Potosí, over 17,000 ha are enlisted under Private Land Conservation projects. Development and implementation of a management plan and monitoring program are part of these projects (Vega and Cruz 2007). Saltillo Grasslands, which span Nuevo León and Coahuila, have become a Natural Protected Area. Pronatura Noreste and The Nature Conservancy's Prairie Wings Program are developing a management plan for the site to develop and implement shortgrass prairie avian conservation goals (Capp and Mehlman 2005).

THREATS: Conversion of grasslands to croplands remains a serious threat in parts of México (Scott-Morales et al. 2004, Scott-Morales et al. 2008). Although the direct effect of prairie dog elimination on Long-billed Curlew wintering populations in Coahuila has not been determined, it may be an impact (Scott-Morales et al. 2004).

MANAGEMENT: Currently only 15% of the land is held as *ejidos* in Coahuila (Askins et al. 2007); generally, privately owned land does not tend to be as intensively grazed as *ejidos* (Desmond and Montoya 2006). Current government programs, which provide incentives for the conversion of habitat only marginally suited for crops, may need to be reevaluated for their effectiveness and balanced against the need for conservation of wintering grassland bird habitat (Askins et al. 2007).

Submitted by Suzanne D. Fellows

Colima

SUMMARY: Long-billed Curlews are common winter visitors. Population estimates and trend data are lacking. Habitat loss and degradation may be the most important threat to Long-billed Curlews.

STATUS: Long-billed Curlews do not have a state designated status in Colima.

TRENDS: Long-billed Curlew trends are not measured in Colima.

North American Breeding Bird Survey (BBS) trends and abundance data: Long-billed Curlews do not breed in Colima.

Christmas Bird Count (CBC): There are no CBC circles established for Colima and no CBC data are available for Long-billed Curlew in the state (National Audubon Society 2006; W. H. Howe, pers. comm.).

RANGE:
Migration:
Approximate timing: Unknown
Locations: Laguna Cuyutlán (19°10'–18°55'N, 104°20'–104°05'W).
Numbers, particularly high counts: 69 Long-billed Curlews (Mellink and de la Riva 2005).

Winter: Same as Migration.

ABUNDANCE AND POPULATION: There is no information on Long-billed Curlew abundance in Colima.

HABITAT: Long-billed Curlews use tidal estuaries and open parts of salt marshes during migration and winter.

MONITORING: There are no known Long-billed Curlew specific monitoring programs.

RESEARCH: There is no research for Long-billed Curlew in Colima

CONSERVATION ACTIVITIES (ONGOING): There are no current population conservation actions or management efforts directed specifically at Long-billed Curlews in the state.

THREATS: Habitat loss and degradation may be the most important threat to Long-billed Curlews in Colima.

MANAGEMENT: There are no Long-billed Curlew specific management recommendations for Colima.

Submitted by Guillermo Fernández

Jalisco

SUMMARY: Long-billed Curlews are poorly studied in the state. Most of the information available comes from general waterbird studies. The species has been recorded at 14 sites, but only 9 sites have available abundance data. In Jalisco, Laguna Sayula, Agua Dulce, and Barra de Navidad are critical sites. Population estimates and trend data are lacking. Major gaps remain in understanding Long-billed Curlew ecology during the non-breeding season, including population structure, survival estimates,

Table 3.3. Abundance of Long-billed Curlews by site in Jalisco.

Site	Location	No. birds	Source
Barra de Navidad	19°11'–19°14'N; 104°37'–104°42'W	131	Hernández-Vázquez 2005b
Tecuan	19°18'–19°20'N; 104°55'–104°58'W	*	Navarro 1993
Chamela	19°25'–19°40'N; 104°57'–105°13'W	*	Arizmendi et al. 1990
Chalacatepec	19°38'–19°42'N; 105°11'–105°16'W	2	Hernández-Vázquez 2005b
Xola-Paramán	19°40'–19°44'N; 105°14'– 105°19'W	51	
		52	Hernández-Vázquez 2005b Esparza-Salas 2001
Majahuas	19°50'–19°53'N; 105°20'–105°23'W	27	Hernández-Vázquez y Mellink 2001
Majahuas		19[1]	Hernández-Vázquez 2005b
El Chorro	19°53'–19°55'N; 105°23'–105°25'W	71	Hernández-Vázquez y Mellink 2001
El Chorro		29[2]	Hernández-Vázquez 2005b
Ermitaño	19°55'–20°00'N; 105°27'–105°30'W	48	Hernández-Vázquez 2005a
Agua Dulce	20°00'–20°05'N; 105°29'–105°32'W	147	Hernández-Vázquez 2005a
El Salado	20°35'–20°40'N; 105°12'–105°15'W	4	Cupul-Magaña 2000
Estuary of Río Ameca	20°39'–20°42'N; 105°15'–105°17'W	*	Martínez-Martínez y Cupul-Magaña 2002
Bahía Banderas	20°15'–20°47'N; 105°15'–105°42'W	*	Howell 1999
Bahía Banderas	20°15'–20°47'N; 105°15'–105°42' W	*	E. E. Martínez-Martínez, pers. comm.
Sayula	19°54'–20°10'N; 103°27'–103°36'W	313	Munguia et al. 2005

[1] 5 November, 2 December, 2 January, 9 February, and 1 September. [2] 2 October, 6 December, 8 January, 8 February, 4 March and 1 April.
*Number of birds unavailable.

migratory connectivity, and habitat use. Habitat loss and degradation may be the most important threats to Long-billed Curlews.

STATUS: Long-billed Curlews do not have a state designated status in Jalisco.

TRENDS: Long-billed Curlew trends are not measured in Jalisco.

North American Breeding Bird Survey (BBS) trends and abundance data: Long-billed Curlews do not breed in Jalisco.

Christmas Bird Count (CBC): There are two CBC circles established in Jalisco, Guadalajara and Laguna de Chapala. Neither of these sites has recorded Long-billed Curlews during the CBC (National Audubon Society 2006; W. H. Howe, pers. comm.).

RANGE:
Migration:
Approximate timing: Migration patterns are unknown; however, there are two important peaks in Long-billed Curlew numbers during the southbound migration, one in August and another between November-December.
Locations: It is possible that Long-billed Curlews use some sites as staging areas during migration but also as a wintering area for a portion of the population (see Table 3.3 and Fig. 3.9).
Numbers, particularly high counts: See Table 3.3 for maximum counts.

Winter:
Approximate timing: In the Laguna de Sayula, Long-billed Curlews were observed from October to May (Munguia et al. 2005). In the coastal sites, they are present from late July to May in Jalisco (Howell and Webb 1995).
Locations: Long-billed Curlews have been recorded at 14 sites (see Table 3.3 and Fig. 3.9).

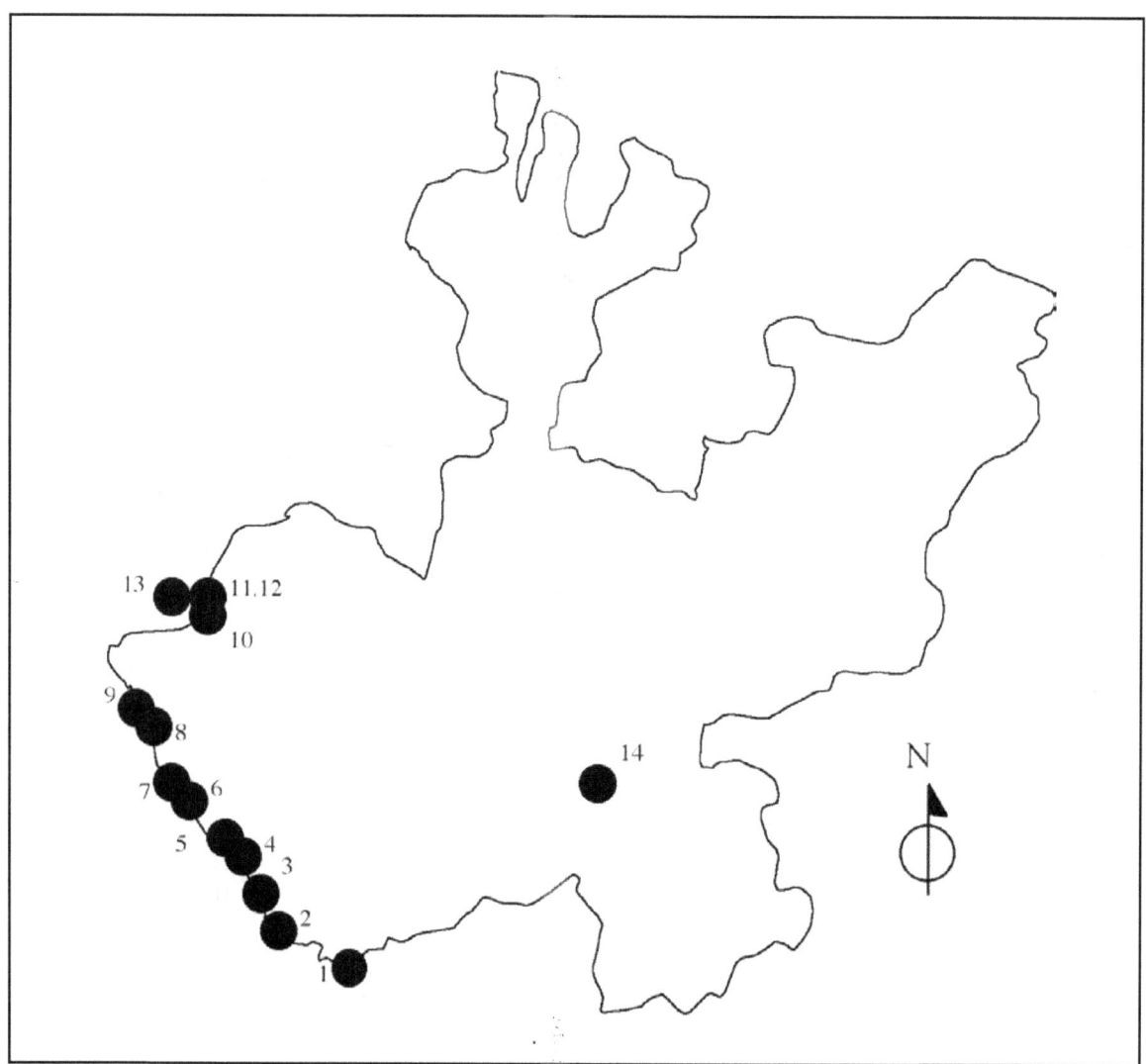

Figure 3.9. Distribution of Long-billed Curlews in Jalisco (S. Hernández-Vásquez and F. G. Cupul Magaña, pers. comm.).

Numbers, particularly high counts: See Table 3.3 for maximum counts.

ABUNDANCE AND POPULATION: There is no population trend for Long-billed Curlews in Jalisco.

HABITAT: The species uses tidal estuaries and open sandy beaches, and commonly roosts in high-elevation mangroves (e.g. Barra de Navidad lagoon) or sandbars and dunes (e.g. Agua Dulce lagoon) during high tide.

MONITORING: All studies in Jalisco in which Long-billed Curlews have been monitored are general waterbird studies. The Universidad de Guadalajara has a monitoring program for waterbirds in the Estero el Salado and Playón de Mismaloya Natural Protected Areas (NPAs). The first published records of Long-billed Curlews are by Schaldach (1963, 1969). Although Schaldach did not indicate the locality, it is possible his records were from the south, near Colima. In the 1990s, there are several inventories recording the occurrence of Long-billed Curlews (e.g. Palomera-García et al. 1994, Howell 1999). Unfortunately, these inventories only indicate that curlews are uncommon. More recently, there have been several studies which report Long-billed Curlew numbers (e.g. Cupul-Magaña 2000, Hernández-Vázquez and Mellink 2001, Hernández-Vázquez et al. 2002, Martínez-Martínez and Cupul-Magaña 2002, Hernández-Vázquez 2005a, b). In general, most studies are limited in seasonality and to the coastal wetlands; information from interior wetlands is still sparse. The only interior study is at the Laguna de Sayula (Munguia et al. 2005).

RESEARCH: There are no research projects in Jalisco for Long-billed Curlews.

CONSERVATION ACTIVITIES (ONGOING): There are no current population or habitat conservation actions or management efforts directed specifically at Long-billed Curlews in Jalisco. There are no education or outreach programs directed specifically at Long-billed Curlews in the state. However, the Departamento de Estudios para el Desarrollo Sustentable de Zona Costera, Universidad de Guadalajara has an environmental education program for the coast, with the primary goal of conserving nesting beaches of sea turtles. As part of this education program, there are several activities for wetlands and shorebird species.

THREATS: Habitat loss and degradation may be the most important threats to Long-billed Curlews in Jalisco. Coastal wetlands have been drained for urban development, tourism, and water-use systems, including the construction of channels, dikes, and piers (Arriaga-Cabrera et al. 1998). Additionally, the quality of water entering wetlands from adjacent urban and agricultural areas has declined in some areas. The untreated sewage waste is discharged directly to some sites (e.g. Barra de Navidad, El Tule, El Chorro, Majahuas, Ermitaño, El Salado),

with unknown consequences to the benthic community and to Long-billed Curlew populations. Chemicals used for agriculture or other purposes could be a potential threat to Long-billed Curlews.

MANAGEMENT: There are no Long-billed Curlew specific management recommendations for Jalisco.

Submitted by Salvador Hernández-Vázquez and Fabio German Cupul-Magaña

Nayarit

SUMMARY: Long-billed Curlews are common winter visitors. Population estimates and trend data are lacking. Habitat loss and degradation may be the most important threat to Long-billed Curlews.

STATUS: Long-billed Curlews do not have a state designated status in Nayarit.

TRENDS: Long-billed Curlew trends are not measured in Nayarit.

North American Breeding Bird Survey (BBS) trends and abundance data: Long-billed Curlews do not breed in Nayarit.

Christmas Bird Count (CBC): There is one CBC circle (San Blas) established in Nayarit. There have only been two counts, one in 2004 and the second in 2005 (National Audubon Society 2006; W. H. Howe, pers. comm.). There are too few data available to develop a CBC population trend.

RANGE:
Migration: Marismas Nacionales (21°30'44"-23°51'59"N, 105°14'13"-106°01'23"W) is the only location identified in Nayarit having Long-billed Curlews.

Winter: Marismas Nacionales is the only winter location for Long-billed Curlews currently identified in Nayrit.

ABUNDANCE AND POPULATION: There is no information on Long-billed Curlew abundance in Nayarit.

HABITAT: During both migration and winter, Long-billed Curlews use tidal estuaries and open parts of salt marshes. It is possible they also use farmlands in the area.

MONITORING: There are no known monitoring programs specific to Long-billed Curlews in Nayarit.

RESEARCH: There are no research projects for Long-billed Curlews in Nayarit.

CONSERVATION ACTIVITIES (ONGOING): There are no current activities specifically aimed at Long-billed Curlew conservation; however, there is formal recognition of the importance of the wetlands and avian resources at Marismas Nacionales. It has been designated as an Important Bird Area, a WHSRN Site of International Importance, and a Ramsar Site (Arizmendi and Márquez Valdelamar 2000).

THREATS: Marismas Nacionales has been drained for urban, agricultural, cattle, and shrimp farming purposes. Chemicals used for agriculture or other purposes could be a potential threat to Long-billed Curlews.

MANAGEMENT: There are no Long-billed Curlew specific management recommendations for Nayarit.

Submitted by Guillermo Fernández

Nuevo León

SUMMARY: Long-billed Curlews are common winter visitors in the shortgrass prairie of the state. The Valle de La Soledad may support over 6,000 individuals during the winter. Within the valley, San Rafael and La Soledad, La Hediondilla, and La Trinidad NPAs are important sites. A statewide population estimate and trend data are unavailable. There has been a monitoring program for Long-billed Curlews at La Soledad, La Trinidad, and Hediondilla NPAs since 2002. Habitat loss and degradation are the most important threats to Long-billed Curlews in the region. Grasslands have been transformed to agricultural land and the economic pressures for habitat reduction still persist.

STATUS: Long-billed Curlews do not have a state designated status in Nuevo León.

TRENDS: Long-billed Curlew trends are not currently measured in Nuevo León.

North American Breeding Bird Survey (BBS) trends and abundance data: Long-billed Curlews do not breed in Nuevo León.

Christmas Bird Count (CBC): There are two CBC circles established in Nuevo León, Cumbres de Monterrey and Valle de la Soledad; however, no Long-billed Curlews have been observed (National Audubon Society 2006; W. H. Howe, pers. comm.).

RANGE:
Migration: Migration routes of Long-billed Curlews populations are not well known. It is possible that Long-billed Curlews use some sites as both a staging area during migration and as a wintering area, at least for a portion of the population.
    Approximate timing: Long-billed Curlews generally arrive in the state between October and November and depart in March.
    Locations: In October, the species has been recorded in La Soledad NPA (24°55'29"N, 100°43'24"W), La Hediondilla NPA (24°59'58"N, 100°41'05"W), and the Rafael-Hedionilla Highway (24°58'47.48"N, 100°41'47.60"W).

Numbers, particularly high counts: Maximum counts are 283 at La Soledad NPA, 3000 at La Hediondilla NPA, and 250 at the Rafael-Hediondilla Highway.

Winter:
    Approximate timing: Long-billed Curlews are present from late November to March in the state. Local movements among sites are unknown. In El Uno (25°00'24"N, 100°38'35"W), San Rafael (25°01'08" N, 100°35'31"W), and the Rafael-Hediondilla Highway, small numbers of Long-billed Curlews (1-4 individuals) have been observed between late-May and July. It is not known whether these birds migrate from other sites and then discontinue their northward migration or spend the entire year at these sites. There is evidence that curlews delay breeding until their second or third year (Redmond and Jenni 1986); thus, it may be that birds remaining at these sites are first- or second-year birds.
    Locations: Long-billed Curlews have been recorded in San Rafael, La Soledad NPA, La Hediondilla NPA, and La Trinidad NPA (24°54'34" N, 100°25'00" W).
    Numbers, particularly high counts: Maximum counts are 300 Long-billed Curlews at La Soledad NPA, 80 curlews at La Hediondilla NPA, and 150 curlews at the Rafael-Hediondilla Highway. Based on number of individuals per transect and area surveyed, the population estimate is 2860 curlews at La Soledad NPA, 85 curlews at La Trinidad NPA, and 232 curlews at Hediondilla Grande NPA. The population estimate for Long-billed Curlews in the Valle de la Soledad (approximately 17,000 ha) is 6392.

ABUNDANCE AND POPULATION: There is no information on Long-billed Curlew abundance or population trends in Nuevo León.

HABITAT: Long-billed Curlews use dry shortgrass prairie with some patches of desert shrub.

MONITORING: Since 2002 Pronatura Noreste, A.C. and the Universidad Autónoma de Nuevo León have conducted a winter monitoring program for Long-billed Curlews and other species such as Mountain Plovers, Worthen's Sparrows, Ferruginous Hawks, and Burrowing Owls (*Athene cunicularia*). The first record of a Long-billed Curlew was in El Tokio (24°41'15" N, 100°14'05" W) on 29 February 1976 (Contreras 1978). The existing monitoring program is based on 25 random transects, each covering 30 ha (1000 m × 300 m).

RESEARCH: There are no research projects in Nuevo León.

CONSERVATION ACTIVITIES (ONGOING): There are no current conservation actions or management efforts directed specifically at Long-billed Curlews in Nuevo León. However, conservation activities which target native habitats can potentially postively affect Long-billed Curlews. Because of its unique physical and ecological conditions, the Mexican Plateau was designated as Important Bird Area and a High-priority Terrestrial Zone for the Comisión Nacional para el Conocimiento y Uso de la Biodiversidad (Arizmendi and Márquez Valdelamar 2000, Arriaga et al. 2000). Pronatura Noreste A.C. is working with Nature Conservancy and WHSRN to foster the protection and long-term management of 10,000 ha, with conservation easements with local private land owners and *ejidatarios* [farmers or ranchers that work on communal property]. These 10,000 ha were designated as a WHSRN Site of International Importance for Long-billed Curlews and Mountain Plovers. In 2002 Nuevo León established three NPAs, La Soledad, La Trinidad, and Hediondilla Grande, which are important for Mexican prairie dogs, Long-billed Curlews, Mountain Plovers, Burrowing Owls, Ferruginous Hawks, and endemic Worthen's Sparrows. Pronatura Noreste A.C., Nature Conservancy, and RARE (a U.S. based conservation organization) are implementing a new education program entitled "*Campaña por el Orgullo*". The main goal of the program is to educate people of the Galeana Municipality about the importance of their natural resources.

THREATS: In Nuevo León, the most important threat for Long-billed Curlews is habitat loss and habitat degradation. In the last 30 years, agriculture and cattle ranching have been the most important economic activities in the Galeana Municipality. Grassland transformation to agricultural land still persists (Avedaño 1999). For example, 23% of the potato crop produced in México comes from this region. Given the intensive characteristics of this type of production, fields become unable to support potato farming in less than three years and new grasslands are transformed into potato fields. Changes in land use and vegetation result in a fragmented landscape; this leads to the loss of endemic species and may negatively influence the survival of Long-billed Curlews.

MANAGEMENT: There are no current management efforts directed specifically at Long-billed Curlews in the state.

Submitted by José Ignacio Gonzalez-Rojas, Miguel Ángel Cruz Nieto, Armando Jiménez-Camacho, Gabriel Ruiz-Ayma, and Irene Ruvalcaba-Ortega

Sinaloa

SUMMARY: Long-billed Curlews are a poorly studied species in the state. They are present year-round in coastal wetlands of Sinaloa, with the highest number occurring during the winter period. They have been recorded at 7 sites, but only 2 sites have abundance data. Statewide population estimates and trend data are lacking. Bahía Santa María and Ensenada Pabellones are critical sites for Long-billed Curlew in Sinaloa. Habitat loss and degradation may be the most important threats to Long-billed Curlews. Most of the coastal wetlands are bordered by

agricultural land where Long-billed Curlews may be exposed to potentially harmful chemicals.

STATUS: Long-billed Curlews do not have a state designated status in Sinaloa.

TRENDS: Long-billed Curlew trends are not measured in Sinaloa.

North American Breeding Bird Survey (BBS) trends and abundance data: Long-billed Curlews do not breed in Sinaloa.

Christmas Bird Count (CBC): There is one CBC circle (El Yugo) established in Sinaloa. The first count was held in January 2008. No Long-billed Curlews were reported (National Audubon Society 2006; W. H. Howe, pers. comm.).

RANGE:
Migration: In Sinaloa, migration patterns are unknown. It is possible that at least a portion of the population of Long-billed Curlews use some sites both as staging areas during migration and also as wintering sites.

Winter:
Approximate timing: The species is present from late July to May in Sinaloa (Howell and Webb 1995). In Bahía Navachistes–San Ignacio, Estero Urias, and other small coastal wetlands near Mazatlan, less than 20 Long-billed Curlews have been observed in June (G. Fernández, pers. comm.). This suggests that the area may be important for younger birds, enabling them to survive and improve their foraging efficiency during summer.
Locations: Long-billed Curlews have been recorded in Bahía Agiabampo (26°15'N, 109°15'W), Bahía Navachistes–San Ignacio (25°29'–25°35'N, 108°40'–108°44'W), Bahía Santa María (24°43'–25°10'N, 107°56'–108°19'W), Ensenada Pabellones (24° 27'N, 107°35'W), Playa Ceuta (24°04'–24°15'N, 107°11'–108°24'W), Estero Urias, and Laguna Huizache–Caimanero (23°04'–22°55'N, 106°10'–105°58'W; Morrison et al. 1992, 1994; Engilis et al. 1998).
Numbers, particularly high counts: Long-billed Curlews occur in small numbers in coastal wetlands of Sinaloa. Maximum counts are 283 Long-billed Curlews in Bahía Santa María and 90 in Ensenada Pabellones (Engilis et al. 1998). Both sites are Importand Bird Areas (Arizmendi and Márquez Valdelamar 2000), and Bahía Santa María is also a Ramsar and WHSRN site of Hemispheric Importance.

ABUNDANCE AND POPULATION: There is no information on Long-billed Curlew abundance or population trends in Sinaloa.

HABITAT: Long-billed Curlews are restricted to the higher, consolidated intertidal flats and mangrove edges (Engilis et al. 1998). Use and importance of agricultural fields during the winter is unknown.

MONITORING: There are no current statewide monitoring programs specific to Long-billed Curlews in Sinaloa. Aerial surveys were conducted in the region by Canadian Wildlife Service and Manomet Center for Conservation Sciences from 1992 to 1994 (Harrington 1992, 1994; Morrison et al. 1992, 1994). Ground surveys of Bahía Santa María and Ensenada Pabellones were conducted by Ducks Unlimited, Inc. and Ducks Unlimited de México, A. C. (Engilis et al. 1998). These surveys indicated Long-billed Curlews were much less numerous in the coastal wetlands of Sinaloa than in other regions of northwestern México, such as the west coast of the Baja California peninsula (Page et al. 1997). Most studies are limited in both seasonality and the areas surveyed.

RESEARCH: No research projects have been conducted in Sinaloa.

CONSERVATION ACTIVITIES (ONGOING): There are no current population conservation actions or management efforts directed specifically at Long-billed Curlews in Sinaloa. However, there are several conservation efforts which focus on wetland habitats and Long-billed Curlews could potentially benefit from these general activities. Bahía Santa María is recognized as Ramsar Site and a WHSRN Site of Hemispheric Importance; Bahía Santa María and Ensenada Pabellones are recognized as Important Bird Areas. Pronatura Noroeste, A.C.–Dirección de Conservación en Sinaloa is working with a coalition of partners to foster the protection and long-term management of Bahía Santa María and Ensenada Pabellones. No education programs are directed specifically at Long-billed Curlews in Sinaloa, although Pronatura Noroeste, A.C.–Dirección de Conservación en Sinaloa has education and outreach programs for wetlands, which include shorebird species.

THREATS: Habitat loss and degradation may be the most important threats to Long-billed Curlews. Across the state, coastal wetlands have been drained for urban development, tourism, agriculture, and shrimp-farming purposes. Most of the coastal wetlands in the state are bordered by agricultural land where Long-billed Curlews may be exposed to potentially harmful chemicals. Chemicals used for agriculture or other purposes, either individually or in combination, have the potential to harm shorebirds on-site or following run-off. Pesticide types and levels in coastal wetlands are unknown. There is growing recreational use of estuarine and other shallow water areas by humans, but the effects of these activities on migrating and/or wintering Long-billed Curlews are unknown. Disturbance from human activities (e.g. pedestrians, motorized vehicles, water crafts, pets, shellfish harvest activities, and hunting) are potential threats to Long-billed Curlews along the coast of Sinaloa. The consequences of human disturbance, in terms of physical condition or survival should be the focus of research.

MANAGEMENT: There are no Long-billed Curlew specific management recommendations for Sinaloa.

Submitted by Guillermo Fernández

Sonora

SUMMARY: Long-billed Curlews are common winter visitors in Sonora, with records throughout the year in the Delta de Río Colorado and adjacent areas. Long-billed Curlews represent 3%-5% of the entire shorebird community at this site. During migration peak numbers are in September and March. Wintering birds are present from November to January. Most of the species information in the state comes from Alto Golfo de California y Delta del Río Colorado. Long-billed Curlews use the intertidal mudflats of Golfo de Santa Clara and Bahía Adahír as foraging and roosting sites. The monitoring efforts in Sonora began relatively recently, thus population estimates and trend data for the state are lacking. Conservation actions include the protection of foraging and roosting sites located in the Biosphere Reserve of the Alto Golfo de California y Delta del Río Colorado, and the development of education and outreach programs for all shorebirds species and wetlands. Major gaps remain in understanding Long-billed Curlew ecology during the non-breeding season, including population structure, survival estimates, migratory connectivity, and habitat use. Habitat loss due to development of the coastal zone for tourism may be the most important threat to Long-billed Curlews.

STATUS: Long-billed Curlews do not have a state designated status in Sonora.

TRENDS:
North American Breeding Bird Survey (BBS) trends and abundance data: Long-billed Curlews do not breed in Sonora.

Christmas Bird Count (CBC): In Sonora, there are several CBC circles where Long-billed Curlews have been recorded including: Puerto Peñasco, Delta del Río Colorado, Yécora, and San Carlos. However, Puerto Peñasco is the only location where counts have been carried out over a long term (1990–2008; Fig. 3.10). Between 1990 and 2005, the average abundance per survey was 157 Long-billed Curlews and average 4.9 curlews per hour per survey. Based on data standardized by effort, the population trend was significantly downward with a rate of decrease of 61% per year ($P = 0.02$). However, the correlation factor is relatively low ($r^2 = 0.29$) and the overall trend is biased by the 1990 survey, when the number of participants greatly influenced the number of birds reported by party hour. If the 1990 survey is excluded, there is a non-significant downward trend ($r^2 = 0.18$, $P = 0.11$).

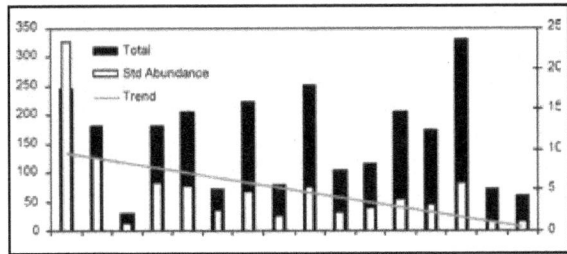

Figure 3.10. Total and standardized abundance (individuals per hour of survey) of Long-billed Curlews during Christmas Bird Counts in Puerto Peñasco, Sonora (M. M. Gómez-Sapiens, O. Hinojosa-Huerta, and E. Soto-Montoya, pers. comm.).

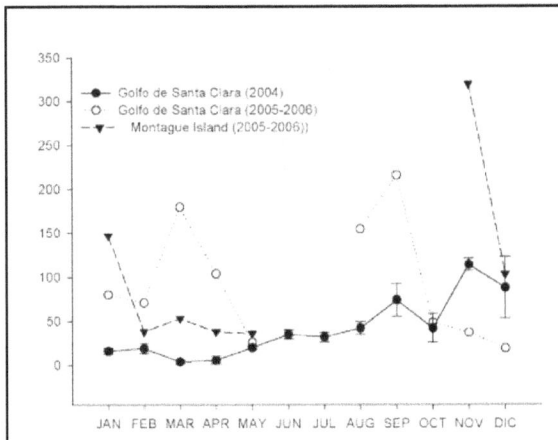

Figure 3.11. Number of Long-billed Curlews in the Golfo de Santa Clara and Isla Montague, Sonora during 2004 – 2006. In 2004, average number (SE) of curlews per month in two transects of 1 km long. In 2005 and 2006, three transects in the Golfo de Santa Clara and two transects in Isla Montague (M. M. Gómez-Sapiens, O. Hinojosa-Huerta, and E. Soto-Montoya, pers. comm.).

RANGE:

Migration:

Approximate timing: Although migration patterns are unknown, the southward migration begins in July, with peak numbers in August–September. The northward migration is from March to May (Russell and Monson 1998).

Locations: There are records of Long-billed Curlews throughout the coast and a few records from the interior of Sonora. Long-billed Curlews probably use some sites as staging areas during migration but also as wintering areas, at least for a portion of the population.

Numbers, particularly high counts: During northward migration, maximum counts are 200 Long-billed Curlews in the Golfo de Santa Clara (31°41'N, 114°30'W) and 50 in Isla Montague (31°43'N, 114°43'W), Municipality of San Luis Río Colorado (Fig. 3.11). During the southward migration, maximum counts are over 200 in the Golfo de Santa Clara (Fig. 3.11). For the Delta del Río Colorado, Mellink et al. (1997) estimated 2478 and 1248 Long-billed Curlews during the northward

and southward migrations respectively. At this site, curlews made up 5% and 24% of the total number of migratory north and southbound shorebirds, respectively (Mellink et al. 1997). The Golfo de Santa Clara, Isla Montague, and Bahía Adahír, Municipality of Puerto Peñasco (31°35'N, 113°55'W) are part of the Biosphere Reserve of the Alto Golfo de California y Delta del Río Colorado, which is also an Important Bird Area (Arizmendi and Márquez Valdelamar 2000).

Winter:

Approximate timing: Long-billed Curlews are present from November to February during the winter (Fig. 3.11). In the area of the Alto Golfo y Delta del Río Colorado, 303 Long-billed Curlews have been observed during the summer (Mellink et al. 1997). Long-billed Curlews may stay throughout the summer at nearby locations such as the Baja California Peninsula, Imperial Valley, and Salton Sea (Patten et al. 2001, Patten et al. 2003). It is possible these birds may have migrated from other sites and then discontinued their northward migration. As Long-billed Curlews delay breeding until their second or third year (Redmond and Jenni 1986) it may be that birds remaining at these sites are first- or second-year birds.

Locations: There are records of Long-billed Curlews throughout the Sonora coast (Howell and Webb 1995, Russell and Monson 1998). In the area of the Alto Golfo y Delta del Río Colorado, Long-billed Curlews are found in the Golfo de Santa Clara, Isla Montague, and Bahía Adahír.

Numbers, particularly high counts: Maximum counts are 300 Long-billed Curlews at Isla Montague, 100 at Golfo de Santa Clara (Fig. 3.11), and 120 at Bahía Adahír (Fig. 3.12). In the area of the Delta del Río Colorado, Long-billed Curlews made up less than 1% of the wintering shorebirds (Mellink et al. 1997). In a more recent shorebird survey (2005-2006) by Biosphere Reserve personnel, Long-billed Curlews made up 5% of the wintering shorebirds in the area.

ABUNDANCE AND POPULATION: There is no information on Long-billed Curlew abundance in Sonora.

HABITAT: Winter and migration habitats are the same for Long-billed Curlews in Sonora. In the area of the Alto Golfo y Delta del Río Colorado, Long-billed Curlews use the intertidal mudflats of the Golfo de Santa Clara and Isla Montague and the beaches and estuaries of Bahía Adahír. The few records from the interior indicated that curlews have been recorded in grasslands, farm fields, and near water dams.

MONITORING: In the Delta del Río Colorado, there have been efforts to survey shorebirds by the Comisión de Ecología y Desarrollo Sustentable del Estado de Sonora (CEDES) since 2004 (Román-Rodríguez 2004) and, since 2003, CBC surveys which are organized by Pronatura Noroeste, A.C., Direccion de Conservacion en Sonora. The

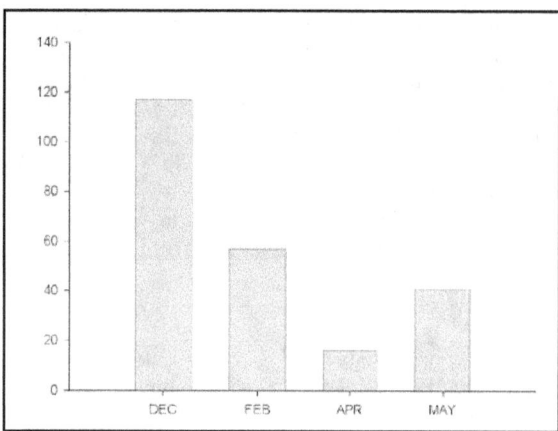

Figure 3.12. Number of Long-billed Curlews in two transects (5 counting points – 400 m between points) in Bahía Adahír (Puerto Peñasco), Sonora from December 2005 to May 2006 (M. M. Gómez-Sapiens, O. Hinojosa-Huerta, and E. Soto-Montoya, pers. comm.).

Biosphere Reserve of the Alto Golfo de California y Delta del Río Colorado also has a shorebird monitoring program in the priority wetlands within and outside the NPA. The main objectives of this monitoring program are to establish patterns of shorebird distribution and abundance and to link this information into the conservation actions of the Biosphere Reserve and the Mexican Shorebird Plan. Moreover, since 2004 there has been a monitoring program for all birds in the Río Colorado region, including the flooded flats and adjacent farm fields (Hinojosa-Huerta et al. 2004). This program is based on point counts of variable distance (Ralph et al. 1996) in 16 transects randomly located in the river flats, with 4 visits per year (one per season). Each transect consist of 8 survey points, with 200 m between each point. Although this monitoring program is not designed to specifically survey shorebirds, there are Long-billed Curlew records during the winter and spring in farm fields. Aerial surveys conducted in Sonora by CWS (Morrison et al. 1992), helped identify and prioritize wetlands for wintering shorebirds. Mellink et al. (1997) studied the distribution and abundance of non-breeding waterbids in the Delta del Río Colorado.

RESEARCH: There has been no Long-billed Curlew research in Sonora.

CONSERVATION ACTIVITIES (ONGOING): There are no current population conservation actions or management efforts directed specifically at Long-billed Curlews in the state. In general, conservation actions are directed to mitigate the consequences of habitat loss due to the development of the coastal zone. In particular, the Golfo de Santa Clara and Isla Montague, locations with the highest abundance of curlews, are part of the area nucleus of the Biosphere Reserve of the Alto Golfo de California y Delta del Río Colorado. No education programs are directed specifically at Long-billed Curlews in Sonora. However, Pronatura Noroeste, A.C.,

Dirección de Conservación en Sonora coordinates the Programa de Involucramiento y Educación which instructs primary school teachers in the region of the Alto Golfo and at coastal wetlands across the state. CEDES and personnel of the Biosphere Reserve of the Alto Golfo de California y Delta del Río Colorado offer workshops to teachers and students on the importance of the birds and coastal wetlands.

THREATS: In Sonora, habitat loss and degradation may be the most important threat to Long-billed Curlews during the non-breeding season. Across the state, coastal wetlands have been drained for urban and tourism development. The construction of the highway from the Golfo de Santa Clara to Puerto Peñasco, from Puerto Peñasco to Bahía Kino, and eventually from Kino to Guaymas may increase the rate of habitat loss. This highway construction is related to the development of the coastal zone for tourism. In the southern portion of Sonora, several coastal wetlands are threatened by shrimp farm development.

MANAGEMENT: There are no Long-billed Curlew specific management recommendations for Sonora.

Submitted by Martha Marina Gómez-Sapiens, Osvel Hinojosa-Huerta, and Eduardo Soto-Montoya

---

Tamaulipas

SUMMARY: Long-billed Curlews can be found at Laguna Madre and coastal grasslands along the Gulf of México, from the Municipality of Matamoros in the north, south to Tampico. It is believed that the conservation status of Long-billed Curlews is stable because most of the habitats used by the species have not been heavily modified. However, the coastal region is coming under increasing pressure and fragmentation from cattle ranching and other agricultural activities. It is not considered a flagship species for local conservationist groups because Long-billed Curlews are not listed under any conservation criteria by the state or federal government.

STATUS: Long-billed Curlews do not have a state designated status in Tamaulipas.

TRENDS: Long-billed Curlew trends are not measured in Tamaulipas.

North American Breeding Bird Survey (BBS) trends and abundance data: Long-billed Curlews do not breed in Tamaulipas.

Christmas Bird Count (CBC): There are four CBC circles established in Tamaulipas which have reported Long-billed Curlew: Rancho Rinco de Anacahuitas, Rancho las Carreras, Rancho los Colorados, and Rio Corona (National Audubon Society 2006; W. H. Howe, pers. comm.). Surveys have not been regular enough at most of the sites to be used to develop a CBC population trend for Long-billed Curlews in the state.

However, 168 Long-billed Curlews were observed at Laguna Madre (Olalla-Kerstupp 2003).

RANGE:
Migration: It is possible that Long-billed Curlews use some sites as both a staging area during migration and as a wintering area, at least for a portion of the population (Table 3.4, Fig. 3.13). Migration patterns are unknown. However, it is believed that Long-billed Curlews move from the north part of the state to the south.

Winter:
  Approximate timing: Long-billed Curlews are present from July to May.
  Locations: They have been recorded at 64 sites (Table 3.4, Fig. 3.13).
  Numbers, particularly high counts: There are no data available across the entire state.

ABUNDANCE AND POPULATION:
There is no information on Long-billed Curlew abundance in Tamaulipas.

HABITAT:
The habitat types used during the winter are the same as those used during migration. Long-billed Curlews use coastal prairies, sand beaches, tidal estuaries, and open parts of salt marshes during low tide. They also use farmlands. Coastal grasslands are probably the most important habitat for wintering Long-billed Curlews.

MONITORING:
There are no current or historic Long-billed Curlew specific monitoring programs in Tamaulipas. Development of techniques for conducting rangewide surveys during migration and winter should be a monitoring priority.

Figure 3.13. Records of Long-billed Curlews in Tamaulipas (Garza-Torres 2006).

Table 3.4. Geographic coordinates of records Long-billed Curlews in Tamaulipas (Garza-Torres 2006).

Municipality	Locality	Latitude	Longitude
Aldama	Rancho Nuevo	23.19472222	-97.79722222
Altamira	Laguna La Culebra-Ejido La Gloria	22.43908333	-98.35475
Gonzalez	Rancho Los Verlages, Presa artificial	22.9002778	-98.57416667
Matamoros	Isla San Juan	25.11305556	-97.50638889
Matamoros	Isla La Florida	25.30033333	-97.61972222
Matamoros	Puerto El Mezquital	25.24072222	-97.44097222
Matamoros	Playa Bagdad	25.82386111	-97.15172222
Matamoros	Norte de la Laguna Madre, a 100 metros del Panteón San Isidro	25.42377778	-97.41330556
Matamoros	Ejido la Capilla (La Puntilla)	25.35591667	-97.44947222
Matamoros	Isla Buenos Aires	25.16944444	-97.49361111
Matamoros	Isla del Coyote	25.22583333	-97.47083333
Matamoros	Rancho Buena Vista	25.31725	-97.71755556
Matamoros	Isla El Ébanal	25.31388889	-97.64583333
Matamoros	Rancho El Chapeño	25.36611111	-97.65916667
Matamoros	Isla El Ranchito	25.284722222	-97.62277778
Matamoros	3 km antes del Ejido Higuerillas, orilla de la Laguna Madre. por la entrada a la playa.	25.288361111	-97.41772222
Matamoros	Isla El Te	25.22583333	-97.4711111
Matamoros	Isla El Toro	25.28638889	-97.53416667
Matamoros	Isla El Amor	25.23611111	-97.45805556
Matamoros	Puente Los Tomates	25.87	-97.47527778
Matamoros	Rancho Los Ébanos	25.34708333	-97.71483333
Matamoros	El faro, playa Bagdad	25.89767222	-98.39748611
Matamoros	La Loma	25.89767222	-98.39748611
Matamoros	Matamoros	25.86180556	-97.50366667
Matamoros	Centro Pesquero Las Higuerillas	25.25602778	-97.43930556
Reynosa	Reynosa	26.07055556	-98.27269444
Río Bravo	Río Bravo	25.97166667	-98.09161111
San Fernando	Bayuco de Oro	24.40138889	-97.79194444
San Fernando	Barra Boca Ciega	25.03505556	-97.58077778
San Fernando	Barra de Jesús María	24.66805556	-97.75916667
San Fernando	Isla El Reloj	24.99969444	-97.68527778
San Fernando	Bayuco de Barsora	25.15638889	-97.69658333
San Fernando	Isla Los Potros	25.24944444	-97.6827778
San Fernando	Escolleras, Barra Santa Isabel	24.41777778	-97.8930556
San Fernando	Ejido Pastores, Carretera San Fernando – El Barrancón	25.04730556	-97.8593056
San Fernando	Bayuco Las Papas	24.55166667	-97.841111
San Fernando	Ejido Francisco J. Mújica (La Poza)	25.26338889	-97.7612222
San Fernando	Centro Pesquero La Ensenada	25.19444444	-97.7047778
San Fernando	Barra Santa Isabel	24.44805556	-97.7405556
San Fernando	Laguna La Nacha, Rancho El Azteca	24.82502778	-97.8388611
San Fernando	Punta de Alambre	24.55086111	-97.7318889
San Fernando	Isla La Playita, Ejido Carboneras (Antes llamada Isla Rincón del Gato)	24.61005556	-97.7152778
San Fernando	Isla La Coyota	24.62361111	-97.7725
San Fernando	Rancho San Antonio, carretera San Fernando - Carboneras km 44	24.65322222	-97.7913056
San Fernando	Rancho Las Malvinas, orilla de La Laguna La Nacha	24.928388889	-97.7725556
San Fernando	Rancho Santa Cecilia	25.897672222	-98.3974861
San Fernando	La Casa Azul, 1 km al sur de la Congregación La Media Luna	25.161027778	-97.6753056
San Fernando	km 37 Carretera San Fernando - El Barrancón	25.249444444	-97.9363889
San Fernando	Isla Las Manecillas	24.991527778	-97.6731667
San Fernando	San Fernando	24.842833333	-98.1546111
San Fernando	Los Lirios	25.897672222	-98.3974861
Soto la Marina	Limite sur de La Laguna Almagre, interconexión con el Río Soto La Marina (La Trozadura)	23.791055556	-97.8021944
Soto la Marina	Barra Soto la Marina, 3 km al norte de la Playa La Pesca.	23.821361111	-97.7338333
Soto la Marina	Vista Hermosa	23.8	-97.9166667
Soto la Marina	Centro Pesquero Congregación Enramadas, Orilla de la Laguna Madre	24.239666667	-97.7569722
Soto la Marina	Los Soldados	23.843055556	-97.7788889
Soto la Marina	Laguna La Sal, Salinas de San Enrique, frente Hotel Hacienda el Contadero, carretera Soto la Marina - La Pesca	23.801916667	-97.8921945
Soto la Marina	Estero La Pesca, Orilla de la Laguna Almagre	23.79175	-97.7869722
Soto la Marina	Laguna La Sal, Salinas de San Enrique, 1 km al este del Ejido Vista Hermosa	23.801916667	-97.8921945
Soto la Marina	Isla El Anillo	24.134166667	-97.7502778
Soto la Marina	Salinas de san Enrique 1.5 km E del Ejido Vista Hermosa	23.801916667	-97.8921945
Soto la Marina	Isla la Jabalina	24.26	-97.7422222
Soto la Marina	Playa La Pesca (Barra Soto la Marina)	23.77325	-97.7371667
Valle Hermoso	Valle Hermoso	25.66405556	-97.8057778

RESEARCH: There are no research activities from Tamaulipas.

CONSERVATION ACTIVITIES (ONGOING): There are no current population conservation actions or management efforts directed specifically at Long-billed Curlews in Tamaulipas. In 2005, the federal government established the NPAs of Laguna Madre and Delta of Rio Bravo, which is important for Long-billed Curlews. Laguna Madre and Delta of Rio Bravo are Important Bird Areas (Arizmendi and Márquez Valdelamar 2000) and WHSRN Sites of International Importance. Pronatura Noreste A.C. is working with Nature Conservancy among other partners to foster the protection and long-term management of Laguna Madre. Pronatura Noreste A.C. has restored coastal wetlands (over 4450 ha) and is working to develop a coastal corridor with conservation easements with local private owners and *ejidatarios*. No education programs are directed specifically at Long-billed Curlews in Tamaulipas. However, Pronatura Noreste A.C. has education and outreach programs for wetlands, which include shorebird species, in the Laguna Madre NPA.

THREATS: Habitat loss and degradation may be the most important threats to Long-billed Curlews. In the coastal zone, cattle ranching and agricultural activities are the most important sources of habitat loss and degradation. There is a low risk of coastal development for urban or tourism purposes.

MANAGEMENT: There are no Long-billed Curlew specific management recommendations for Tamaulipas.

Submitted by Alfonso Banda-Valdez

Veracruz

SUMMARY: Long-billed Curlews are common winter visitors at interior and coastal wetlands of Veracruz. The species is not given any special conservation status by the state or federal government. Usually, Long-billed Curlews have been recorded in small flocks (about 20 birds) or as single birds and in association with other shorebird species.

STATUS: Long-billed Curlews do not have a state designated status in Veracruz.

TRENDS: Long-billed Curlew trends are not measured in Veracruz.

North American Breeding Bird Survey (BBS) trends and abundance data: Long-billed Curlews do not breed in Veracruz.

Christmas Bird Count (CBC): There is one CBC circle (Coast of Central Veracruz, Municipality of Actopan) established in Veracruz. The first count was held in December 2003. Small numbers (2-26, average 10) have been reported in each of the five survey years (National Audubon Society 2006; W. H.

Howe, pers. comm.). There are too few data available to develop a population trend based on the CBC.

RANGE:
Migration:
    Approximate timing: Migration patterns are unknown.
    Location of staging areas: Long-billed Curlews have been observed along the coast and in interior wetlands. It is possible that Long-billed Curlews use some sites as staging areas during migration as well as for wintering areas for at least a portion of the population. Coffey (1960) reported 12 on 31 May 1957 along Laguna Chila, Cacalilao, which suggests that some Long-billed Curlews may not migrate to northern breeding grounds.
    Numbers, particularly high counts: Maximum counts are 20.

Winter:
    Locations: The locations used during the winter are the same as those used during migration.
    Approximate timing: Long-billed Curlews are present from August to April (Howell and Webb 1995).
    High Counts: Maximum counts are 26 Long-billed Curlews in the Municipality of Actopan.

ABUNDANCE AND POPULATION: There is no information on Long-billed Curlew abundance in Veracruz. There are no long term surveys which can be used to determine the population trend of Long-billed Curlews in the state.

HABITAT: Long-billed Curlews use interior (e.g. lakes and rivers) and coastal (e.g. sandy beaches, estuaries, and coastal lagoons) wetlands in Veracruz during both winter and migration.

MONITORING: There are no current statewide Long-billed Curlew specific monitoring programs. Populations of all avian species are monitored in different surveys carried out by personnel of Pronatura Veracruz, A. C. and Instituto de Ecología, A. C.

RESEARCH: No research is available in the state.

CONSERVATION ACTIVITIES (ONGOING): There are no current population conservation actions or management efforts directed specifically at Long-billed Curlews in the state. Several locations that are used by Long-billed Curlews, such as Tamiahua, Tampamachoco, La Mancha-El Llano, Alvarado, Sontecomapan, could be proposed to the Ramsar Convention Bureau as Sites of International Importance for conserving biological diversity. Some sites are NPAs at the state or federal government level. It is necessary to implement local conservation plans to secure additional critical habitats for Long-billed Curlews at these sites. Pronatura Veracruz, A. C. and Nature Conservancy are working in a conservation planning process for the coastal zone that will guide conservation actions designed to protect these sites. There are no education or outreach programs specifically directed at Long-billed Curlews within the state. However, Pronatura Veracruz, A. C. has education and outreach programs for wetlands that include general shorebird conservation and ecology.

THREATS: Habitat loss and degradation may be the most important threats to Long-billed Curlews. The degree and consequences of these conservation threats varies among sites.

However, overall development along the coast is increasing. Across the state coastal wetlands have been drained for urban, agricultural, and cattle ranching purposes. Changes in agricultural and cattle ranching practices have caused an overall significant reduction in available shorebird habitat.

A considerable loss of habitat for tourism development has also influenced the coastal zone. The quality of several wetlands has been degraded through development of water-use systems, including the construction of channels and dikes. Deforestation in the upper basin may increase erosion resulting in habitat changes in the coastal zone. Oil spills pose local threats to Long-billed Curlews almost every where along the coast of Veracruz. Untreated sewage and industrial waste is discharged directly into some sites as well.

MANAGEMENT: There are no Long-billed Curlew management recommendations for Veracruz.

Submitted by Elisa Peresbarbosa-Rojas

Literature Cited

Ackerman, D. S. 2007. Distribution, abundance, and habitat associations of the Long-billed Curlew in southwestern North Dakota. M.S. thesis. University of North Dakota, Grand Forks.

Adamus, P. R., K. Larsen, G. Gillson, and C. R. Miller. 2001. Oregon breeding bird atlas. Oregon Field Ornithologists, Eugene, Oregon.

Allen, A. A. 1937. The shore birds, cranes, and rails: willets, plovers, stilts, phalaropes, sandpipers, and their relatives deserve protection. Pages 257-296 *in* G. Grosvenor, and A. Wetmore, editors. The book of birds: the first work presenting in full color all the major species of the U.S. and Canada. National Geographic Society, Washington, D.C.

Allen, J. N. 1980. The ecology and behavior of the Long-billed Curlew in southeastern Washington. Wildlife Monographs 73:1-67.

American Ornithologists' Union. 1957. Check-list of North American birds. 5th Edition. American Ornithologists' Union, Washington, D.C.

American Ornithologists' Union. 1998. Check-list of North American birds. 7th Edition. American Ornithologists' Union, Washington, D.C.

Andrei, A. E., L. M. Smith, D. A. Haukos, and J. G. Surles. 2006. Community composition and migration chronology of shorebirds using the saline lakes of the Southern Great Plains, USA. Journal of Field Ornithology 77:372-383.

Andrews, R., and R. Righter. 1992. Colorado birds: a reference to their distribution and habitat. Denver Museum of Natural History, Denver, Colorado.

Animal and Plant Health Inspection Service. 2003. Grasshoppers and Mormon cricket fact sheet. U.S. Department of Agriculture, Animal and Plant Health Inspection Service, Washington, D.C. <http://www.aphis.usda.gov/lpa/pubs/fsheet_faq_notice/fs_phgrasshoppersmc.html> (accessed 23 August 2006).

Arizmendi, M. C., H. Berlanga, L. Márquez, L. Navarijo, and F. Ornelas. 1990. Avifauna de la región de Chamela, Jalisco. Cuadernos del Instituto de Biología 4. UNAM, Distrito Federal, México.

Arizmendi, M. C., and L. Márquez Valdelamar, editors. 2000. Áreas de Importancia para la Conservación de las Aves en México. Consejo Internacional para la Preservación de las Aves en México (CIPAMEX), Distrito Federal, México.

Arriaga, L., J. M. Espinoza, C. Aguilar, E. Martínez, L. Gómez, and E. Loa, editors. 2000. Regiones terrestres prioritarias de México. Comisión Nacional para el Conocimiento y Uso de la Biodiversidad, México, Distrito Federal, México.

Arriaga-Cabrera, L., E. Vázquez-Domínguez, J. González-Cano, R. Jiménez-Rosenberg, E. Muñoz-López, and V. Aguilar-Sierra, editors. 1998. Regiones marinas prioritarias de México. Comisión Nacional para el Conocimiento y Uso de la Biodiversidad, México, Distrito Federal, México.

Askins, R. A., F. Chávez-Ramírez, B. C. Dale, C. A. Haas, J. R. Herkert, F. L. Knopf, and P. D. Vickery. 2007. Conservation of grassland birds in North America: understanding ecological processes in different regions. Ornithological Monographs 64:1-46.

Avedaño, J. J. 1999. Análisis socioeconómico de las comunidades aledañas a colonias de perro de las praderas (*Cynomys mexicanus*) en el noreste de México. Reporte Técnico World Wildlife Fund. Programa del Desierto Chihuahuense. Monterrey, Nuevo León, México.

Bailey, A. M., and R. J. Niedrach. 1967. Pictorial checklist of Colorado birds. Denver Museum of Natural History, Denver, Colorado.

Bart, J., B. Andres, S. Brown, G. Donaldson, B. Harrington, H. Johnson, V. Johnston, S. L. Jones, R. I. G. Morrison, M. Sallaberry, and S. K. Skagen. 2005. The program for regional and international shorebird monitoring (PRISM). Pages 983-901 *in* C. J. Ralph, and T. D. Rich, editors. Bird conservation implementation and integration in the Americas: Proceedings of the Third international Partners in Flight conference. General Technical Report PSW-GTR-191, U.S. Department of Agriculture Forest Service, Albany, California.

Baumgartner, F. M., and A. M. Baumgartner. 1992. Oklahoma bird life. University of Oklahoma Press, Norman, Oklahoma.

Behle, W. H. 1985. Utah birds: geographic distribution and systematics. Utah Museum of Natural History Occasional Publication 5:1-147.

Behle, W. H., E. D. Sorensen, and C. M. White. 1985. Utah birds: a revised checklist. Utah Museum of Natural History, University of Utah, Salt Lake City, Utah.

Bicak, T. K. 1977. Some eco-etholgoical aspects of a breeding population of Long-billed Curlews (*Numenius americanus*), in Nebraska. M.S. thesis, University of Nebraska, Omaha.

Blachly, C. P. 1880. Ornithology of Riley County, Kansas. Transactions of the Kansas Academy (1872-1880) 7:102-111.

Blanchan, N. 1904. Birds that hunt and are hunted: life histories of one hundred and seventy birds of prey, game birds and water-fowls. Grosset & Dunlap, New York, New York.

Blus, L. J., C. J. Henny, and A. J. Krynitsky. 1985. Organochlorine-induced mortality and residues in Long-billed Curlews from Oregon. Condor 87:563-565.

Brabata, G. 1995. Presencia y conducta alimenticia de cuatro especies de playeros (Scolopacidae) en la Ensenada de La Paz, B.C.S. B.Sc. thesis, Universidad Autónoma de Baja California Sur, La Paz, México.

Brabata, G., and R. Carmona. 1999. Conducta alimentaria de cuatro especies de aves playeras (Charadriiformes:Scolopacidae) en Chametla, B.C.S., México. Revista de Biología Tropical 47:239-243.

British Columbia Ministry of Environment. 2001. Habitat atlas for wildlife at risk, species profiles - Long-billed Curlew. British Columbia Ministry of Environment, Victoria, British Columbia, Canada. <http://wlapwww.gov.bc.ca/sir/fwh/ wld/atlas/species/species_index.html> (accessed 23 January 2007).

British Columbia Ministry of Environment. 2007. British Columbia conservation data centre - species summary: *Numenius americanus*. British Columbia Ministry of Environment, Victoria, British Columbia, Canada. <http://srmapps.gov. bc.ca/ apps/eswp/> (accessed 22 January 2007).

British Columbia Ministry of Environment. Undated. British Columbia's wildlife at risk: Long-billed Curlew. British Columbia Ministry of Environment, Victoria, British Columbia, Canada. <http://wlapwww.gov.bc.ca/ wld/documents/ curlewfa_s.pdf> (accessed 22 January 2007).

Brown, C. R., M. B. Brown, P. A. Johnsgard, J. Kren, and W. C. Scharf. 1996. Birds of Cedar Point Biological Station area, Keith and Garden counties, Nebraska: seasonal occurrence and breeding data. Transactions of the Nebraska Academy of Sciences 23:91-108.

Brown, S., C. Hickey, B. Harrington, and R. Gill, editors. 2001. U.S. shorebird conservation plan. 2nd Edition. Manomet Center for Conservation Sciences, Manomet, Massachusetts.

Brown, S. M. 1986. The influences of cattle grazing on avian distribution in a seasonal wetland. M.S. thesis, University of Idaho, Moscow.

Bruner, L., R. H. Wollcott, and M. H. Swenk. 1904. A preliminary review of the birds of Nebraska, with synopses. Klopp and Bartlett, Omaha, Nebraska.

Brusati, E. D., P. J. DuBowy, and T. E. Lacher, Jr. 2001. Comparing ecological functions of natural and created wetlands for shorebirds in Texas. Waterbirds 24:371-380.

Brush, T. 2005. Nesting birds of a tropical frontier. Texas A&M University Press, College Station, Texas.

Bry, E. 1986. Buffaloberry patch. North Dakota Outdoors 3:25.

Buchanan, J. B. 2005. Long-billed Curlew (*Numenius americanus*). Pages 147-148 *in* T. R. Wahl, B. Tweit, and S. G. Mlodinow, editors. The birds of Washington. Oregon State University Press, Corvallis, Oregon.

Busby, W. H., and J. L. Zimmerman. 2001. Kansas breeding bird atlas. University Press of Kansas, Lawrence, Kansas.

Butler, A. W. 1898. Birds of Indiana. Indiana Department of Geology and Natural Resources Annual Report 22: 515-1187.

Cable, T. T., S. Seltman, and K. J. Cook. 1996. Birds of Cimarron National Grassland. U.S. Dept. of Agriculture, Forest Service, Rocky Mountain Forest and Range Experiment Station Gen. Tech. Rep. RM-GTR-281, Fort Collins, Colorado.

California Department of Fish and Game. 1992. Bird species of special concern. Unpublished list, July 1992, California Department of Fish and Game, Sacramento, California.

Campbell, R. W. 1972. Coastal records of the Long-billed Curlew for British Columbia. Canadian Field-Naturalist 86:167-168.

Campbell, R. W., N. K. Dawe, I. McTaggart-Cowan, J. M. Cooper, G. W. Kaiser, and M. C. E. McNall. 1990. The birds of British Columbia. Volume 2. University of British Columbia Press, Vancouver, British Columbia, Canada.

Canadian Wildlife Service. 2007. Habitat Stewardship Programs 2005-2006, Canadian Wildlife Service, Prairie and Northern Region. Environment Canada, Canadian Wildlife Service, Prairie and Northern Region, Saskatoon, Saskatchewan, Canada. <http://www.cws-scf.ec.gc.ca/hsppih/default.asp?lang=en&n =E3E4A23A> (accessed 24 June 2006).

Cannings, R. J. 1999. Status of the Long-billed Curlew in British Columbia. British Columbia Ministry of Environment, Lands and Parks Wildlife Working Report No. WR-96, Victoria, British Columbia, Canada.

Capp, J. C., and D. Mehlman, 2005. A new conservation partnership: conserving migratory birds in the Americas. Pages 1138-1142 *in* C. J. Ralph, and T. D. Rich, editors. Bird conservation implementation and integration in the Americas: Proceedings of the Third international Partners in Flight conference. General Technical Report PSW-GTR-191, U.S. Department of Agriculture Forest Service, Albany, California.

Carmona, R. 1995. Distribución temporal de aves acuáticas en la playa El Conchalito, Ensenada de La Paz, B.C.S. Investigaciones Marinas CICIMAR 10:S1-S21.

Casey, D. 2000. Partners in Flight bird conservation plan Montana Version 1.0. Montana Partners in Flight, Kalispell, Montana. <http://www.partnersinflight.org/bcps/pl_mt_10.pdf> (accessed 11 August 2006).

Cavallaro, R. 2006. Conservation and management of Long-billed Curlews and waterbirds in the Foster's Slough wetland complex, Teton Valley, Idaho. Wader Study Group Bulletin 109:32.

Cerovski, A. O., M. Grenier, B. Oakleaf, L. Van Fleet, and S. Patla. 2004. Atlas of birds, mammals, amphibians, and reptiles in Wyoming. Wyoming Game and Fish Department Nongame Program, Lander, Wyoming. <http://gf.state.wy.us/ downloads/pdf/nongame/WYBirdMammHerpAtlas04.pdf> (accessed 1 December 2006).

Chisholm, G., and L. A. Neel. 2002. Birds of Lahontan Valley: a guide to Nevada's wetland oasis. University of Nevada Press, Reno, Nevada.

Clark, T. W., and A. H. Harvey. 1989. Rare, sensitive, and threatened species of the greater Yellowstone ecosystem. Northern Rockies Conservation Cooperative, Jackson, Wyoming.

Clarke, J. N. 2006. Reproductive ecology of Long-billed Curlews breeding in grazed landscapes of western South Dakota. M.S. thesis, South Dakota State University, Brookings.

Clarke, J. N., and K. C. Jensen. 2006. Nesting success, brood survival, and habitat use of Long-billed Curlews in grazed landscapes of western South Dakota. Wader Study Group Bulletin 109:31.

Cochrane, J. F. 1983. Long-billed Curlew habitat and land-use relationships in western Wyoming. M.S. thesis, University of Wyoming, Laramie.

Coffey, B. B, Jr. 1960. Late North American spring migrants in Mexico. Auk 77:288-297.

Cole, T., and R. S. Sharpe. 1976. The effects of grazing management on a sandhills prairie community. III. Breeding bird density and diversity. Proceedings of the Nebraska Academy of Sciences 86:12.

Colorado Division of Wildlife. 2006. Colorado's comprehensive wildlife conservation strategy and wildlife action plans. Denver, Colorado. <http://wildlife.state.co.us/WildlifeSpecies/ComprehensiveWildlife ConservationStrategy/> (accessed 14 February 2007).

Colwell, M. A. 2006. Abundance, spatial distributions, and social system of Long-billed Curlews in coastal northern California. Wader Study Group Bulletin 109:32.

Colwell, M. A., and R. L. Mathis. 2001. Seasonal variation in territory occupancy of non-breeding Long-billed Curlews in intertidal habitats. Waterbirds 24:208-216.

Colwell, M. A., R. L. Mathis, L.W. Leeman, and T. S. Leeman. 2002. Space use and diet of territorial Long-billed Curlews (*Numenius americanus*) during the non-breeding season. Northwestern Naturalist 83:47-56.

Colwell, M. A., and K. D. Sundeen. 2000. Shorebird distributions on ocean beaches of northern California. Journal of Field Ornithology 71:1-14.

Committee on the Status of Endangered Wildlife in Canada. 2002. COSEWIC assessment and update status report on the Long-billed Curlew *Numenius americanus* in Canada. Environment Canada, Canadian Wildlife Service, Ottawa, Ontario, Canada.

Contreras, A. 1998. Birds of Coos County, Oregon: status and distribution. Cape Arago Audubon Society and Oregon Field Ornithologist Special Publication 12, Eugene, Oregon.

Contreras, B. A. 1978. Estudio comparativo de la ornitofauna en tres áreas representativas de las tres regiones fisiográficas del sur de Nuevo León, México. B.Sc. thesis, Facultad de Ciencias Biológicas, Universidad Autónoma de Nuevo León, Monterey, Nuevo León, México.

Contreras-Balderas, A. J., J. H. López-Soto, J. M. Torres-Ayala, and S. Contreras-Arquieta. 2004. Additional records of birds from Cuatro Ciénegas Basin Natural Protected Area, Coahuila, México. Southwestern Naturalist 49:103-109.

Corman, T. E., and C. Wise-Gervais, editors. 2005. Arizona breeding bird atlas. University of New Mexico Press, Albuquerque, New Mexico.

Coues, E. 1874. Birds of the Northwest. Ayer Company Publishers, Manchester, New Hampshire.

Cupul-Magaña, F. G. 2000. Aves acuáticas del estero El Salado, Puerto Vallarta, Jalisco. Huitzil 1:3-8.

Dahl, T. E. 1990. Wetland losses in the U.S. 1780s to 1980s. U.S. Department of the Interior, Fish and Wildlife Service, Washington, D.C.

Dale, B., M. Norton, C. Downes, and B. Collins. 2005. Monitoring as a means to focus research and conservation – the Grassland Bird Monitoring example. Pages 485-495 *in* C. J. Ralph, and T. D. Rich, editors. Bird conservation implementation and integration in the Americas: Proceedings of the Third international Partners in Flight conference. General Technical Report PSW-GTR-191, U.S. Department of Agriculture Forest Service, Albany, California.

Danemann, G. D., R. Carmona, and G. Fernández. 2002. Migratory shorebirds in the Guerrero Negro Saltworks, Baja California Sur, México. Wader Study Group Bulletin 97:36-41.

Danufsky, T., and M. A. Colwell. 2003. Winter shorebird communities and tidal flat characteristics at Humboldt Bay, California. Condor 105:117-129.

Davis, C. A., and L. M. Smith. 1998. Ecology and management of migrant shorebirds in the Playa Lakes Region of Texas. Wildlife Monographs 140:5-45.

Davis, C. V. 1961. A distributional study of the birds of Montana. Ph.D. dissertation. Oregon State University, Corvallis.

De Smet, K. 1992. Status report on the Long-billed Curlew *Numenius americanus* in Canada. Committee on the Status of Endangered Wildlife in Canada, Environment Canada, Canadian Wildlife Service, Ottawa, Ontario, Canada.

Dechant, J. A., M. L. Sondreal, D. H. Johnson, L. D. Igl, C. M. Goldade, P. A. Rabie, and B. R. Euliss. 2003. Effects of management practices on grassland birds: Long-billed Curlew. U.S. Department of Interior, U.S. Geological Survey, Northern Prairie Wildlife Research Center, Jamestown, North Dakota. <http://www.npwrc. usgs.gov/resource/literatr/ grasbird/Long-billed Curlews/Long-billedCurlews.htm> (accessed 12 December 2003).

del Hoyo, J., A. Elliott, and J. Sargatal, editors. 1996. Handbook of the birds of the world. Vol 3. Hoatzin to Auks. Lynx Edicions, Barcelona, Spain.

DeLuca, T. H. 2007. Environmental benefits and consequences of biofuels development in the U.S. The Wilderness Society, Washington, D.C. <http://wilderness.org/files/biofuels-development. pdf> (accessed 29 September 2008).

Desmond, M. 2004. Effects of grazing practices and fossorial rodents on a winter avian community in Chihuahua, México. Biological Conservation 116:235-242.

Desmond, M., and J. A. Montoya. 2006. Status and distribution of Chihuahuan Desert grasslands in the U.S. and México. Pages 17-21 *in* X. Basurto, and D. Hadley, editors. Grasslands ecosystems, endangered species, and sustainable ranching in the Mexico-U.S. borderlands: conference proceedings. U.S. Department of Agriculture Forest Service, Rocky Mountain Research Station, Fort Collins, Colorado, RMRS-P-40.

Dice, L. R. 1918. The birds of Walla Walla and Columbia counties, southeastern Washington. Auk 35:40-51.

Dick-Peddie, W. A. 1993. New Mexico vegetation: past, present, and future. University of New Mexico Press, Albuquerque, New Mexico.

Dieni, J. S., W. H. Howe, S. L. Jones, P. Manzano-Fischer, and C. P. Melcher. 2003. New information on wintering birds of northwestern Chihuahua. American Birds 57:26-31.

Dirk, C. N. G. 2003. North Dakota animal species of concern. Unpublished list. North Dakota Natural Heritage Program, Bismarck, North Dakota.

Donaldson, G. M., C. Hyslop, R. I. G. Morrison, H. L. Dickson, and I. Davidson. 2000. Canadian shorebird conservation plan. Environment Canada, Canadian Wildlife Service Special Publication CW69-15 / 5-2000E, Ottawa, Ontario, Canada.

Drewien, R. C., W. M. Brown, and D. S. Benning. 1996. Distribution and abundance of sandhill cranes in México. Journal of Wildlife Management 60:270-285.

Driver, E. A. 1992. Grassland bird study in southwestern Saskatchewan. Environment Canada, Canadian Wildlife Service, Ecological Research Studies, Saskatoon, Saskatchewan, Canada.

Dronen, N. O., and J. E. Badley. 1979. Helminths of shorebirds from the Texas Gulfcoast. I. digenetic trematodes from the Long-billed Curlew, *Numenius americanus*. Journal of Parasitology 65:645-649.

Dronen, S. I. 1984. Windbreaks in the Great Plains. Northern Journal of Applied Forestry 1:55-59.

Ducey, J. E. 1988. Nebraska birds: breeding status and distribution. Simon-Boardman Books, Omaha, Nebraska.

Ducey, J. E. 2000. Birds of the untamed west: the history of birdlife in Nebraska, 1750 to 1875. Making History, Omaha, Nebraska.

Dugger, B. D., and K. M. Dugger. 2002. Long-billed Curlew (*Numenius americanus*). *In* A. Poole, and F. Gill, editors. The Birds of North America, No. 628. Academy of Natural Sciences, Philadelphia, Pennsylvania; American Ornithologists' Union, Washington, D.C.

Dugger, B. D., and K. M. Dugger. 2003. Long-billed Curlew. Pages 224-226 *in* D. B. Marshall, M. G. Hunter, and A. L. Contreras, editors. Birds of Oregon: a general reference. Oregon State University Press, Corvallis, Oregon.

eBird. 2008. eBird: an online database of bird distribution and abundance [web application]. Version 2. eBird, Ithaca, New York. <http://www. ebird.org> (accessed 8 September 2008).

Elphick, C. S., and L. W. Oring. 1998. Winter management of California rice fields for waterbirds. Journal of Applied Ecology 35:95-108.

Engilis, A. Jr., L. W. Oring, E. Carrera, J. W. Nelson, and A. Martinez-Lopez. 1998. Shorebird surveys in Ensenada Pabellones and Bahia Santa Maria, Sinaloa, México: critical winter habitats for Pacific flyway shorebirds. Wilson Bulletin 110:332-341.

Environment Canada. 2004. Consultation on amending the list of species under the Species at Risk Act: March 2004. Environment Canada, Canadian Wildlife Service, Gatineau, Québec, Canada.

Erickson, W. 2006. Direct impacts to birds. Pages 12-13 *in* D. S. Klute, editor. Conference on wind power and wildlife in Colorado, 23-25 January 2006. Fort Collins, Colorado. < http://wildlife.state.co.us/LandWater/Energy/WindPowerWildlifeSymposium.htm> (accessed 23 August 2006).

Esparza-Salas, R. 2001. Avifauna acuática de la laguna Xola-Paramán, Jalisco, México. Tesis Profesional. Departamento de Estudios para El Desarrollo Sustentable de Zona Costera, Universidad de Guadalajara, Guadalajara, Jalisco, México.

Floyd, T., C. S. Elphick, G. Chisholm, K. Mack, E. M. Ammon, and J. D. Boone. 2007. Atlas of the breeding birds of Nevada. University of Nevada Press, Reno, Nevada.

Ford, E. R. 1956. Birds of the Chicago region. Chicago Academy of Sciences, Chicago, Illinois.

Forsythe, D. M. 1972. Observations on the nesting biology of the Long-billed Curlew. Great Basin Naturalist 32:88-90.

Foster-Willfong, J. M. 2003. Census methodology and habitat use of Long-billed Curlews (*Numenius americanus*) in Saskatchewan. M.S. thesis, University of Regina, Saskatchewan, Canada.

Garza de León, A., I. Morán, F. Valdés, and R. Tinajero. 2007. Coahuila. Pages 98-136 *in* Avifaunas Estatales de México. R. Ortiz-Pulida, A. Navarro-Sigüenza, H. Gómez de Silva, O. Rojas-Soto, and T. A. Peterson, editors. CIPAMEX, Pachuca, Hidalgo, México. <http://www.huitzil. net/coahuila.pdf> (8 September 2008).

Garza-Torres H. A. 2006. Aves de importancia para la conservación en Tamaulipas: Diagnostico y estrategias para su conservación. Instituto de Ecología y Alimentos, Universidad Autónoma de Tamaulipas, Ciudad Victoria, Tamaulipas, México.

Georgia Department of Natural Resources Wildlife Resources Division. 2005. A comprehensive wildlife conservation strategy for Georgia. Social Circle, Georgia. <http://www1.gadnr.org/cwcs/Documents/strategy.html> (accessed 11 October 2008).

Gillihan, S. W. 1999. Best management practices for select bird species of the Comanche National Grassland. U.S. Department of Agriculture, U.S. Forest Service, Cimarron and Comanche National Grasslands, Pueblo, Colorado. <http://www.fs.fed. us/r2/Nebraska/gpng/tes_projects/comanchebmp. htm> (accessed 23 August 2006).

Goldie, K. 2005. Long-billed Curlew monitoring surveys: population estimates, trend analysis, and habitat associations. A final report to U.S. Fish and Wildlife Service, Region 1, Richland, Washington.

Goldman, E. A. 1926. Breeding birds of a White Mountains lake. Condor 28:159-164.

Gorrell, J. V., M. E. Andersen, K. D. Bunnell, M. F. Canning, A. G. Clark, D. E. Dolsen, and F. P. Howe. 2005. Utah comprehensive wildlife conservation strategy. Utah Division of Wildlife Resources, Salt Lake City, Utah. <http://www. wildlife. utah.gov/cwcs/utah_cwcs_strategy.pdf> (accessed 12 October 2006).

Granlund, J., G. A. McPeek, and R. J. Adams. 1994. Birds of Michigan. Indiana University Press, Bloomington, Indiana.

Gratto-Trevor, C. L. 2000. Use of managed and natural wetlands by upland breeding shorebirds in southern Alberta. Pages 252-259 *in* J. Thorpe, T. A. Steeves, and M. Gollop, editors. Proceedings of the fifth prairie conservation and endangered species conference, February 1998, Saskatoon, Saskatchewan. Provincial Museum of Alberta Natural History Occasional Paper No. 24. Saskatoon, Saskatchewan, Canada.

Gratto-Trevor, C. L. 2006. Upland nesting prairie shorebirds: use of managed wetland basins and accuracy of breeding surveys. Avian Conservation and Ecology. 1:2-20. <http://www.ace-eco.org/vol1/iss2/art2/> (accessed 10 January 2007).

Grinnell, J. 1921. Concerning the status of the supposed two races of the Long-billed Curlew. Condor 23:21-27.

Gullion, G. W. 1951. Birds of the southern Willamette Valley, Oregon. Condor 53:129-149.

Hagen, S. K., P. T. Isakson, and S. R. Dyke. 2005. North Dakota comprehensive wildlife conservation strategy. North Dakota Game and Fish Department. Bismarck, North Dakota <http://gf.nd.gov/conservation/cwcs.html> (accessed 12 October 2006).

Hall, F. S. 1934. Studies in the history of ornithology in the state of Washington (1792-1932) with special reference to the discovery of new species. Part III. Murrelet 15:3-19.

Hand, K. D., and L. L. Cadwell. 1994. 1993 Study of Long-billed Curlews on the Yakima Training Center. Report to the U.S. Department of the Army. PNL-9465. Pacific Northwest Laboratory, Richland, Washington.

Hands, H. M. 2008. Shorebird (Charadriiformes) migration at selected sites throughout Kansas during 2002-2006. Transactions of the Kansas Academy of Science 111:61-78.

Hanni, D. J., and M. M. McLachlan. 2004. Section-based monitoring of breeding birds within the Shortgrass Prairie Bird Conservation Region (BCR 18). Rocky Mountain Bird Observatory, Brighton, Colorado. <http://rmbo.org/public/monitoring/downloads.aspx> (accessed 9 October 2006).

Harrington, B. A. 1992. A coastal, aerial winter shorebird survey on the Sonora and Sinaloa coasts of México, January 1992. A final report to Manomet Bird Observatory, Manomet, Massachusetts.

Harrington, B. A. 1994. A coastal, aerial winter shorebird survey on the Sonora, Sinaloa and Nayarit, México, January 1994. A final report to Manomet Bird Observatory, Manomet, Massachusetts.

Harrington, B. A., S. C. Brown, J. Corven, and J. Bart. 2002. Collaborative approaches to the evolution of migration and the development of science-based conservation in shorebirds. Auk 119:914-921.

Hartman, C. A., and L. W. Oring. 2006a. Long-billed Curlew nest-site selection and nest survival at large and small spatial scales. Wader Study Group Bulletin 109:31.

Hartman, C. A., and L. W. Oring. 2006b. Population ecology of Long-billed Curlews breeding in north-eastern Nevada. Wader Study Group Bulletin 109:31.

Hatch, P.L. 1892. Notes on the birds of Minnesota. Geological and Natural History Survey of Minnesota, University of Minnesota Press, Minneapolis, Minnesota.

Hayward, C. L., C. Cottam, A. M. Woodbury, and H. H. Frost. 1976. Great Basin naturalist memoirs: birds of Utah. Brigham Young University Press, Provo, Utah.

Hernández-Vázquez, S. 2005a. Aves acuáticas de la laguna de Agua Dulce y esteros El Ermitaño, Jalisco, México. Biología Tropical/International Journal of Tropical Biology and Conservation 53:229-238.

Hernández-Vázquez, S. 2005b. Aves acuáticas de la costa de Jalisco: análisis de la comunidad, reproducción e identificación de las áreas prioritarias para la conservación de las aves. Tesis Doctorado. Instituto Politécnico Nacional. Centro Interdisciplinario de Ciencias Marinas. La Paz, Baja California Sur, México.

Hernández-Vázquez, S., H. de la Cueva S., and J. Rojo-Vázquez. 2002. Análisis comparativo de la avifauna del estero Majahuas (Jalisco, México) entre un evento El Niño y un año no Niño. Boletín del Centro de Investigaciones Biológicas. 1:94-112.

Hernández-Vázquez S., and E. Mellink. 2001. Coastal waterbirds of El Chorro and Majahuas, Jalisco, México, during the non-breeding season, 1995-1996. Revista de Biología Tropical 49:357-365.

Hill, D. P. 1998. Status of the Long-billed Curlew (Numenius americanus) in Alberta. Alberta Environmental Protection, Fisheries & Wildlife Management Division, and Alberta Conservation Association, Wildlife Status Report No. 16, Edmonton, Alberta, Canada.

Hinojosa-Huerta, O., H. Iturribarría-Rojas, Y. Carrillo-Guerrero, M. de la Garza-Treviño, and E. Zamora-Hernández. 2004. Bird conservation plan for the Colorado River Delta. Pronatura Noroeste, Dirección de Conservación Sonora. San Luis Río Colorado, Sonora, México.

Howell, S. N. G. 1999. A bird-finding guide to México. Cornell University Press, Ithaca, New York.

Howell, S. N. G., and S. Webb. 1995. A guide to the birds of México and Northern Central America. Oxford University Press, New York, New York.

Hoy, P.R. 1853. Notes on the ornithology of Wisconsin. Transactions of the Wisconsin State Agricultural Society 2:341-364.

Hubbard, J. P. 1978. Revised check-list of the birds of New Mexico. New Mexico Ornithological Society Publication No. 6. McLeod Printing Co., Albuquerque, New Mexico.

Hunter, W. C. 2006. Conservation priority bird species of the Atlantic Coast. Page 6 in M. P. Guilfoyle, R. A. Fischer, D. N. Pashley, and C. A. Lott, editors. Summary of the first regional workshop on dredging, beach nourishment, and birds on the south Atlantic Coast. U.S. Army Corps of Engineers, Washington, DC. <http://el.erdc.usace.army.mil/elpubs/pdf/trel06-10.pdf> (accessed 17 October 2006).

Idaho Department of Fish and Game. 2005. Idaho comprehensive wildlife conservation strategy. Idaho Conservation Data Center, Idaho Department of Fish and Game, Boise, Idaho. <http://fishandgame.idaho.gov/cms/tech/CDC/cwcs.cfm> (accessed 13 October 2006).

Igl, L. D., and B. M. Ballard. 1999. Habitat associations of migrating and overwintering grassland birds in southern Texas. Condor 101:771-782.

Inskipp, T., and H. J. Gillett, editors. 2005. Checklist of CITES species and Annotated CITES Appendices and reservations. Compiled by UNEP-WCMC. CITES Secretariat, Geneva, Switzerland and UNEP-WCMC, Cambridge, England. <http://www.cites. org/common/resources/2005_CITES_Checklist.pdf> (accessed 23 August 2006).

Jenni, D. A., R. L. Redmond, and T. K. Bicak. 1981. Behavioral ecology and habitat relationships of Long-billed Curlew in western Idaho. A final report to U.S. Department of the Interior, Bureau of Land Management, Boise District, Boise, Idaho.

Jewett, S. G. 1929. Limicolae of the State of Oregon. Auk 46:214-222.

Johnson, D. H. 2006. Disturbance and fragmentation: indirect and cumulative impacts. Page 14 *in* D. S. Klute, editor. Conference on wind power and wildlife in Colorado, 23-25 January 2006. Fort Collins, Colorado. < http://wildlife.state.co.us/LandWater/Energy/WindPowerWildlifeSymposium.htm> (accessed 23 August 2006).

Johnson, D. H., and J. A. Shaffer. 2006. Assessing the avoidance impacts of wind generators on grassland breeding birds. Pages 18-19 *in* D. S. Klute, editor. Conference on wind power and wildlife in Colorado, 23-25 January 2006. Fort Collins, Colorado. < http://wildlife.state.co.us/LandWater/Energy/WindPowerWildlifeSymposium.htm> (accessed 23 August 2006).

Jones, S. L., C. S. Nations, S. D. Fellows, and L. L. McDonald. 2008. Breeding abundance and distribution of Long-billed Curlews (*Numenius americanus*) in North America. Waterbirds 31:1-14.

Jones, S. L., T. R. Stanley, S. K. Skagen, and R. L. Redmond. 2003. Long-billed Curlew (*Numenius americanus*) rangewide survey and monitoring guidelines. Final study plan. Administrative report. U.S. Department of Interior, Fish and Wildlife Service, Denver, Colorado. <http://mountain-prairie.fws.gov/species/birds / longbilled_curlew/LONG-BILLED CURLEWS%20study%20plan-photos%2012-2003.pdf> (accessed 14 September 2006).

Jorgensen, J. G. 2006. The Long-billed Curlew (*Numenius americanus*) in Nebraska: status, trends and conservation needs. A final report to Nebraska Game and Parks Commission, Lincoln, Nebraska.

Jurek, R. M. 1973. California shorebird survey, 1969-74. Special Wildlife Investigation Project Final Report. California Department of Fish and Game, Sacramento, California.

Kale, H. W., II, and D. S. Maehr. 1990. Florida's birds: a handbook and reference. Pineapple Press, Sarasota, Florida.

Kennicott, R. 1854. Catalogue of animals observed in Cook County, Illinois. Illinois State Agricultural Society Transactions for 1853-1854 1:577-595.

Kent, T. H., and J. J. Dinsmore. 1996. Birds in Iowa. Privately printed, Iowa City and Ames, Iowa.

King, R. 1978. Habitat use and related behaviors of breeding Long-billed Curlews. M.S. thesis, Colorado State University, Fort Collins, Colorado.

Kingery, H. E., editor. 1998. Colorado breeding bird atlas. Colorado Bird Atlas Partnership and Colorado Division of Wildlife, Denver, Colorado.

Knick, S. T., D. S. Dobkin, J. T. Rotenberry, M. A. Schroeder, W. M. Vander Haegen, and C. van Riper III. 2003. Teetering on the edge or too late? Conservation and research issues for avifauna of sagebrush habitats. Condor 105:611-634.

Kreil, R. 1987. Long-billed Curlew survey results: 1986. North Dakota Outdoors 49:16.

Kumlein, L., and N. Hollister. 1903. Birds of Wisconsin. Bulletin of the Wisconsin Natural History Society 3:1-143.

Leeman, T. S., and M. A. Colwell. 2005. Coastal pasture use by Long-billed Curlew at the northern extent of their non-breeding range. Journal Field Ornithology 76:33-39.

Leeman, L. W., M. A. Colwell, T. S. Leeman, and R. L, Mathis. 2001. Diets, energy intake, and kleptoparasitism of nonbreeding Long-billed Curlews in a northern California estuary. Wilson Bulletin 113:194-201.

Lehman, P. E. 1994. The birds of Santa Barbara County, California. Vertebrate Museum, University of California, Santa Barbara, California.

Lenard, S., J. Carlson, J. Ellis, C. Jones, and C. Tilly. 2003. P. D. Skaar's Montana bird distribution, 6th ed. Montana Audubon Society, Helena, Montana.

Lenard, S., J. Carlson, P. Hendricks, and C. Currier. 2006. Grassland bird surveys in North Valley county, Montana: progress report. Department of Interior, Bureau of Land Management. Montana Natural Heritage Program, Helena, Montana.

Littlefield, C. D. 1990. Birds of Malheur National Wildlife Refuge, Oregon. Oregon State University Press, Corvallis, Oregon.

Lockwood, M. W. 2001. Birds of the Texas hill country. University of Texas Press, Austin, Texas.

Lockwood, M. W., and B. Freeman. 2004. The Texas ornithology society handbook of Texas birds. Texas A&M University Press, College Station, Texas.

Long, L. L., and C. J. Ralph. 2001. Dynamics of habitat use by shorebirds in estuarine and agricultural habitats in northwestern California. Wilson Bulletin 113:41-52.

Maimone-Celorio, M. R., and E. Mellink. 2003. Shorebirds and benthic fauna of tidal mudflats in Estero Punta Banda, Baja California, México. Bulletin Southern California Academy of Sciences 102:26-38.

Manzano-Fischer, P., R. List, and G. Ceballos. 1999. Grassland birds in prairie-dog towns in northwestern Chihuahua, México. Studies in Avian Biology No. 19:263-271.

Manzano-Fischer, P., R. List, G. Ceballos, and J. E. Cartron. 2006. Avian diversity in a priority area for conservation in North America: the Janos-Casas Grandes Prairie Dog Complex and adjacent habitats in northwestern México. Biodiversity and Conservation 15:3801-3825.

Martínez-Martínez, B. Z., and F. G. Cupul-Magaña. 2002. Listado actualizado de las aves acuáticas de la desembocadura del Río Ameca, Bahía de Banderas, México. Ciencia y Mar 6:38-43.

Mathis, R. L., M. A. Colwell, L. W. Leeman, and T. S. Leeman. 2006. Long-billed Curlew distributions in intertidal habitats: scale-dependent patterns. Western Birds 37:156-168.

McCallum, D. A., W. D. Graul, and R. Zaccagnini. 1977. The breeding status of the Long-billed Curlew in Colorado. Auk 94:599-601.

McNeil, R., S. J. Ramón Rodriquez, and F. Mercier. 1985. Winter range expansion of the Long-billed Curlew (*Numenius americanus*) to South America. Auk 102:174-175.

Mellink, E., and G. de la Riva. 2005. Non-breeding waterbirds at Laguna Cuyutlán and its associated wetlands, Colima, México. Journal of Field Ornithology 76:158-167.

Mellink, E., E. Palacios, and S. González. 1997. Non-breeding waterbirds of the Delta of the Río Colorado, México. Journal of Field Ornithology 68:113-123.

Merrill, J. C. 1897. Notes on the birds of Fort Sherman, Idaho. Auk 14:347-357.

Mollfhoff, W. J. 2001. The Nebraska breeding bird atlas 1984-1989. Nebraska Ornithologists' Union Occasional Paper No. 7/Nebraska Technical Series No. 20. Nebraska Game and Parks Commission, Lincoln, Nebraska.

Monson, G., and A. Phillips. 1981. Annotated checklist of the birds of Arizona. University of Arizona Press, Tucson, Arizona.

Montana Fish, Wildlife and Parks. 2005. Montana's comprehensive fish and wildlife conservation strategy. Montana Fish, Wildlife and Parks, Helena, Montana.

Montanta Natural Heritage Program, Montana Audubon, and Montana Fish, Wildlife and Parks. undated. online version Montana bird distribution database. Missoula, Montana. <http://nhp.nris.mt.gov/> (accessed 10 March 2007).

Morrison, R. I. G., R. E. Gill, Jr., B. A. Harrington, S. K. Skagen, G. W. Page, C. L. Gratto-Trevor, and S. M. Haig. 2001. Estimates of shorebird populations in North America. Environment Canada, Canadian Wildlife Service Occasional Paper no. 104, Ottawa, Ontario, Canada.

Morrison, R. I. G., B. J. McCaffery, R. E. Gill, S. K. Skagen, S. L. Jones, G. W. Page, C. L. Gratto-Trevor, and B. A. Andres. 2006. Population estimates of North American shorebirds, 2006. Wader Study Group Bulletin 111:67-85.

Morrison, R. I. G., R. K. Ross, and J. P. Guzmán. 1994. Aerial surveys of Nearctic shorebirds wintering in México: preliminary results of surveys on the southern half of the Pacific coast, Chiapas to Sinaloa. Environment Canada, Canadian Wildlife Service Progress Notes No. 209, Ottawa, Ontario, Canada.

Morrison, R. I. G., R. K. Ross, and S. M. Torres. 1992. Aerial surveys of Nearctic shorebirds wintering in México: some preliminary results. Environment Canada, Canadian Wildlife Service Progress Report No. 201, Ottawa, Ontario, Canada.

Muckleston, K., and R. W. Highsmith, Jr. 1978. Center pivot irrigation in the Columbia Basin of Washington and Oregon: dynamics and implications. Water Resources Bulletin 14:1121-1128.

Mumford, R. E., and C. E. Keller. 1984. The birds of Indiana. Indiana University Press, Bloomington, Indiana.

Munguia, P., P. López, and I. Fortes. 2005. Seasonal changes in waterbird habitat and occurrence in Laguna de Sayula, Western México. Southwestern Naturalist 50:318-322.

National Audubon Society. 2006. Christmas bird count historical results [online]. <http://www.audubon.org/bird/cbc> (accessed 14 November 2006).

NatureServe. 2006. NatureServe Explorer: an online encyclopedia of life. Version 4.7. NatureServe, Arlington, Virginia. <http://www.natureserve.org/explorer> (accessed 23 August 2006).

Navarro, M. T. 1993. Estudio preliminar de las aves de la laguna El Tecuan (albufera La fortuna) municipio de la Huerta, Jalisco. Tesis de licenciatura, Universidad de Guadalajara, Guadalajara, Jalisco, México.

Nehls, H. B. 1994. Oregon shorebirds, their status and movements. Oregon Department of Fish and Wildlife, Wildlife Diversity Program, Salem, Oregon. Technical Report No. 94-1-02.

Nelson, E. W. 1876. Birds of northeastern Illinois. Essex Institute Bulletin 8:90-155.

Nevada Department of Wildlife. 2005. Nevada's wildlife action plan. Nevada Department of Wildlife, Reno, Nevada. <http://www.ndow.org/wild/conservation/cwcs/index.shtm#plan> (accessed 20 January 2008).

New Mexico Department of Game and Fish. 2006. Comprehensive wildlife conservation strategy for New Mexico. New Mexico Department of Game and Fish. Santa Fe, New Mexico. <http://fws-nmcfwru.nmsu.edu/cwcs/documents/CWCS_NM_Feb142006.pdf> (accessed 25 January 2007).

Nicholoff, S. H., editor. 2003. Wyoming Partners In Flight: Wyoming bird conservation plan, v. 2.0. Wyoming Game and Fish Department, Lander, Wyoming. <http://www.blm.gov/wildlife/plan/WY/menu.htm> (accessed 1 December 2006).

Oberholser, H. C. 1974. The bird life of Texas. University of Texas Press, Austin, Texas.

Ohanjanian, I. A. 1985. The long-billed curlew, *Numenius americanus*, on Skookumchuck Prairie - status report and enhancement plan. British Columbia Ministry of Environment, Wildlife Branch, Cranbrook, British Columbia, Canada.

Ohanjanian, I. A. 1992. Numbers, distribution and habitat dynamics of Long-billed Curlews in the East Kootenay. British Columbia Ministry of Environment, Wildlife Branch, Cranbrook, British Columbia, Canada.

Olalla-Kerstupp, A. 2003. Aves playeas de la Laguna Madre, Tamauilas, México. B.Sc. thesis, Universidad Autónoma de Nuevo León, San Nicolás de los Garza, México.

Oregon Department of Fish and Wildlife. 2005. Oregon conservation strategy. Oregon Department of Fish and Wildlife, Salem, Oregon.

Oring, L. W. 2006. Long-billed Curlew symposium. Wader Study Group Bulletin 109:30.

Oring, L. W., and C. A. Hartman. 2006. Hayfields in the American west: critical habitat for highly imperiled Long-billed Curlews. Wader Study Group Bulletin 109:31.

Oring, L. W., L. Neel, and K. E. Oring. 1999. U.S. national shorebird conservation plan: Intermountain West regional shorebird plan. Department of Interior, U.S. Fish and Wildlife Service, Portland, Oregon.

Otte, C. 2006. The Kansas county checklist project, 20 April 2006. Kansas Ornithological Society, Manhattan, Kansas. <http://www.ksbirds.org/checklist/maps/LBCU.jpg> (accessed 8 June 2006).

Page, G. W., and R. E. Gill, Jr. 1994. Shorebirds in western North America: late 1800s to late 1900s. Studies in Avian Biology 15:147-160.

Page, G. W., E. Palacios, A. Lucia, S. Gonzalez, L. E. Stenzel, and M. Jungers. 1997. Numbers of wintering shorebirds in coastal wetlands of Baja California, México. Journal of Field Ornithology 68:562-574.

Page, G. W., L. E. Stenzel, and J. E. Kjelmyr. 1999. Overview of shorebird abundance and distribution in wetlands of the Pacific coast of the contiguous U.S. Condor 101:461-471.

Palacios, E., A. Escofet, and D. H. Loya-Salinas. 1991. El Estero de Punta Banda, B.C., México, como eslabón del "Corredor del Pacifico": abundancia de aves playeras. Ciencias Marinas 17:109-131.

Palomera-García, C., E. Santana, and R. Amparan-Salido. 1994. Patrones de distribución de la avifauna en tres estados del occidente de México. Anales del Instituto de Biología, Universidad Nacional Autónoma de México, Serie Zoología 65:137-175.

Pampush, G. J. 1980a. Breeding chronology, habitat utilization and nest-site selection of the Long-billed Curlew in northcentral Oregon. M.S. thesis. Oregon State University, Corvallis, Oregon.

Pampush, G. J. 1980b. Status report on the Long-billed Curlew in the Columbia and northern Great Basins. Unpublished report, Department of Interior, U.S. Fish and Wildlife Service, Portland, Oregon.

Pampush G. J., and R. G. Anthony 1993. Nest success, habitat utilization and nest-site selection of Long-billed Curlews in the Columbia Basin, Oregon. Condor 95:957-967.

Parrish, J. R., F. P. Howe, and R. E. Norvell. 2002. Utah Partners in Flight avian conservation strategy Version 2.0. Utah Division of Wildlife Resources Publication No. 02-27, Salt Lake City, Utah. <http://www.wildlife.utah.gov/publications/pdf/utah_partners_in_flight.pdf> (accessed 15 November 2006).

Paton, P. W. C., and J. Dalton. 1994. Breeding ecology of Long-billed Curlews at Great Salt Lake, Utah. Great Basin Naturalist 54:79-85.

Patten, M. A., G. McCaskie, and P. Unitt. 2003. Birds of the Salton Sea. University of California Press, Berkeley, California.

Patten, M. A., E. Mellink, H. Gómez de Silva, and T. E. Wurster. 2001. Status and taxonomy of the Colorado Desert Avifauna of Baja California. Monographs in Field Ornithology 3:29-63.

Paulson, D. 1993. Shorebirds of the Pacific Northwest. University of Washington Press, Seattle, Washington.

Pemberton, J. R. 1922. A large tern colony in Texas. Condor 2:37-48.

Peterson, J., and B. R. Zimmer. 1998. Birds of the trans-Pecos. University of Texas Press, Austin, Texas.

Peterson, R. A. 1995. The South Dakota breeding bird atlas. South Dakota Ornithologists' Union, Aberdeen, South Dakota.

Pfister, C., B. A. Harrington, and M. Lavine. 1992. The impact of human disturbance on shorebirds at a migration staging area. Biological Conservation 60:115-126.

Pimentel, D., R. Zuniga, and D. Morrison. 2005. Update on the environmental and economic costs associated with alien-invasive species in the U.S. Ecological Economics 52:273-288.

Playa Lakes Joint Venture Landbird Team. 2007. Playa Lakes Joint Venture Landbird Team Report (a working document), version 2.0., November 2007. Playa Lakes, Joint Venture, Lafayette, Colorado. <http://www.pljv.org/cms/technical-documents> (accessed 12 September 2008).

Playa Lakes Joint Venture Shorebird Team. 2007. Shorebird conservation plan for the Playa Lakes Joint Venture (draft July 2007). Playa Lakes Joint Venture, Lafayette, Colorado. <http://www.pljv.org/cms/technical-documents> (accessed 12 September 2008).

Prairie Conservation Action Plan Partnership. 2003. Saskatchewan Prairie Conservation Action Plan 2003-2008. Canadian Plains Research Center, University of Regina, Regina, Saskatchewan, Canada.

Prairie Conservation Forum. 2006. Alberta Prairie Conservation Action Plan: 2006-2010. Prairie Conservation Forum, Lethbridge, Alberta, Canada.

Prairie Habitat Joint Venture. 2000. Prairie Canada shorebird conservation plan. Environment Canada, Canadian Wildlife Service, Prairie and Northern Region, Saskatoon, Saskatchewan, Canada.

Putnam, C., and G. Kennedy. 2005. Montana birds. Lone Pine Publishing, Edmonton, Alberta, Canada.

Ralph, C. J., G. R. Geupel, P. Pyle, T. E. Martin, D. F. DeSante, and B. Mila. 1996. Manual de métodos de campo para el monitoreo de aves terrestres. U.S. Department of Agriculture, Forest Service, Pacific Southwest Research Station, General Technical Report PSW-GTR-159, Albany, California.

Ramsar Convention on Wetlands. 2008. Additional Ramsar sites in México. Ramsar Convention on Wetlands, Gland, Switzerland <http://ramsar.org/wn/w.n.mexico_april08.htm> (accesssed 7 September 2008).

Redmond, R. L., and D. A. Jenni. 1982. Natal philopatry and breeding area fidelity of Long-billed Curlews (*Numenius americanus*): patterns and evolutionary consequences. Behavioral Ecology and Sociobiology 10:277-279.

Redmond, R. L., and D. A. Jenni. 1986. Population ecology of the Long-billed Curlew (*Numenius americanus*) in western Idaho. Auk 103:755-767.

Renaud, W. E. 1980. The Long-billed Curlew in Saskatchewan: status and distribution. Blue Jay 38:221-237.

Rivers, J. W., and T. T. Cable. 2003. Evaluation of farmed playa wetlands as avian habitat using survey data and tow rapid assessment techniques. Transactions of the Kansas Academy of Science 106:155-165.

Robbins, S. D., Jr. 1991. Wisconsin birdlife. University of Wisconsin Press, Madison, Wisconsin.

Robel, R. J. 2006. Potential impacts of human activity and energy development on Lesser Prairie-Chicken populations. Pages 19-20 *in* D. S. Klute, editor. Conference on wind power and wildlife in Colorado, 23-25 January 2006. Fort Collins, Colorado. < http://wildlife.state.co.us/LandWater/Energy/WindPowerWildlifeSymposium.htm> (accessed 23 August 2006).

Roberts, T. S. 1932. The birds of Minnesota. University of Minnesota Press, Minneapolis, Minnesota.

Román-Rodríguez, M. J. 2004. Plan de monitoreo y difusión de los humedales prioritarios de la Reserva de la Biósfera Alto Golfo de California y Delta del Río Colorado y su zona de influencia. Reporte Parcial. Instituto del Medio Ambiente y el Desarrollo Sustentable del Estado de Sonora, México.

Rosche, R. R. 1982. The birds of northwestern Nebraska and southwestern South Dakota. Published by the author, Chadron, Nebraska.

Rosche, R. R. 1994. Bird of the Lake McConaughy area and the North Platte River Valley, Nebraska. Published by the author, Chadron, Nebraska.

Rosenberg, K. V., R. D. Ohmart, W. C. Hunter, and B. W. Anderson. 1991. Birds of the Lower Colorado River Valley. University of Arizona Press, Tucson, Arizona.

Royal British Columbia Museum. 2002. Living landscapes 4.17, Long-billed Curlew: *Numenius americanus* (Bechstein). Royal British Columbia Museum, Victoria, British Columbia, Canada. <http://www.livinglandscapes.bc.ca/cbasin/endangered/long-bil.htm> (accessed 22 January 2007).

Ruiz-Campos, G., E. Palacios, J. A. Castillo-Guerrero, S. González-Guzmán, and E. H. Batche- González. 2005. Spatial and temporal composition of the avifauna from small coastal wetlands and adjacent habitats in northwestern Baja California, México. Ciencias Marinas 31:553-576.

Russell, R. P. 2006. The early history of the Long-billed Curlew (*Numenius americanus*) in the Midwest. Wader Study Group Bulletin 109:30.

Russell, S. M., and G. Monson, 1998. The birds of Sonora. The University of Arizona Press, Tucson, Arizona.

Saalfeld, S. T., W. C. Conway, D. A. Haukos, and M. Rice. 2008. Local and geospatial landscape analysis of habitat use by Long-billed Curlews (*Numenius americanus*) breeding in the United States. Final report to U.S. Fish and Wildlife, Region 6, Denver, Colorado.

Sadler, T. S., and M. T. Myres. 1976. Alberta birds 1961-1970. Provincial Museum of Alberta, Natural History Occasional Paper No. 1. Alberta Culture, Historical Resources Division, Edmonton, Alberta, Canada.

Salt, W. R., and J. R. Salt. 1976. The birds of Alberta. Government of Alberta, Edmonton, Alberta, Canada.

Sauer, J. R., J. E. Hines, and J. Fallon. 2008. The North American Breeding Bird Survey, results and analysis 1966-2008. Version 5.15.2008. U.S. Department of Interior, Geological Survey, Patuxent Wildlife Research Center, Laurel, Maryland. <http://www.mbr-pwrc.usgs.gov/bbs/> (accessed 8 September 2008).

Saunders, E. J. 2001. Population estimate and habitat associations of the Long-billed Curlew (*Numenius americanus*) in Alberta. Alberta Species at Risk Report No. 25. Edmonton, Alberta. <http://mountain-prairie.fws.gov/species/birds/ longbilled_curlew/LONG-BILLED CURLEWS -Alberta.pdf> (accessed 14 September 2006).

Schaldach, W. J. 1963. The avifauna of Colima and adjacent Jalisco, México. Proceedings of the Western Foundation of Vertebrate Zoology 1:1-100.

Schaldach, W. J. 1969. Further notes in the avifauna of Colima and adjacent Jalisco, México. Anales del Instituto de Biología, Serie Zoología 2:299-316.

Scharlemann, J. P. W., and W. F. Laurance. 2008. How green are biofuels? Science 319:43-44.

Schneider, R., M. Humpert, K. Stoner, and G. Steinauer. 2005. The Nebraska natural legacy project: a comprehensive wildlife conservation strategy. Nebraska Game and Parks Commission, Lincoln, Nebraska.

Scott-Morales, L., E. Estrada, F. Chávez-Ramírez, and M. Cotera. 2004. Continued decline in geographic distribution of the Mexican prairie dog (*Cynomys mexicanus*). Journal of Mammalogy: 85:1095-1101.

Scott-Morales, L., J. Nocedal, M. Cotera, and J. Canales-Delgadillo. 2008. Worthen's Sparrow (*Spizella wortheni*) in the northern Mexican plateau. Southwestern Naturalist 53:91-95.

Secchi, S., and B. A. Babcock. 2007. Impact of high crop prices on environmental quality: a case of Iowa and the Conservation Reserve Program. Working Paper 07-WP 447 Center for Agricultural and Rural Development, Iowa State University, Ames, Iowa <http://www.card.iastate.edu> (accessed 12 September 2008).

Secretaria de Medio Ambiente y Recursos Naturales. 2002. Norma Oficial Mexicana NOM-059-ECOL-2001, Protección ambiental – especies nativas de México de flora y fauna silvestres – categorías de riesgo y especificaciones para su inclusión, exclusión o cambio – lista de especies en riesgo. Distrito Federal, México. <http://www.sedarh.gob.mx/vidasilvestre/archivos/NOM-059-ecol-2001.pdf> (accessed 23 August 2006).

Semenchuk, G. P. 1992. The atlas of breeding birds of Alberta. Federation of Alberta Naturalists, Edmonton, Alberta, Canada.

Senner, N. R. 2006. First record of Long-billed Curlew (*Numenius americanus*) in Peru and other observations of Nearctic waders in the Virilla estuary. Cotinga 26:39-42.

Sessions, L. 1901. Changes in the bird fauna of the prairies in the last thirty years. Proceedings of the Nebraska Ornithologists' Union 2:71-73.

Seyffert, K. D. 2001a. Birds of the Texas panhandle: their status, distribution, and history. Texas A&M University Press, College Station, Texas.

Seyffert, K. D. 2001b. Long-billed Curlew. The Texas breeding bird atlas. Texas A&M University Press, College Station, Texas. <http://tbba.cbi. tamucc.edu> (accessed 12 July 2001).

Shackford, J. S. 1994. Nesting of Long-billed Curlews on cultivated fields. Bulletin Oklahoma Ornithological Society, 27:17-20.

Shane, T. G. 2005. A significant midcontinental stopover site for the Long-billed Curlew. Kansas Ornithological Society Bulletin 56:33-37.

Shane, T. G., and S. J. Shane. 2006. The spring 2006 Long-billed Curlew migration in the Finney County, Kansas region [abstract]. Horned Lark 33:4-5.

Sharpe, R. S., W. R. Silcock, and J. G. Jorgensen. 2001. Birds of Nebraska: their distribution and temporal occurrence. University of Nebraska Press, Lincoln, Nebraska.

Shuford, W. D., and T. Gardali, editors. 2008. California bird species of special concern 2006: a ranked assessment of species, subspecies, and distinct populations of birds of immediate conservation concern in California. Studies of Western Birds. Western Field Ornithologists, Lawrence, Kansas.

Shuford, W. D., G. W. Page, J. G. Evens, and L. E. Stenzel. 1989. Seasonal abundance of waterbirds at Point Reyes: a coastal California perspective. Western Birds 20:137-265.

Shuford, W. D., G. W. Page, and L. E. Stenzel. 2002b. Patterns of distribution and abundance of migratory shorebirds in the intermountain west of the U.S. Western Birds 33:134-174.

Shuford, W. D., N. D. Warnock, and R. L. McKernan. 2004. Patterns of shorebird use of the Salton Sea and adjacent Imperial Valley, California. Studies in Avian Biology 27:61-77.

Shuford, W. D., N. D. Warnock, K. C. Molina, and K. K. Sturm. 2002a. The Salton Sea as critical habitat to migratory and resident waterbirds. Hydrobiologia 473:255-274.

Silcock, W. R. 2004. Summer field report, June-July 2004. Nebraska Bird Review 72:44-61.

Silcock, W. R., and J. G. Jorgensen. 1997. Summer field report, June-July 1997. Nebraska Bird Review 65:102-115.

Silloway, P. M. 1900. Notes on the Long-billed Curlew. Condor 2:79-82.

Skagen, S. K., and F. L. Knopf. 1993. Toward conservation of mid-continental shorebird migration. Conservation Biology 7:533-541.

Skagen, S. K., P. B Sharpe, R. G. Waltermire, and M. B. Dillon. 1999. Biogeographical profiles of shorebird migration in midcontinental North America. Biological Science Report USGS/BRD/BSR-2000-0003. U.S. Government Printing Office, Denver, Colorado.

Smith, A. R. 1996. Atlas of Saskatchewan birds. Saskatchewan Natural History Society, Special Publication No. 22, Regina, Saskatchewan, Canada.

Smith, G. A. 2004. Long-billed Curlew (*Numenius americanus*). Pages 152-153 *in* D. L. Reinking, editor. Oklahoma breeding bird atlas. University of Oklahoma Press. Norman, Oklahoma.

Smith, M. R., P. W. Mattocks, Jr., and K. M. Cassidy. 1997. Breeding birds of Washington State: location data and predicted distributions. Seattle Audubon Society, Seattle, Washington.

Smith, V. J., J. A. Jenks, C. R. Berry, Jr., C. J. Kopplin, and D. M. Fecske. 2002. The South Dakota gap analysis project. Final Report. Research work order No. 65, Department of Wildlife and Fisheries Science, South Dakota State University, Brookings, South Dakota.

South Carolina Department of Natural Resources. 2006. Comprehensive wildlife conservation strategy. South Carolina Department of Natural Resources, Columbia, South Carolina. <http://www.dnr.sc.gov/cwcs/ index.html> (accessed 24 January 2007).

South Dakota Department of Wildlife. 2006. Rare, threatened or endangered animals tracked by the South Dakota Natural Heritage program. South Dakota Natural Heritage Program, Pierre, South Dakota. <http://www.sdgfp.info/Wildlife/Diversity/index.htm> (accessed 18 January 2007).

South Dakota Ornithologists' Union. 1991. The birds of South Dakota. South Dakota Ornithologists' Union, Aberdeen, South Dakota.

Sparks, R. A., and D. J. Hanni. 2006. Section-based monitoring of breeding birds within the Shortgrass Prairie Bird Conservation Region (BCR 18). Rocky Mountain Bird Observatory, Brighton, Colorado. <http://rmbo.org/public/monitoring/downloads.aspx> (accessed 9 October 2006).

Sparks, R. A., D. J. Hanni, and M. McLachlan. 2005. Section-based Monitoring of Breeding Birds within the Shortgrass Prairie Bird Conservation Region (BCR 18). Rocky Mountain Bird Observatory, Brighton, Colorado. <http://rmbo.org/public/monitoring/downloads.aspx> (accessed 9 October 2006).

Spomer, R. 1981. Long-billed Curlews and Sprague's Pipits near Pierre. South Dakota Bird Notes 33:78.

Stanley, T. R., and S. K. Skagen. 2007. Estimating the breeding population of Long-billed Curlew in the U.S. Journal of Wildlife Management 71:2556-2564.

Stenzel, L. E., H. R. Huber, and G. W. Page. 1976. Feeding behavior and diet of the Long-billed Curlew and Willet. Wilson Bulletin 88:314-332.

Stepniewski, A. 1999. The birds of Yakima County, Washington. Yakima Valley Audubon Society, Yakima, Washington.

Stewart, G. B., A. S. Pullin, and C. F. Coles. 2007. Poor evidence-base for assessment of windfarm impacts on birds. Environmental Conservation 34:1-11.

Stewart, R. E. 1975. Breeding birds of North Dakota. Tri-College Center for Environmental Studies, Fargo, North Dakota.

Stralberg, D., V. Toniolo, G. W. Page, and L. E. Stenzel. 2004. Potential impacts of non-native *Spartina* spread on shorebird populations in South San Francisco Bay. Point Reyes Bird Observatory Report to California Coastal Conservancy (contract #02-212). Point Reyes Bird Observatory Conservation Science, Bolinas, California.

Strickland, D. 2006. Broad perspective on relative impacts of wind power development on wildlife as well as information needs. Pages 9-10 *in* D. S. Klute, editor. Conference on wind power and wildlife in Colorado, 23-25 January 2006. Fort Collins, Colorado. < http://wildlife.state.co.us/LandWater/Energy/WindPowerWildlifeSymposium.htm> (accessed 23 August 2006).

Stubbs, M. 2007. Congressional research service report for Congress: land conversion in the Northern Plains. Report prepared for members and committees of Congress, Order Code RL 33950 <http://or.ducks.org/Media/Conservation/Farm%20Bill/_documents/CRSSodbusterReport.pdf> (accessed 12 September 2008).

Sutton, G. M. 1967. Oklahoma birds: their ecology and distribution, with comments on the avifauna of the southern great plains. University of Oklahoma Press, Norman, Oklahoma.

Tallman, D. A., D. L. Swanson, and J. S. Palmer. 2002. Birds of South Dakota. South Dakota Ornithologists' Union, Aberdeen, South Dakota.

Texas Ornithological Society. 1995. Checklist of the birds of Texas, 3rd edition. Capital Printing, Austin, Texas.

Texas Parks and Wildlife Department. 2005. Texas comprehensive wildlife conservation strategy 2005-2010. Texas Parks and Wildlife Department, Austin, Texas. <http://www.tpwd.state.tx.us/business/grants/wildlife/cwcs/> (accessed 12 October 2006).

Thompson, M. C., and C. Ely. 1989. Birds of Kansas Volume I. University of Kansas Museum of Natural History, University Press of Kansas, Lawrence, Kansas.

Timken, R. L. 1969. Notes on the Long-billed Curlew. Auk 86:750-751.

U.S. Coast Guard. 2003. Statistics of oil spills in U.S. waters (annual data and graphics) 1969-2000. U.S. Department of Homeland Security, U.S. Coast Guard, Washington, D.C. <http://www.uscg.mil/hq/g-m/nmc/response/stats/ac.htm> (accessed 23 August 2006).

U.S. Department of Energy. 2008. U.S. – wind resources map. U.S. Department of Energy, National Renewable Energy Laboratory, Golden, Colorado. <http://www.windpoweringamerica.gov/wind_maps.asp> (accessed 8 September 2008).

U.S. Fish and Wildlife Service. 2002. Birds of conservation concern 2002. Administrative Report. U.S. Department of Interior, Fish and Wildlife Service, Division of Migratory Bird Management, Arlington, Virginia. <http://migratorybirds.fws.gov/reports/ bcc2002.pdf> (accessed 23 August 2006).

U.S. Fish and Wildlife Service. 2006. Hanford Reach National Monument draft comprehensive conservation plan and environmental impact statement. U.S. Department of Interior, Fish and Wildlife Service, Richland, Washington.

U.S. Fish and Wildlife Service. 2007. McNary and Umatilla National Wildlife Refuges comprehensive conservation plan and environmental assessment. U.S. Department of Interior, Fish and Wildlife Service, Richland, Washington.

U.S. Fish and Wildlife Service. 2008a. Migratory Bird Treaty Act of 1918. U.S. Department of Interior, Fish and Wildlife Service, Washington, D.C. <http://www.fws.gov/migratorybirds/intrnltr/treatlaw.html#mbta > (accessed 22 December 2008).

U.S. Fish and Wildlife Service. 2008b. Endangered Species Act. U.S. Department of Interior, Fish and Wildlife Service, Washington, D.C. <http://www.fws.gov/endangered/wildlife.html> (accessed 22 December 2008).

U.S. Fish and Wildlife Service. 2008c. Birds of conservation concern 2008. Administrative Report. U.S. Department of Interior, Fish and Wildlife Service, Division of Migratory Bird Management, Arlington, Virginia. <http://www.fws.gov/migratorybirds/reports/BCC2008/BCC2008.pdf> (accessed 12 May 2009).

U.S. Fish and Wildlife Service. 2008d. Division of Bird Habitat Conservation 2008 Neotropical Grants. U.S. Department of Interior, Fish and Wildlife Service, Washington, D.C. <http://www.fws.gov/birdhabitat/Grants/NMBCA/ 2008.shtm> (accessed 7 September 2008).

U.S. Forest Service. 2005a. Amendment number 30: establish an updated list of Management Indicator Species (MIS), August 2005. U.S. Department of Agriculture, U.S. Forest Service, Cimarron and Comanche National Grasslands, Pueblo, Colorado. <http://www.fs.fed.us/ r2/psicc/publications/ amendments/amend_30_mis.pdf> (accessed 13 June 2006).

U.S. Forest Service. 2005b. Draft Cimarron and Comanche National Grasslands land management plan. December 2005. U.S. Department of Agriculture, U.S. Forest Service, Cimarron and Comanche National Grasslands, Pueblo, Colorado. <http://www.fs.fed.us/r2/psicc/projects/forest_ revision> (accessed 13 June 2006).

U.S. Shorebird Conservation Plan. 2004. High priority shorebirds – 2004. U.S. Department of Interior, Fish and Wildlife Service, Arlington, Virginia. <http://www.fws.gov/shorebirdplan/ downloads/ShorebirdPriorityPopulationsAug04. pdf> (accessed 19 June 2006).

Utah Division of Wildlife Resources. 2003. Utah sensitive species list. Utah Division of Wildlife Resources, Salt Lake City, Utah. <http://dwrcdc. nr.utah.gov/ucdc/> (accessed 4 February 2009).

Utah Division of Wildlife Resources. 1999. Utah Gap Analysis: an environmental information system: DWR neotrops revision. USDI National Biological Service and Utah State University, Salt lake City, Utah. <http://dwrcdc.nr.utah.gov/rsgis2/Search/ Map.asp?Id=329> (accessed 4 February 2009).

Vega, X., and M. A. Cruz. 2007. Conservación de tierras privadas: un nuevo y práctico mecanismo legal para la conservación de las aves playeras. Wader Study Bulletin 113:3.

Walters, R. E., and E. Sorenson. 1983. Utah bird distribution: latilong study. Utah Division of Wildlife Resources Publication No. 83-10, Salt Lake City, Utah.

Wells, K. M., J. P. McCarty, and L. L. Wolfenbarger. 2005. Final Report: 2004 Long-billed Curlew Survey. Nebraska Game and Parks Commission, Lincoln, Nebraska.

Western Hemisphere Shorebird Reserve Network. 2006. Cape Romain National Wildlife Refuge site description. Manomet Center for Conservation Sciences, Manomet, Massachusetts. <http://www. whsrn.org> (accessed 25 January 2007).

Williams, S. O., III. 2005. The winter season: New Mexico. North American Birds 59:303.

Wilson, M. H, and D. A. Ryan. 1997. Conservation of Mexican wetlands: role of the North American Wetlands Conservation Act. Wildlife Society Bulletin 25:57-64.

Wolfe, L. R. 1931. The breeding Limnicolae of Utah. Condor 33:49-59.

World Wildlife Fund. 2001. Okanagan dry forests (NA0522). World Wildlife Fund, Washington, D.C. <http://www.worldwildlife.org/wildworld/profiles/ terrestrial/na/na0522_full.html> (accessed 22 January 2007).

Wyoming Game and Fish Department. 2005. A comprehensive wildlife conservation strategy for Wyoming. Wyoming Game and Fish Department, Cheyenne, Wyoming. <http://gf.state.wy.us/ wildlife/CompConvStrategy/index.asp> (accessed 12 October 2006).

Wyoming Game and Fish Department. 2006. Nongame program species of special concern. Wildlife Division, Lander, Wyoming. <http://gf.state.wy.us/wildlife/nongame/ SpeciesofSpecialConcern/> (accessed 1 December 2006).

Yocom, C. F. 1956. Re-establishment of breeding populations of Long-billed Curlews in Washington. Wilson Bulletin 68:228-231.

Zárate-Ovando, B., E. Palacios, H. Reyes-Bonilla, E. Amador, and G. Saad. 2006. Waterbirds of the lagoon complex Magdalena Bay-Almejas, Baja California Sur, Mexico. Waterbirds 29:350-364.

Long-billed Curlew, High Island. Bob Gress©.

U.S. Department of the Interior
U.S. Fish & Wildlife Service
Route 1, Box 166
Shepherdstown, WV 25443

http://www.fws.gov

July 2009

www.ingramcontent.com/pod-product-compliance
Lightning Source LLC
Chambersburg PA
CBHW081222280526
45787CB00006B/2489